Dr. R.K. Suneja MD, DCH is an eminent pediatrician of India. He was formerly Consultant & Head, Department of Pediatrics and Medical Superintendent, Hindu Rao Hospital, Delhi and had the distinction of being appointed as an Honorary Physician to the President of India.

He also worked as Child Health Consultant to the Municipal Corporation of Delhi; Consultant, Integrated Child Development Services Scheme, Government of India and Member, Consultative Committee, Child Guidance Centre, Delhi School of Social Work. He received a special award in 1989 in recognition of his outstanding work and immense contribution to the development of child health and medical services in Delhi. He is presently a practising Pediatric Consultant in New Delhi and is a Member of the Committee of National Children's Fund, Delhi.

Praise for *Baby & Child Care*

A must for mothers. Practical and handy. *Baby & Child Care* by eminent paediatrician Dr. R.K. Suneja deals with valuable information on baby care and emotional changes in the new mother. Interestingly, unlike other child care books, this book takes you even beyond the first year to the formative age...

Bogged by queries ... pick up Dr. Suneja's book and you'll get the answers.

The Hindustan Times (Metropolitan)

India's answer to the legendary Dr. Spock. A must have for new parents to be as well as child care givers. Simple and easily comprehendible. The book provides information without overloading readers with medical jargon. The book talks not only of the physical aspects of child care but also of the mental development of the growing child.

Delhi Mid-Day

Written from a proudly Indian perspective. Dr. Suneja provides succour in all departments of child-rearing, from feeding a newborn to development milestones, from behavioural problems to hiring the right ayaḥ. Parents can finally take it easy.

The Indian Express

Swadeshi Ben Spock. Counsellor from before conception to after birth. Useful tips such as against force-feeding.

India Today

BABY & CHILD CARE

A handy and complete guide for parents and parents-to-be

Dr. R. K. Suneja

Rupa . Co

First in Rupa Paperback 1998
Nineth Impression 2007
Revised and updated Edition 2009
Twelfth Impression 2011

Published by
Rupa Publications India Pvt. Ltd.
7/16, Ansari Road, Daryaganj,
New Delhi 110 002

Sales Centres:

Allahabad Bengaluru Chennai
Hyderabad Jaipur Kathmandu
Kolkata Mumbai

Illustrations by Sandip Sinha
Typeset in Baskerville and Corporate Black

Printed in India by
Saurabh Printers Pvt. Ltd.
A-16, Sector-IV
Noida 201 301

Illustrations nos. 1.1 and 1.11 are adapted from *New Pregnancy Book*, nos. 1.2, 1.3, 1.4, 1.5, 1.8, 1.9, 12.1, 13.1 from First Year of Life and no. 1.10 from *Myles Textbook for Midwives*.

Affectionately dedicated to
Amrit, our parents and children

CONTENTS

ACKNOWLEDGMENTS

I owe the publication of this book to my parents and my wife, Amrit, who gave me the inspiration and strength to undertake this venture. This endeavour has received immeasurable support from our children, their wives and our other family members. This book could not have been what it is without them.

I am indebted to Dr. H. C. Goyal, Dr. Suvira, Mrs. S. Mathur and several other colleagues for their valuable suggestions. Some illustrations in this book carry the imprint of ideas derived from different sources and the same are gratefully acknowledged with sincere apologies for any inadvertent omission in giving individual credit. I am particularly grateful to the publishers for their excellent cooperation and special interest in this volume.

INTRODUCTION

For all intelligent and caring parents and parents-to-be, having a child is not only exciting and enjoyable but also means a big responsibility. Children are dependent on parents for their sustenance and the quality of care given to them in childhood has a profound influence on their physical, emotional and intellectual development. Few parents, however, possess adequate knowledge about the appropriate manner in which children should be taken care of. It is not uncommon for a child's health, growth or learning problems to remain unnoticed by parents till it assumes major proportions. Many children suffer from avoidable nutritional deficiencies, physical ailments and inappropriate development due to inadequate care by uninformed parents. On the other hand, some overanxious parents suffer from constant, unwarranted worry about their child's health, even when he is healthy and growing normally.

It is not enough for parents to merely depend on the professional medical attention as and when the child appears to be obviously ill. Children require well-informed vigil and appropriate day-to-day care. The absence of grandparents and their advice in modern nuclear families has added to the problems of parenting.

Parents are often faced with unexpected and baffling situations such as, the baby crying in the middle of the night for no apparent reason, refusing feeds or having a sudden bout of vomiting. They may sometimes be required to deal with an acute medical emergency at home at an odd hour, such as a sudden high fever, fits or an accidental injury. The quality and promptness of immediate care given by them in such emergency situations may be crucial in preventing a major crisis or in determining the final outcome of the child's subsequent treatment by medical experts.

This book provides very useful knowledge to parents about the steps to be taken before and during pregnancy to help them have a healthy, normal baby. It informs about the process of conception and the baby's development in the mother's womb. It will further take you along on an exciting, happy journey of discovery, stage by stage, from the time of a child's birth to early adulthood.

As an everyday companion guide, it will provide answers to your child's day-to-day as well as emergency problems, ranging from the minor to the more serious ones. Special attention has been paid to problems encountered particularly by parents in the Indian subcontinent. It will help you to detect the onset of an illness or an abnormal deviation in your child's development at an early stage. Author seeks the reader's indulgence for the 'child' being referred to in this book as 'he' and not as 'he/she' for the sake of readability.

The book will enhance both your joy in rearing your children and add to your confidence in giving them quality care. It is also hoped that besides parents and parents-to-be, for whom it is primarily meant, this book will also serve as a useful guide to students, teachers and practitioners of child health and nutrition, home science and child psychology and development.

1

FOR A HEALTHY START TO A NEW LIFE

UNDERSTANDING YOUR BODY

Every prospective mother is excited at the idea of giving birth to a baby of her own. This feeling is, however, often tinged with fears and doubts about her own ability to go through the hardships of pregnancy and labour. She is also sometimes, apprehensive about the possibility of her baby having some abnormality at birth.

To overcome such distressing anxieties it is desirable that, as a first step, she should possess some basic knowledge of the processes involved in getting pregnant, the changes that occur during pregnancy, the way a baby develops in the womb and the process of childbirth.

A woman's body has a womb (uterus) which lies midline in the lower part of the abdomen (pelvis) (Fig.1.1).

Two egg tubes (Fallopian tubes) are attached to the upper part of the uterus, one on the right, and the other on its left side. There are two ovaries, the right ovary and the left. The right ovary is placed close to the open, free end of the right egg tube and the left one, close to the free end of the left egg tube. Each walnut-sized ovary contains millions of unripe eggs (ova).

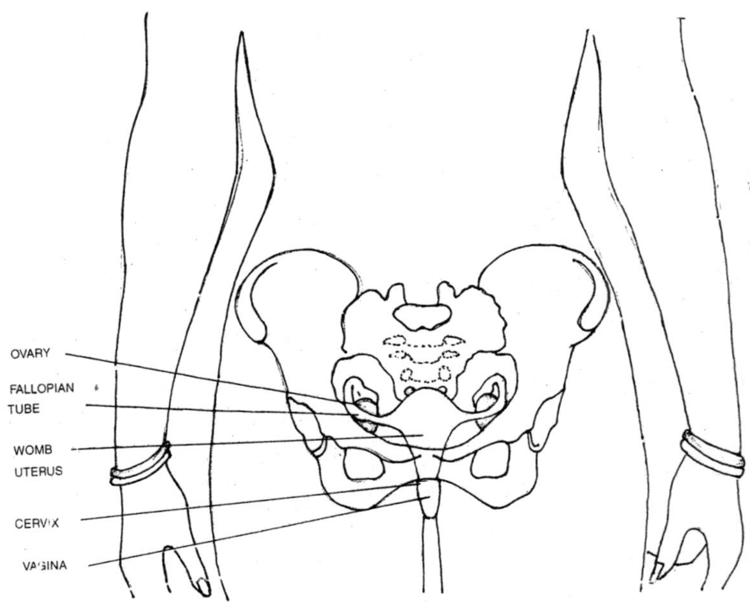

(Fig. 1.1)

Every month just one egg ripens and is released from one of the two ovaries (Fig.1.2). After discharge, the ripe egg soon finds its way into the egg tube whose open end is lying close to it. It then starts travelling through the tube towards the womb to meet the male sperm which may be coming towards it from the vagina (Fig.1.3). Millions of sperms contained in the semen are lodged by the male in the vagina during sexual intercourse. The pear-sized uterus with thick muscular walls, is highly expandable to enable it to accommodate the growing baby. Its inner lining, which is soft and rich in blood supply, undergoes great changes during each menstrual cycle. A narrow neck (cervix) connects the uterus at its lower end with the vagina. The vagina is about 10 cm (4 inches) long and its outer opening lies slightly below the external opening of the urinary passage. It is very elastic, so as to permit the passage of the baby during labour.

THE NORMAL MENSTRUAL CYCLE

Once a month, when a ripe ovum (egg) is released from an ovary, the inner lining of the uterus prepares itself for nesting (implantation) of the fertilized ovum by becoming thicker and richer in blood supply. This preparation is done in the expectation that the ovum will get fertilized by the male sperm (Fig. 1.4). If fertilization of the ovum (i.e., penetration of ovum by the sperm and their union) does not occur, the ovum dies. The prepared thickened lining of the womb is then shed (cast off) resulting in bleeding, which appears as the monthly period (Fig. 1.5). The same cycle of changes are repeated every month till pregnancy occurs or menopause ensues. All these changes occur under the influence of various body hormones.

Menstrual cycles ranging between 21 and 36 days are quite normal. While the cycles are fairly regular in most women, for some these are relatively irregular.

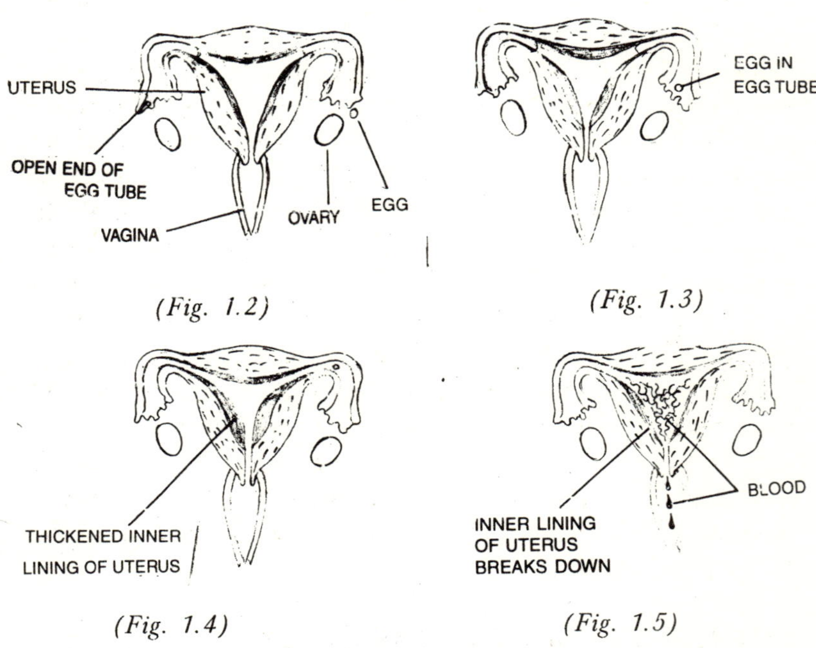

(Fig. 1.2) *(Fig. 1.3)*

(Fig. 1.4) *(Fig. 1.5)*

WHEN ARE THE CHANCES OF BECOMING PREGNANT HIGHEST?

The actual time of release of the ovum from the ovary (ovulation) and timing of sexual intercourse are vital from the point of view of the chances of becoming pregnant. This is so because of the short lives of the ovum and the male sperm. The egg lives for only 18-24 hours. The sperms remain active for about 36 hours, but they take about 6 hours to travel from the vagina to the Fallopian tube, where they try to penetrate and fertilize the ovum. The chances of the sperm meeting the ovum and subsequent occurrence of conception are therefore best when sexual intercourse takes place on the day before ovulation. In this situation, the sperm would have reached and be waiting in the egg tube as the ovum is released from the ovary and enters the tube.

In practice, however, it is extremely difficult to predict the actual time of the release of the ovum. Its timing after the beginning of any menstrual period is very variable. To help find it, the doctor may advise maintaining a daily temperature chart. While the daily morning 'resting' body temperature remains more or less steady during the earlier part of the menstrual cycle, it suddenly rises by about 0.5°C (1°F) at or just around the time of ovulation. Subsequently, the body temperature continues to stay at a higher level till the beginning of the next cycle.

CONCEPTION: BEGINNING OF LIFE

The number of sperms ejaculated by the male in his semen into the vagina during one sexual intercourse varies between 100 million to 300 million. While some leak out of the vagina, others try to swim up through the cervix into the uterus and then into the Fallopian tubes. Although so many of them try, only one sperm may succeed in penetrating the egg and fertilizing it. When this occurs, conception is said to have taken place and it means the beginning of pregnancy (Fig. 1.6).

(Fig. 1.6)

AM I PREGNANT?

MISSED PERIOD

The first and most reliable sign for women who have a regular monthly cycle, is a missed period. It is however, not until 10 days or more after the time of the expected onset of the menstrual period that the absence of menses is an indication of pregnancy. But if a woman who has routinely very irregular periods develops such a delay, one has to be cautious and watch over a longer period before interpreting it as a sign of pregnancy. The menstrual cycles may also, sometimes, become temporarily erratic in a woman (who generally has regular cycles) on account of illness or undue mental stress.

HOW TO BE SURE

In the very early stages of pregnancy, the doctor is not able to detect it through a physical examination, as the recognizable physical changes appear later. He needs to perform a pregnancy test on a sample of the woman's urine.

THE PREGNANCY TEST

This test is generally performed six weeks after the first day of the last menstrual period. A sample of urine passed first thing in the morning is tested for the presence of the HcG hormone. The HcG hormone is produced by the placenta during pregnancy and its presence in the urine indicates pregnancy.

A positive pregnancy test is almost always correct (98 times out of 100) in diagnosing presence of pregnancy. One cannot, however, be absolutely sure about the absence of pregnancy if the result is negative. If negative, the test must be repeated after one week. More sophisticated diagnostic tests have now become available which allow earlier confirmation of pregnancy, much before the expiry of six weeks.

OTHER SYMPTOMS AND FEATURES OF PREGNANCY

Later, certain symptoms and features of pregnancy appear due to hormonal changes and increase in the size of the womb. These are:

1. Breast changes
   (i) swelling of the breasts;
   (ii) tingling, throbbing or even a hurting sensation in the breasts;
   (iii) prominence of veins on the surface of the breasts;
   (iv) increase in the size of nipples and the surrounding area.

Simultaneously, there is darkening of colour, in both nipples and the areolar region.

2. Morning sickness: nausea, with or without vomiting, especially in the morning.
3. Passing urine more frequently, especially at night.
4. Constipation.
5. Changes in taste. Developing a distaste for some foods like tea, coffee, etc., and a craving for things like tamarind (*imli*), clay, chalk, etc.
6. Changes in feelings. Some women may feel depressed or anxious, or may feel like crying for no particular reason.

HOW DOES THE BABY DEVELOP?

The baby starts life as a minute fertilized egg which is invisible to the human eye. Soon after fertilization, it starts dividing and subdividing rapidly into 2,4,8,16 parts and so on. It develops into a solid ball of cells by the third day (Fig.1.7) and undergoes further changes as it moves slowly through the Fallopian tube to the uterus. It embeds itself in the inner lining of the uterus by the 7th day and soon becomes the embryo (Fig.1.8). The outer layer of the embryo subsequently forms the placenta, while the inner layer will form the baby (Fig.1.9). Within 6 weeks the embryo assumes the general form of a miniature human being, about 1.25 cm (½ inch) in length. It is amazing but true that the basic structures of the heart, brain, lungs, limbs and most other organs are already formed and the heart is beating in a 6-week-old, mere 4 cm (1½ inch) long embryo. From 8 weeks onward, the developing baby is called a foetus (meaning 'young one'). Just 12 weeks after conception, the foetus has all its organs, muscles, limbs and bones. Although only 8 cm (3 inches) long, it can kick, turn its head and swallow amniotic fluid (Fig.1.10). From then on, it mainly grows in size and matures in its functional capacities. At 14 weeks, the baby's heartbeat is strong enough to be picked

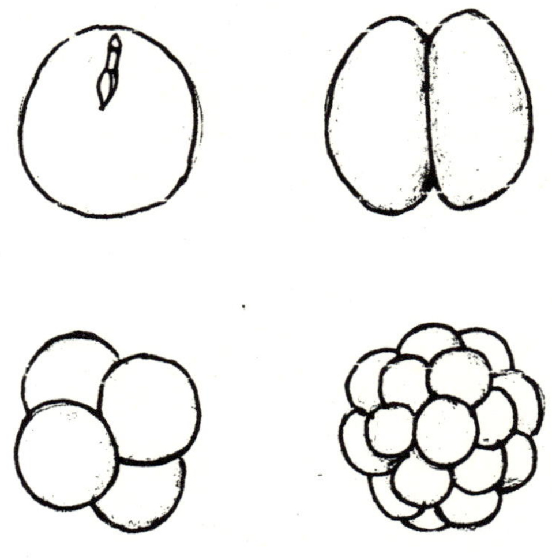

(Fig. 1.7)

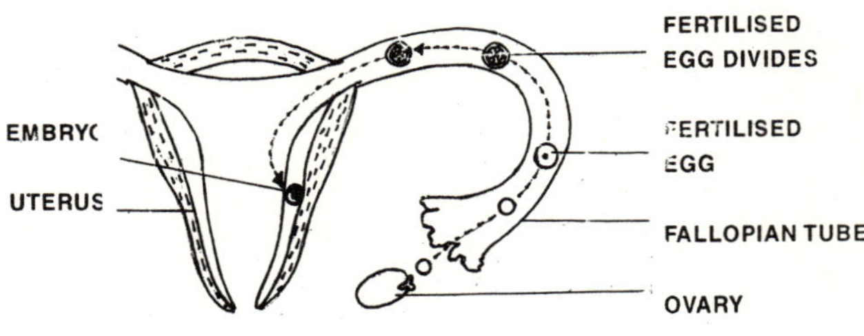

(Fig. 1.8)

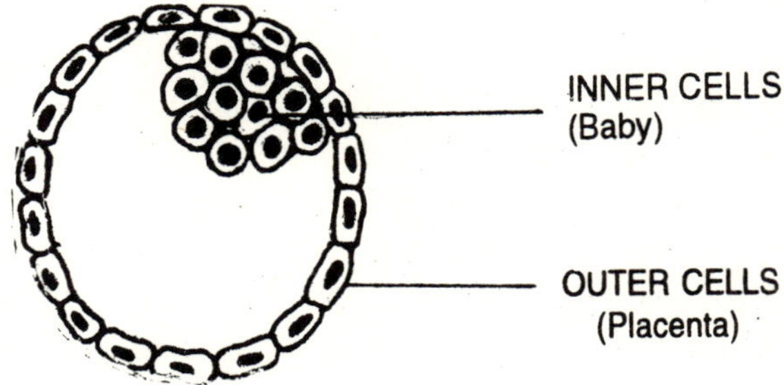

(Fig. 1.9)

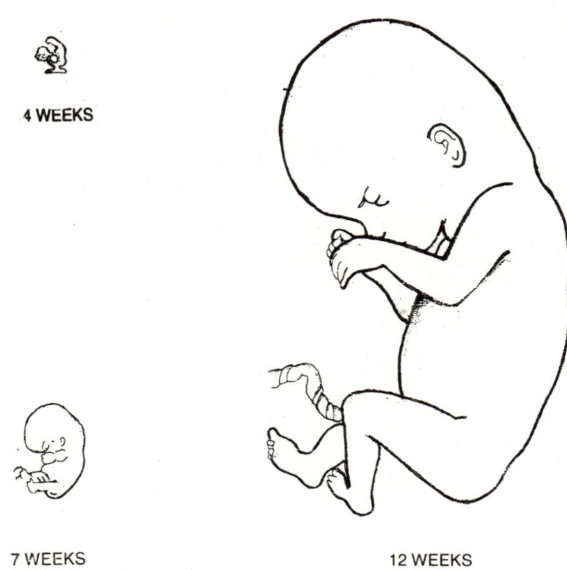

(Fig. 1.10)

up with the help of an ultrasound machine. The mother may now just begin to look pregnant to outsiders.

In the second trimester (2nd three-month period) of pregnancy, the baby grows fast. The mother usually first feels the baby's movements inside her womb at around 18 weeks. At 28 weeks of pregnancy the foetus weighs 1kg and is considered viable. This means that the baby is now considered to have a chance of survival, if born. During the last 3 months of pregnancy, he grows significantly bigger particularly the size of his brain. At around 40 weeks, the baby moves into position in the pelvis ready for delivery. He is now about 50 cm (20 inches) long and weighs 3 kg (Fig. 1.11).

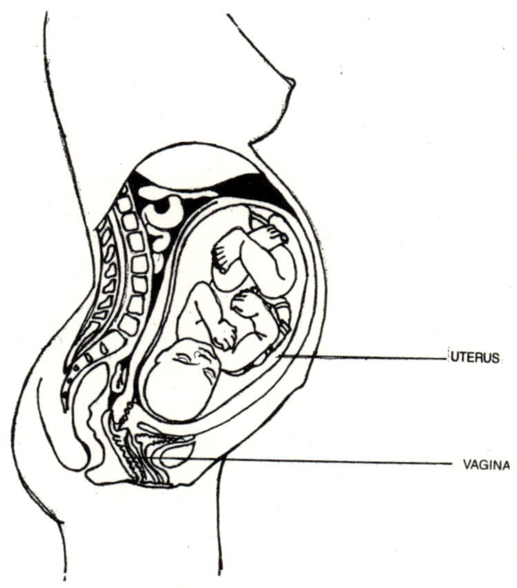

(Fig. 1.11)

MEDICAL CHECKUPS DURING PREGNANCY

It is necessary for the mother to have regular checkups during pregnancy to make sure that she and her baby are healthy, that the baby is developing properly and to prevent any complications during pregnancy, childbirth and soon thereafter.

THE FIRST CHECKUP

HOW SOON SHOULD I GET IT DONE?

You should consult your doctor as soon as you suspect that you are pregnant. Firstly, the pregnancy would need to be confirmed. Secondly, you would need special advice at this critical stage of your baby's development in the womb with regard to your intake of medicines, exposure to X-rays and some viral diseases which can cause serious birth defects in your baby. Thirdly, you should be carefully examined and get certain essential laboratory tests done.

PHYSICAL EXAMINATION

The doctor will check your heart, lungs and other body systems to ensure that you are physically fit. Your blood pressure and body weight will be checked and the doctor will look for any swelling around your ankles and over your fingers to exclude high blood pressure and kidney disease. Special examinations will also be conducted to assess the progress of your baby's growth (by measuring the height of your uterus) and the presentation and position of your baby.

LABORATORY TESTS

The following tests are generally performed as a part of routine medical checkups:

I. **Urine tests:** Routine and microscopic examination.

II. **Blood tests:**

(i) Haemoglobin estimation (Hb)
(ii) Blood grouping (A,B,O or AB)
(iii) Rh typing (Rh + ve or Rh – ve)
(iv) Blood sugar
(v) Serologic test for syphilis (STS)

III. **Other blood tests:**

The following tests are also now considered important as the concerned diseases are becoming increasingly significant:

(i) Blood test for Hepatitis B
(ii) Blood test for immunity against rubella (German measles)
(iii) Blood test for HIV (if you have been at risk for AIDS)

Urine tests

(a) Sugar. Urine is examined for the presence of sugar. If present, your blood sugar estimation would first be done on empty stomach and again 2 hours after you have taken a measured amount of glucose (generally 75 g) by mouth. While mild diabetes may respond to a change in diet, you may need insulin injections for severe diabetes.

(b) Protein/albumin. This is chiefly done to exclude a somewhat serious condition known as 'pregnancy-induced hypertension' (also called 'toxaemia of pregnancy'). A small amount of albumin is also detected in patients with urinary infection.
(c) Microscopic examination. The first morning specimen of urine is examined for the presence of pus cells to exclude infection in the urinary tract.

Blood tests
(i) Haemoglobin (Hb). A haemoglobin level below 10 g/dl in pregnant women (and below 12 g/dl in non-pregnant women) indicates anaemia. If you are found to be anaemic, you would be investigated for the cause of anaemia and treated accordingly.

(ii) Blood grouping (A,B,AB,O). The doctors need to know and keep a record of your blood group as it is required for arranging suitable blood transfusion for you, if needed.

(iii) Whether Rh positive or negative. In India, about 85 % individuals possess the Rh factor in their blood, and they are termed as being Rh positive. If you do not have the Rh factor (i.e., you are Rh negative), there is a risk of your baby developing 'haemolytic disease of the newborn' soon after birth. This disease may manifest itself as severe jaundice and anaemia. To prevent this disease in the baby, an intramuscular injection of anti-Rh(D) globulin would be given to you within 72 hours of delivery or abortion.

Strict precautions are also taken to ensure that Rh negative women in the child bearing age-group are given only Rh negative blood transfusion, if and when needed.

(iv) Blood test for syphilis (STS). The detection of

syphilis in the mother (if present) at an early stage and its effective treatment will help prevent the baby from getting infected by this bad disease. Syphilis can be extremely damaging to a baby's vital organs like the heart, brain, bones, eyes, etc.

(v) Blood test for Hepatitis B. Hepatitis B infection in the mother can get transmitted to the baby in the womb. The baby may subsequently suffer from chronic liver damage. If this viral infection is detected in a pregnant mother, prophylactic treatment of her newborn baby is started soon after his birth to protect him against acquiring this disease. (For details, see under Immunization.)

(vi) HIV blood test. If you think that you may have been at risk of getting AIDS, seek your doctor's advice in confidence, who will help you.

(vii) Test for immunity to German measles (rubella). This blood test will show whether you have already become immune due to the rubella vaccine given to you in early childhood or because of your having suffered from rubella earlier. If found immune nothing needs to be done. But if you are not immune you would need to be watched, especially during the first four months of your pregnancy, to look for possible occurrence of this infection. You cannot however, be given the rubella vaccine for your protection at this stage because it is not safe during pregnancy.

FOLLOW-UP MEDICAL VISITS

It is recommended that you should see your doctor every month till 28 weeks of pregnancy, every 2 weeks between 28 and 36 weeks and then every week from 36 weeks onwards. These visits are required to maintain a regular check on the well-being and growth of your baby and your own medical fitness. Your blood pressure, heart condition, and urinary status are kept under regular supervision for early detection of any complications. If not detected and controlled in time they can seriously harm your baby and become life threatening for you, too.

It is also important that your weight gain during pregnancy is appropriate. Normally, you should have a total weight gain of about 1 kg. over the first three-month period, and then 1.7 kg. every month during the next six months. Your aggregate gain during the whole pregnancy should be around 11 kg. Excessive weight gain may mean that you are accumulating excess fluids, which would need to be carefully looked into by your doctor. You may also be getting unduly fat due to inappropriate eating and poor physical activity. Less than the expected gain in the mother's body weight may mean inadequate growth of the baby in the womb, besides your own malnutrition. The doctor would then arrange suitable investigations to check it up.

CAN I LOSE MY PREGNANCY?

When a pregnant mother happens to spontaneously lose her baby during pregnancy, in lay terms it is called a 'miscarriage'. On the other hand, when a pregnancy is terminated by medical personnel (say, for purposes of family planning), it is deemed to be an 'abortion'. However, in medical terms, whether a pregnancy ends spontaneously or it is terminated by a doctor before the foetus is sufficiently developed to survive, if born – both are termed as abortion. Formerly, babies born before 28 weeks of pregnancy were not considered viable. But with the availability of higher levels of specialized care for premature babies in USA and some other developed countries, babies born there at 20 weeks of pregnancy are now considered to be viable.

An overwhelming majority of pregnancies develop normally but occasionally things can go wrong, especially during the early weeks. The commonest cause of miscarriage during the first 12 weeks is the death of a grossly abnormal embryo. This is nature's mechanism of avoiding the birth of seriously defective babies.

WHAT SHOULD I DO?

While there is no cause for you to worry unnecessarily, you should take the following precautions:

1. If you notice even a slight spotting during your pregnancy, you should immediately take bed rest and seek advice from your doctor. In early pregnancy, bleeding may sometimes be due to a miscarriage or an ectopic pregnancy (where the baby begins to grow in the egg tube and not in the uterus). But many women who bleed at this stage stop doing so after a while and subsequently complete their pregnancy and have a healthy baby. You should however, not take any chances, particularly if the bleeding is accompanied by pain in the abdomen or backache.
2. You should take suitable medical treatment for any infectious illness, particularly during early pregnancy.
3. Avoid smoking and drinking because they are known to enhance the risk of miscarriage. The increase in risk is in direct proportion to the number of cigarettes smoked and the frequency and amount of alcohol consumed.
4. If you are diabetic, you must keep it well under control, especially during the first month after conception.
5. The risks of miscarriage are higher in a woman who has had trouble in becoming pregnant, in pregnant women who are over 35 years of age and in those who had two miscarriages earlier. You should be extra careful if you fall into any one of these categories. In such circumstances, it is advisable to avoid undue jerks during travelling and to limit sexual activity. Sometimes, miscarriages are caused

by hormonal disturbance. Hormones, and bed rest are then recommended. In a few cases, a weak cervix is responsible for recurrent miscarriages at around 20 weeks and this may need some corrective surgical measures.

SEX DURING PREGNANCY

You should not harbour any undue fears that sexual intercourse in pregnancy may harm your baby. It is safe and normal to continue to have sex during this period. However, towards the end of pregnancy when the abdomen is large, the common man-on-top position may be rather inconvenient and some different mutually convenient positions may be adopted.

But, if you have had a previous miscarriage, you should avoid intercourse in the early months. If any bleeding is seen at any stage, you should abstain and seek medical advice. Similarly, in a case where the process of delivery (labour) starts in a mother prematurely and it is successfully controlled by the doctor, couples should avoid having sex.

WHEN IS MY BABY DUE ?

The average duration of pregnancy is 280 days (40 weeks) from the first day of the last menstrual period. It can, however, vary between 37 and 42 weeks. You can work out when your baby is due by calculating 280 days from the beginning of your last period. The following simple formula makes this task easier. Add 7 days to the date when your last period began. Then count back 3 months. This will give you the expected date of delivery. For example, if your last period began on 16th July, add 7 days to 16, which gives you 23. Count back 3 months from July–June, May, April. Thus your baby would be born on 23rd April next year. However, considering the normal variation in the duration of pregnancy, your baby may be born any time within 2 weeks on either side of 23rd April, i.e., between 9th April and 7th May. If you are not sure about the date of your last period, an ultrasound scan of your abdomen would help establish your baby's present approximate intrauterine age. The expected date of delivery can then be worked out.

BOY OR GIRL?

WHO DECIDES?

In most Indian homes, it is still wrongly believed that it is the female who is responsible when she gives birth to a girl. Actually, it is the character of the sperm of the male which fertilizes the ovum, that decides whether the baby is going to be a male or a female. All female eggs contain only one kind of sex chromosome – the 'X' sex chromosome. On the other hand, there are two types of male sperms. One type of male sperm has the 'Y' sex chromosome and the second type has the 'X' sex chromosome. When a male sperm containing 'Y' sex chromosome unites with an egg having 'X' sex chromosome, the resultant baby embryo would have 'XY' sex chromosomes and it would develop into a male. If, on the other hand, a male sperm containing 'X' sex chromosome fertilizes the egg (which always contains 'X' chromosomes), a female baby with 'XX' sex chromosomes would be born.

CAN I CHOOSE?

Although innumerable magic potions and supposedly very clever methods have been handed out to overanxious parents, mostly to ensure the birth of a male baby (and occasionally a girl), nothing has yet been found to succeed. You must avoid falling prey to any such unscientific and unprincipled procedures. In fact, some of them may even harm you or your baby.

WILL MY BABY BE NORMAL?

You need not be unduly worried about your baby being abnormal since the chances of that happening are, in general, extremely low (2.5 %). Further, in about 1/3rd of such cases the abnormalities can be partly or completely corrected. Some important abnormalities can also now be detected at an early stage of pregnancy by special techniques like the amniocentesis, ultrasound, chorionic villus biopsy and foetal blood examination. Where the baby's defect is considered to be of a serious nature (e.g., mongolism, thalassemia), the mother is offered the option of terminating her pregnancy by undergoing abortion.

AVOIDING BIRTH OF AN ABNORMAL BABY

PRE-PREGNANCY CONSULTATION AND CHECKUP

Ideally, every prospective mother should consult her doctor before becoming pregnant. But you must surely do it, if the following circumstances exist in your case:

1. A close family member has an abnormal baby at birth or where the baby has developed evidence of an inherited (genetic) disorder like thalassemia, haemophilia (both blood disorders) and muscular dystrophy later in life.
2. Your previous baby had an abnormality at birth (e.g., mongolism) or suffered from a genetic disorder later.
3. You or another member of your family is suffering from diabetes.
4. If you are suffering from epilepsy, high blood pressure, kidney disease, thyroid disorder, tuberculosis, syphilis or any other long-standing disease or are receiving some long-term drug treatment.

If there is a family history of mongolism,

thalassemia, or other genetic disorders on your side or that of your husband, your doctor will refer you to an expert in hereditary diseases (geneticist) for detailed checks. After thorough assessment, he will discuss with you and your husband the degree of risk of your baby being abnormal. This will enable you to take an enlightened, well-considered decision about becoming pregnant. In the event of your going ahead with the pregnancy, your obstetrician will arrange some appropriate special checks (like amniocentesis, ultrasound, chorionic villus biopsy and foetal blood examination) within the first few weeks for early detection of any abnormality in your baby.

Diabetic mothers carry a high risk of their babies being born with congenital defects. Because the developmental defects in the baby largely occur at a very early stage of the diabetic mother's pregnancy, it is important for her to ensure that her diabetes is well under control before she becomes pregnant.

High blood pressure, thyroid disorders, syphilis, epilepsy, tuberculosis and kidney disorders must also be adequately treated and kept under control, both before and during pregnancy. Safe drugs which are known to be harmless to the developing baby should be used.

Ideally, every mother should ensure that she is protected against German measles before becoming pregnant. If she develops this viral disease during the first four months of her pregnancy, the causative virus may go across the placenta and damage the baby's developing organs leading to birth abnormalities like heart defects, mental retardation and deafness. Immunization with rubella vaccine or MMR vaccine (which contains vaccines against rubella, measles and mumps) is therefore done in childhood to provide later protection against these potentially serious diseases. A simple blood test will show whether your body possesses an adequate level of protective antibodies. If you are not immune, you should take a dose of rubella vaccine to build up your immunity. In that case you would need to avoid pregnancy for a period of three months after you have received the vaccine to avoid any risks to your baby.

CARE DURING PREGNANCY

Avoid drugs

You should avoid taking any drugs during your pregnancy, especially during the first three months. If it becomes very essential, these may be taken as little as possible with the express permission of your doctor. Some drugs taken by you can go across the placenta to your baby and damage his developing organs, leading to various defects in his heart, brain, eyes, ears, etc. The drugs which are not considered safe for the pregnant mother include tetracycline and streptomycin (both antibiotics) and some of the drugs used for the treatment of diabetes, high blood pressure, epilepsy, thyroid disorders, hormonal disturbances and cancer. You must therefore, inform your doctor as soon as you suspect that you may be pregnant so as to avoid the possible use of any unsafe drug.

Regular antenatal checkup

You should have regular antenatal checkups during pregnancy so that diseases like high blood pressure, diabetes, syphilis, malnutrition and complications of pregnancy (e.g., toxaemia of pregnancy) can be detected and properly managed in time. If untreated, they can lead to various diseases, abnormalities, premature birth and low birth-weight in the newborn baby.

WHAT SHOULD I EAT?

It is not necessary for you to follow any special dietary regime during pregnancy. But you do need to take an adequate, well-balanced, varied diet consisting of food items belonging to each of the different food groups (explained below) so as to provide proper nutrition to you as well as to your baby. The diet should contain sufficient proteins, vitamins and minerals, chiefly folic acid calcium and iron. Calcium and vitamin D are required for the formation of the baby's bones and teeth and you are liable to develop anaemia in the absence of sufficient supplies of iron.

Deficiency of folic acid during the first 3 month of pregnancy is closely associated with the development of neural tube defects (defects in brain and spinal cord) in the baby. As such, daily intake of 400 ug of folic acid as tablets (singly or in combination with appropriate dose of iron, vitamins and minerals) is recommended.

You should continue to eat chapaties, rice, bread or cereals in any form in sufficient quantities. They chiefly provide energy, starch, dietary fibre and B vitamins.

The other food group consisting of *dals*, peas, beans, egg, fish meat and poultry is rich in proteins and your meals should contain good helpings of any of these food items.

Milk, yoghurt, cheese and milk products provide calcium, phosphorus and vitamin D beside proteins and vitamin A. If you do not relish taking milk, you may take it in any other more palatable form like ice cream, milk shake, *khoya*, or dessert made with milk.

You should eat plenty of fruits and vegetables. Oranges, *mosambi* and other citurs fruits are rich sources of vitamin C. Mangoes, papayas, carrots and other red and orange coloured fruits and vegetables provide a lot of vitamin A. Leafy green vegetables like spinach, cabbage and salads are excellent sources of iron, vitamins and minerals.

You should, however, cut down on your intake of sugar and sugary foods, such as, Indian sweets, biscuits, chocolates, jams, and sugary drinks. Intake of food preparations like *halwa, pinnies,* pastry, cakes, *paratha,* and fatty meats, which contain a lot of fat must also be reduced to avoid overweight and later risk of heart disease.

CAN I CONTINUE WITH SMOKING AND ALCOHOL?

Smoking cigarettes during pregnancy increases the chances of your baby being born with disproportionately low birth-weight. Low birth weight babies suffer from difficulty in breathing, feeding and combating infections and are liable to develop complications involving several vital systems. You should, therefore, stop smoking completely in the interest of your baby. It is also advisable that you should not expose yourself to tobacco smoke released by other smokers at home or at work.

Heavy daily drinking of alcohol by the mother throughout her pregnancy is now known to cause several serious birth defects in the baby like mental retardation, heart malformations, spine and limb defects and growth retardation. Less serious effects have been noticed with those who are not heavy drinkers. It may be safe to take a small drink once a week or so but no safe limit has yet been established scientifically. It would therefore be better to stop alcohol consumption completely during your pregnancy.

WHAT IS LABOUR?

Labour is a process by which the baby and his placenta are expelled from the mother's uterus. The onset of labour is indicated by the following signs:

1. Regular, frequent uterine contractions.
The mother begins to have uterine contractions frequently at regular intervals of 15 to 30 minutes. To begin with, these are mild and brief, lasting for half a minute or so. They progressively become more frequent, strong, and painful and last for a longer period.
2. The 'show'.
During pregnancy a protective plug of mucus blocks the cervix (the passage between the vagina and the uterus). At the onset of labour this mucus plug loosens and is discharged through the vagina

along with a small amount of blood. This phenomenon, called the 'show' indicates the onset of labour.
3. Breaking of the 'water bag'.
When the cervix dilates at the beginning of labour, the water bag (amniotic sac) surrounding the baby in the womb comes down and the bulge can be felt by the doctor or the nurse. When it breaks, there is a sudden gush of watery fluid or a slow trickle down the vagina.

When the onset of labour has got established, it is advisable for you to go to the hospital or make arrangements for delivery at home as per plans finalized earlier in consultation with your doctor.

WHAT HAPPENS IN LABOUR?

The process occurs in three stages. The first stage is the stage of preparation, one prior to the actual process of birth (Fig. 1.12). During this phase, the mother gets regular uterine contractions every 3 to 5 minutes and the lower portion of the uterus and the cervix dilate so as to allow subsequent easy passage of the foetus during the delivery. The duration of the first stage generally varies between 8 and 16 hours in mothers who are having their first baby and between 4 and 8 hours during subsequent pregnancies.

During the second stage, strong uterine contractions, aided by the mother's own 'bearing down' efforts bring expulsion of the baby (Fig. 1.13). In cases with head presentation (baby's head lying lowermost in the uterus opposite the opening of the birth canal) the baby's head is the first part of his body to appear and emerge out of the vagina as labour progresses. To avoid ragged perineal tears and damage to the mother during delivery, the doctor may sometimes find it necessary to make a small cut in the perineum, which is medically termed as episiotomy. This cut is later stitched and it heals quite well subsequently. After delivery, the baby's cord is clamped and cut. Mucus is sucked out of the baby's nose and mouth, his body dried and he is wrapped in a towel or blanket. The second stage lasts 1 to 2 hours in the case of the first baby; in subsequent deliveries it is shorter and may be as little as 10 to 15 minutes.

The third stage of labour is the stage of afterbirth, when the placenta and the membranes are expelled sometime after delivery of the baby. This may take about 20 minutes. If delayed, the process is speeded up with the help of suitable drugs.

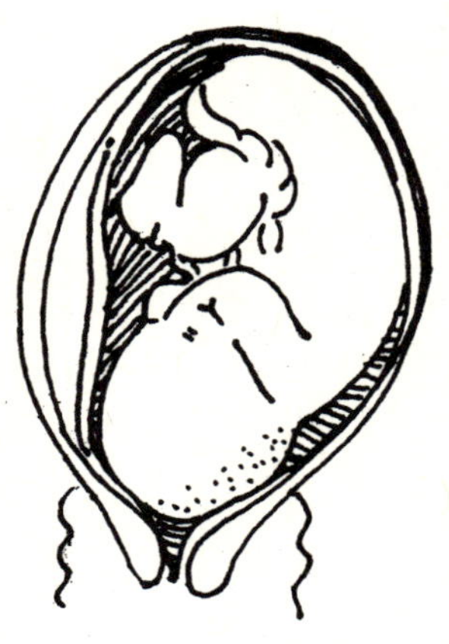

BEFORE START OF LABOUR

(Fig. 1.12)

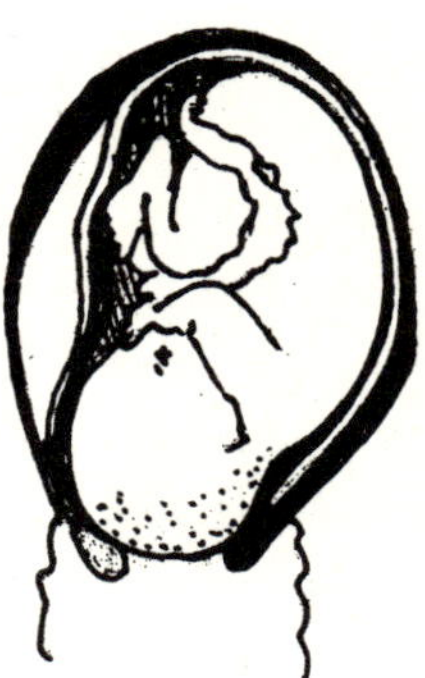

FIRST STAGE OF LABOUR

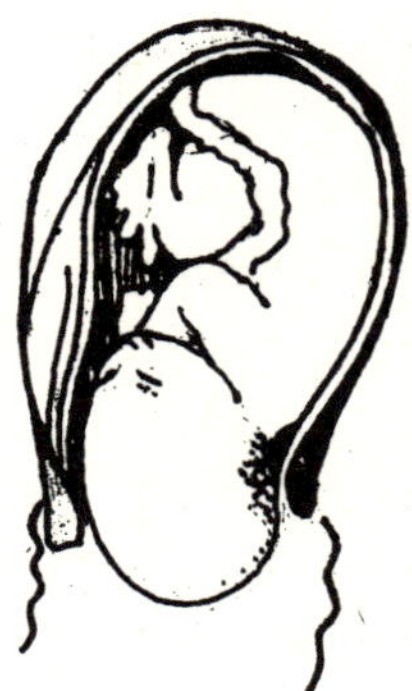

SECOND STAGE OF LABOUR

(Fig. 1.13)

DELIVERY: NORMAL, FORCEPS OR CAESAREAN

During normal labour, the forceful contractions of the mother's uterus push the baby through her passage and deliver him out of the vagina without any external aid. But if the contractions are not strong enough, or the baby gets stuck in a difficult position or if he starts showing signs of distress, the baby is delivered by forceps or vacuum extraction.

Both these techniques are quite safe. The blades of the forceps or the rubber cups of the vacuum extractor are applied to the baby's head and the baby is gently pulled out by the use of well-controlled, firm force. After birth the baby may show marks at the site of forceps or vacuum extractor application for a few days after which they fade away.

BREECH DELIVERY

Generally the baby is delivered with his head first. This is so because the head is the largest part of the baby's body and as it keeps passing through the birth passage during labour, the rest of the body follows comfortably.

Sometimes near the expected time of delivery, the baby assumes breech position, i.e., his bottom (not the head) presents towards the lower opening of the uterus. The doctors try to 'turn' the baby in the womb before labour begins so that the head becomes lower-most but these efforts may not always succeed.

There is, however, no cause for anxiety in expert hands. A large number of babies are born in this manner and are perfectly normal and healthy.

CAESAREAN DELIVERY

WHAT IS IT? IS IT GOOD OR BAD?

When delivering the baby in the normal manner can be harmful to your baby or to you, the doctor may decide delivering your baby through Caesarean operation. In this case, a cut is made in your lower abdominal wall and your womb and the baby is taken out. The cut parts are stitched back into their earlier position.

You should not feel unduly upset if you are told either in advance (because of your having an unduly small passage for safe normal delivery) or at the very last moment that you must have a Caesarean. If the progress of labour is unsatisfactory and the baby starts showing signs of lack of oxygen supply (foetal distress), which can be critically damaging for the baby, emergency Caesarean has to be done. Sometimes it may have to be done in the interest of the mother, when her health status is poor on account of high blood pressure or other complications.

This operation is done primarily in your interest and that of your baby. It has saved a large number of babies from death or serious damage during a difficult delivery. In Britain about one in every ten babies and in USA one in every six babies are born by Caesarean operation. You should therefore, not be unduly anxious and leave the decision to the good judgement of your doctor.

AFTER THE OPERATION?

The stitches or the metal clips used to stitch together the cut edges of your skin wound are taken out between five and eight days after the operation. The wound may be painful for a few days and you may be given pain relieving drugs for one to two days. The doctor will advise you about the amount of rest to be taken at home and about the postnatal exercises that you must do to get your muscles back in shape.

ONCE A CAESAREAN, ALWAYS A CAESAREAN?

Not necessarily. While the chances of repeat Caesarean after one operation are relatively high, the doctor would judge the need for Caesarean in each subsequent pregnancy on its own merit. Many women have normal vaginal delivery subsequent to an earlier Caesarean. On the other hand, some women have three or more Caesareans without any difficulty.

SPECIAL TESTS: WHY AND WHEN?

ULTRASOUND SCAN EXAMINATION

In this test, sound waves are used to create pictures of the baby (and his various parts) in the mother's womb. No X-rays are involved and it is quite safe and painless. It is usually done at about 16-20 weeks of pregnancy and thereafter as and when necessary. This test is employed chiefly for the following purposes:

(i) To check the baby's age and the process of his growth from time to time.

(ii) To exclude twin pregnancy.

(iii) To look for some important abnormalities, like absence of brain development (anencephaly), large head (hydrocephalus), defects of the spine and major heart defects. In some incurable conditions like anencephaly, termination of pregnancy is recommended.

AMNIOCENTESIS

During the test some amniotic fluid is withdrawn from the amniotic sac (water bag) surrounding the baby inside the mother's womb. It is done with the help of ultrasound scan at a few well developed medical centres. It is usually conducted around 16 weeks of pregnancy.

Chromosome analysis, chemical and other examinations performed on this fluid help in early detection of mongolism (a type of mental deficiency), spina bifida (a defect of the spine and the spinal cord) and some other important inherited diseases. Early recognition of the presence or absence of these diseases in the foetus enable the mother and the doctor to decide on the continuation or termination of pregnancy. This test is specially important if the mother or her family has a past history of genetic disorders.

TESTS FOR THALASSEMIA AND SICKLE-CELL ANAEMIA

Thalassemia in children is a form of hereditary anaemia. It is an extremely disturbing lifelong problem, requiring blood transfusions almost every month and constant daily care. Either you or your husband can be a thalassemia trait carrier without having any significant symptoms and without your knowing about its existence. But if both of you are carriers, there is a 25% chance in each pregnancy that your baby may suffer from full-fledged thalassemia with all its problems and complications.

It is, therefore, particularly important that if any of your or your husband's close relatives suffer from thalassemia or if either one of you is known to be a carrier or a patient of this disease, discuss the matter at once with your doctor who will advise you to consult an expert in hereditary inherited disorders (geneticist) at a major medical centre at around 8-9 weeks of pregnancy. The geneticist will arrange specialized tests both for you and your baby in the womb. These tests will help determine whether your unborn baby has thalassemia major or not.

Different types of tests may be performed. Chorionic villus sampling (CVS) is done by an obstetrician at 9-12 weeks of pregnancy and the villus tissue is subjected to DNA studies by the geneticist. Alternatively, foetal blood samples may be taken around 18 weeks of pregnancy and analysed. The diagnosis made by these techniques is accurate. If the unborn baby is found to be having thalassemia, you can take a decision regarding termination of pregnancy, which can be done safely at this stage.

A list of some well developed centres where the aforementioned genetic studies can be carried out is placed at appendix 8.

2

UNDERSTANDING YOUR NEWBORN BABY

Every mother is keen that her baby should remain healthy and that he should attain excellent growth and development, both physical and intellectual. But as you begin to look after him, you often feel diffident about the best way to handle him. The expert professional advice of a doctor is not always readily available and you seem to need it ever so often, practically everyday. You do not know what to do when your baby refuses to take his scheduled feeds or suddenly starts crying inconsolably in the evening or throws up in the middle of the night.

The so-called counsel of 'experience' offered by the illiterate old *ayah* (nursemaid), the ever obliging neighbours or the grand old lady of the house is unreliable and can be misleading. Hence it is necessary that you must yourself know some basic facts about the physical make up and body functioning of your baby and the common problems which you are likely to encounter in his day-to-day care. It will help you to look after your baby better and with greater confidence.

Prior to his birth, your baby was living in a highly protected environment inside your womb. He was deriving his essential supplies of oxygen and nutrients directly from you through the placenta and he was also disposing off the waste products of his own body through the same route.

Now, he is on his own and is breathing by himself. His lungs are performing the function of oxygenation of his blood. He would be taking and digesting his own feeds, and excreting his body waste products through his urine and stools. Despite his tiny and frail looking body, he is capable of performing all these important functions and much more.

In India, the birth weight of a full-term newborn baby ranges between 2.5kg and 3.5kg with an average of 3kg. His average length is 50 cm (20 inches) and he has a head circumference of 35 cm (14 inches).

SOME ODD FEATURES AND MINOR PROBLEMS

You may notice certain odd features in your newborn baby, which, though minor in nature, may cause you unnecessary alarm and anxiety.

1. THE HEAD

(I) THE SOFT SPOT

A diamond shaped soft area felt on top of the baby's head (medically termed fontanelle) may be wrongly assumed to be a birth defect (Fig. 2.1). It may even be seen to bulge when the baby cries lustily. There is however, no reason to worry. In this area the neighbouring skull bones have not united with each other before birth. This happens so as to allow moulding of the baby's head as it passes through the rather narrow birth canal at the time of delivery. Although soft to the touch, it is not a weak spot liable to injury, because below its skin there lies a tough membrane which fully protects the brain. This soft spot will gradually diminish in size and disappear between 1 and 1½

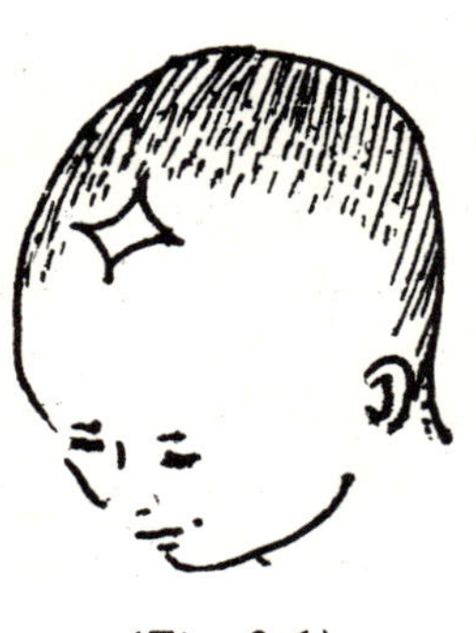

(Fig. 2.1)

years of age as the skull bones slowly get united.

(II) BUMPS, LUMPS AND BRUISES

Various types of bumps and lumps may be seen and felt on the head of a newborn baby for different reasons. A smooth, diffused, sometimes bluish, boggy swelling may be felt on a part of the head. This swelling (medically termed as caput) is the result of pressure on the baby's head during a difficult delivery as the baby is born with his head coming out first. It generally does not require any treatment and disappears in a few days. In babies delivered by forceps, reddish or bluish discolouration and bruises over the skin may be seen over the head or face at the site of application of forceps. These are also transient and subside in a few days.

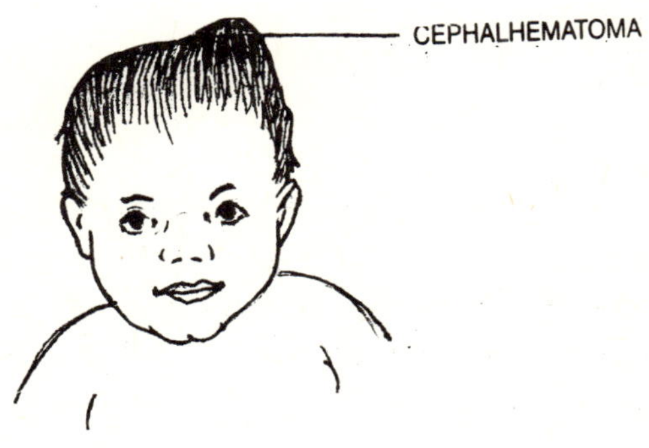

(Fig. 2.2)

In a few babies, a well-defined fairly large lump may be seen on one side of the head a few hours after birth. This occurs due to bleeding under the outer covering of one of the skull bones. In medical terms it is called cephalhematoma (Fig. 2.2). Although it may look alarming, it does not require any treatment and it gradually subsides over the next few weeks.

(III) THE 'CRADLE CAP'

Thick white or yellowish crusts and scales may be seen on the scalp which cannot be removed easily. This is a type of dandruff of the scalp. You should wash the baby's head regularly. If the rash persists or it spreads to the face, behind and inside the ears, neck, armpits or groin, you should consult your doctor. The rash responds quickly to local application of cortisone ointments but has a tendency to recur.

2. THE FACE

(I) 'MILIA'

Very often babies have 1-2 mm sized, pearly-white, raised spots scattered over the face, chiefly around the nose, chin and forehead. These lesions, called 'milia', are the result of blocked sebaceous glands. Do not try to squeeze them. They usually disappear without any treatment by the time the baby is one month old.

3. THE MOUTH

(I) SUCKING BLISTERS

A baby may have thick button-like, firm, whitish blisters over the centre of his upper lip. These are the result of the baby's sucking efforts while in the mother's womb. These gradually subside on their own.

(II) TONGUE-TIE

Many mothers get overconcerned if the baby does not stick his tongue out appreciably. Their anxiety about the baby having future problems with speech and difficulties in feeding are, however, misplaced and unwarranted. As the tongue grows with age, it does so predominantly in the front portion, with the result that it assumes a normal appearance later. The cord attached to the under surface of the tongue hardly ever needs to be cut. However, if the mother continues to be anxious about it, the doctor may be consulted.

(III) 'PEARLS'

You may notice a few little white, raised spots near the mid-line on the roof (palate) of the baby's mouth. These are harmless cysts, medically called the 'Epstein pearls' and may also sometimes be seen on the gums. No treatment is required.

4. THE EYES

(I) THE 'WET' EYE

Normally the tears which form in the eyes to prevent the eye surface from becoming dry keep flowing through a narrow duct into the nose. In about 2 % of babies there is an inborn narrowing or obstruction in the tear passage in one or both eyes. In such cases the eyes of a few days old baby look constantly wet or full of tears. In some there may be constant overflow of tears, or persistent collection of clear or yellowish, thick discharge. The skin around the eyelids may sometimes become red and cracked.

This condition is managed by doing light massage over the inner angle of the eye near its junction with the nose two to three times a day, taking care to avoid injuring the eyes. This is done with a view to assist in the natural process of gradual clearing up of the blocked passages. You may seek a doctor's advice regarding the correct massage procedure. The eyelids should be frequently cleaned with warm water, using a sterile cotton swab. Antibacterial eye drops may also be instilled in the eye as advised. In most cases, the problem settles down within a few months. If it persists, it may be necessary to open the blocked duct passage by syringing and probing.

It must, however, be borne in mind that another distinct eye disorder called conjunctivitis can occur in babies with normal eyes which causes pus discharge from the eyes and needs early treatment by a doctor.

(II) BLOOD STREAKS IN THE EYES

An observant mother may sometimes notice thin moon-shaped streaks of blood in the eyes of her baby, located near the outer angles. This is seen in many normal babies and there is no cause for concern. The blood gets absorbed spontaneously in a few days.

5. MONGOLIAN OR BLUE SPOTS

A baby may have quite large bluish or slate-grey patches of skin discolouration on the lower back, buttocks, thighs, abdomen and even shoulders. These areas of pigmentation are called 'mongolian spots' and they disappear on their own over the next few months.

6. BIRTH MARKS

Many normal newborn babies have little pink or red spots looking like 'stork bite' marks on their face and nape of the neck due to dilated blood vessels. On the face they occur mainly over the eyelids, the middle part of forehead and the upper lip. The patches over the face disappear in a few months. Those over the back of the neck may persist but later get covered over by hair.

Another type of dark red, bunch-like, slightly raised marks called the 'strawberry marks' may appear in some babies several days or weeks after birth. They initially become bigger over a period of 6 to 9 months. Later they spontaneously regress and most disappear by 9 years of age.

Some other types of patches due to a variety of malformations of skin blood vessels may also appear. Regular follow-up under supervision of a doctor is advisable. Some of them may require active treatment, either when they become large and impinge on neighbouring vital structures (like the eye, feeding and respiratory passages) or when they develop some complications.

7. JAUNDICE

A number of babies develop a yellow skin colour and a yellowishness in the whites of their eyes due to jaundice on about the third day after birth. It may increase over the next 2 or 3 days and then it subsides by the 7th to 10th day. This type of jaundice, called 'physiological' jaundice, is harmless. If the jaundice appears within 24 hours after birth or becomes severe or continues to persist beyond 10 days, the baby would require proper investigations and treatment. Most moderate cases respond to 'phototherapy' during which the baby is kept under blue lights. Cases of severe jaundice, (usually due to Rh haemolytic disease), may require exchange blood transfusion.

8. THE BREASTS

Quite often the baby's breasts, in both boys and girls, are a little swollen and may even ooze some milk. This is the result of mother's hormones which have passed through the placenta to the baby before his birth. This condition is normal and temporary. You should leave the breasts alone and not try to squeeze them. The swellings will subside in a few days without any active treatment.

9. THE UMBILICUS (NAVEL)

Immediately after birth, the umbilical cord is cut and tied. The remaining cord stump takes about a week to 10 days to shrivel and drop off. You should keep the navel clean and dry by leaving it exposed to air. Clean it with spirit twice daily or apply triple-dye as advised by your doctor. If you notice any redness around the umbilicus or yellow discharge, consult your doctor.

Some babies later develop a swelling close to the navel which bulges out when the baby cries or strains. This is called umbilical hernia. It must not be strapped with a coin placed over it or in any other manner. Leave it alone. In an overwhelming majority of babies, this hernia subsides on its own by one year of age. If the hernia persists beyond one year, consult your doctor.

10. THE GENITALS

A. MALE

The foreskin of the penis (prepuce) in male newborn babies is normally tight and adherent. You must not try to forcibly loosen it. It will gradually become mobile by itself by the age of 3 years. The opening at the tip of the penis is also normally pinpoint in size and may only be seen with difficulty. Nothing needs to be done as long as the baby passes urine freely. The erection of a baby's penis off and on is quite normal at this stage and has no significance.

B. FEMALE

You may notice a thin greyish-white discharge or even a small amount of bleeding from the vagina in the first few days after birth due to the effect of the mother's hormones. Along with it there may be some swelling of the labia (skin folds) covering the vagina. Both these features pass off without treatment.

11. BOW LEGS

When the legs of a normal baby are straightened out, they look curled with their convexity outwards, giving an appearance of bowed legs. It is normal at this age. You need not worry about the baby possibly having any bone deformity or disease.

SOME COMMONLY ASKED QUESTIONS BY MOTHERS

(I) MY BABY HAS A STRONG GRIP AND HE IS EVEN TRYING TO WALK. CAN HE?

No. He is not capable of performing these tasks voluntarily. However, if you hold him upright and allow his feet to touch a table top or some hard surface and lean him forward he will, through reflex, raise his foot and then place one foot after another as if he is trying to take steps. This is only a 'false walking' and this automatic reflex activity will normally stop in about 3 months time as the baby matures.

The newborn baby, also by reflex, grips your fingers or any other object placed in the palm of his hands. So firm is his grasp that you may even lift him off his bed. This grasp reflex is also an automatic activity which will gradually fade away in about 3 months time.

(II) MY BABY IS STARTLED BY SUDDEN NOISE. IS IT NORMAL?

When there is a sudden loud noise or the baby's cot is suddenly jerked he will immediately fling out both his arms and raise up his legs as if in panic and will instinctively look for support. This automatic response, called 'Moro's reflex' is normal in the newborn baby and passes off at around 3 months of age.

(III) CAN MY BABY SEE AND HEAR?

Your little baby can not only see or hear but can also do a lot more. He can see your face while you breast-feed him and the bright, coloured objects at a distance of 9 inches (22 cm) or so. Distant objects, however, are just a blur to him. He reacts to the tone of your voice. He is happy when you talk softly and soothingly and he may feel frightened and cry when he hears sharp, harsh speech. He feels contented when held close and firm with affection and may prefer the hug of one to that of another. He soon learns to recognize the distinctive smell of your body and breast milk. While he can sense heat and cold, he needs extra protection against an excessively cold and hot environment because of his limited capacity to regulate his own body temperature. He dislikes bitter and sour tastes and prefers very sweet to just sweet.

SPECIAL CHARACTER AND FREQUENCY OF STOOL IN A NEWBORN

For the first two to three days after birth, the baby passes sticky, dark green stool called meconium. This consists of bile and bowel debris which has got collected in the baby's bowels while he was in the mother's womb. After the baby starts taking milk feeds, the colour of the stool gradually changes to greenish-brown and then in another three to four days time, to yellow. Almost all babies pass meconium within 24 hours after birth. If a baby fails to pass it within 24 hours or if the colour of his stool does not subsequently change to greenish brown and then yellow as explained above, a doctor must be consulted immediately.

The frequency of stool largely depends upon the number of times a baby takes his feed. To begin with most babies pass stool soon after almost every feed. The stool of breast-fed babies are generally soft, small in size, yellow and not so smelly, whereas bottle-fed babies have comparatively larger, more firm, brownish and more smelly stool. While most babies pass stool three to five times a day, some may do it only once a day or even once in two to three days. As long as the stool are reasonably soft, nothing needs to be done. There may be some variation in your baby's stool from day to day. But if you notice any of the following, consult your doctor urgently.

1. Stool have become very frequent or watery; or very foul smelling.
2. There is blood or mucus in the stool.

3. Baby looks ill, does not take feeds properly, is lethargic or has fever.
4. He is vomiting and is unable to retain his feeds.
5. He passes urine less frequently than usual.

PINK URINE IN A NEWBORN

The nappy of a newborn baby may sometimes look light pink as the urine dries out. This is due to urate salts passed in the urine and is quite normal.

BABY'S SLEEP PATTERN

Babies vary a great deal in their sleeping patterns; some sleep much more than others. While some generous ones sleep through the night, others seem to enjoy keeping their mothers awake the whole night. Your baby will develop his own distinct pattern of waking and sleeping, which may be quite different from that of your neighbour's baby. For peaceful coexistence you would need to adjust to your own baby's sleep pattern. The newborn baby may sleep for a total of 17 to 18 hours in a day, distributed in patches of varying duration. The amount of time spent in sleep goes down to about 14 to 16 hours by about 4 months of age. By 12 to 18 months, they sleep for about 10 hours at night with additional daytime naps of 1 to 2 hours. All babies do not follow this pattern; many healthy babies sleep less.

HOW TO PUT HIM TO BED

After watching your baby for some time, you will begin to recognize when your baby is ready for sleep. Try the following to help him to go to sleep and to form a night sleep pattern.

1. When he is trying to sleep in the evening, darken the room and arrange for extra comfort and a quiet environment.
2. When he wakes up for feeds at night, just feed him

and try to get him back to sleep. Do not play with him or distract him. Some babies may, however, be most alert at this time. You would have to adjust till things improve.

3. Your baby may sleep better after a feed.

4. There is no need to impose a total curfew on all sounds in the house, when your baby has gone off to sleep. Let him get used to the routine household noises. Loud, sudden noises may however wake him up.

CRYING

WHY DOES HE CRY SO MUCH?

All babies cry; some less than the others. This is the only way they can express their discomfort and unfulfilled needs. In the beginning, you may find it difficult to make out the cause of your baby's crying. He may be crying either because he is hungry, has a wet nappy, feeling uncomfortably hot or cold, is tired and sleepy, feeling pain because of a mosquito bite or an injection given earlier. He may be crying due to colic in his tummy or a general body illness. This should be suspected especially if he is also lethargic, not taking his feeds properly and does not stop crying despite your efforts.

WHAT SHOULD BE DONE?

First try to understand the reason for his crying. Giving feeds to a hungry baby would quieten him. You should also check and remove any obvious cause for his physical discomfort like wetting etc. When there is no such obvious cause, soothing talk, singing and soft music comfort some babies. Most of them feel better after a gentle swaying, rocking or on being taken out for a ride in a pram or in a car. Try to bounce your baby gently in your arms or in his baby cot. Some like to be held snugly in the arms, or against the shoulder and walked around. Others like to be wrapped around tightly while in bed or kept in a sling. You would need to try and find the best technique for your baby and different methods may succeed on different occasions.

If you find that the baby's cry is different from the crying indicating hunger or discomfort, or that you suspect him to be unwell or that he is refusing to get comforted, consult your doctor. Your baby may be physically ill. Colic, a common cause of crying in small babies, has been discussed at length separately in the section on Common Illnesses in Children.

PREMATURE AND LOW BIRTH-WEIGHT BABIES

Any baby who is born before the completion of 37 weeks of pregnancy is termed a premature baby. In India, about 10 % of all births are premature. Malnutrition, infection, high blood pressure, toxaemia of pregnancy, diabetes and severe heart and lung diseases in the mother are common causes leading to premature births. Sometimes, a baby may have to be delivered prematurely by the doctor, if the baby is detected to be suffering from a lack of proper oxygen supply in the mother's womb (foetal distress). Preterm babies have a low birth weight due to the inadequate time available to their various organs for full growth in the mother's womb prior to their delivery.

In some cases, certain birth defects and infections in the baby and in some others, poor ability of the placenta to provide adequate food and oxygen to the developing baby result in his poor growth and disproportionately low birth weight. There is a comparatively high incidence of premature births and a disproportionate low birth weight of newborn babies when there is close spacing between pregnancies, the mother has borne more than four previous children, pregnancy occurs during teenage or at over 35 years of age and when the mother has been smoking and consuming alcohol during pregnancy. A baby with a birth weight less than 2.5 kg is termed as 'low birth weight' baby.

A baby becomes particularly vulnerable when his weight is less than 2 kg.

The earlier the premature babies are born and lower the birth weight, greater is the severity of the handicaps of these babies and their need for help. A very premature baby is likely to have difficulties in breathing, maintenance of his body temperature and feeding. He, therefore, has to be nursed in an incubator. The incubator's inside temperature and the humidity and oxygen content of its air can be carefully controlled and adjusted according to the baby's needs. His nutritional requirements are met through intravenous feeding or feeding through a tube passed into his stomach. These babies are also liable to suffer from complications involving lungs, heart, nervous system and kidneys because of the immaturity of these and other organs. Their ability to maintain their blood glucose level and regulate other metabolic functions is also deficient. Their immune system is also not well developed and they have poor resistance against infections. For these reasons, such babies need to be carefully monitored and nursed in a special Intensive Care Unit. They are discharged only after they are completely well and stabilized, are taking feeds by mouth and showing steady gain in their body weight. They need special care at home, which has been explained in the next section.

OBESE BABIES

The old dictum, "too much of anything is bad" also holds true with respect to a baby's feeding and his undue weight gain. A baby should get enough food to grow well but not so much that he accumulates a large superfluous store of fat. A fat baby is more likely to become a fat adult with the attendant risks of developing heart disease and other disorders. It is also more difficult for a fat baby who has gone on to become a fat adult to lose weight in adulthood as compared to a fat adult who was normal as a baby and grew fat later. This is because when a baby is overfed a larger number of fat storage cells get formed under his skin as compared to those present in a thin baby. On account of the higher number of fat storage cells in his skin, such a baby becomes fat quicker during his adulthood and it is harder for him to lose weight. You should therefore, be careful in preventing your baby from getting fat. If your baby has a tendency to get fat his intake of starchy and sweet foods should be cut down. He should be offered fruits and raw vegetables as a snack between meals instead of biscuits, sweets, chocolates and crisps. Consult your doctor if the problem persists.

3

CARE OF THE NEWBORN

Your baby needs close loving care with due attention to his feeding, body hygiene, clothing and environmental temperature. Premature and low birth-weight babies require special care because of the immaturity of their various organs. While taking day-to-day care of your baby, it is extremely important for you to be alert and to keep a close eye on him for any early signs of disease. Newborn babies have relatively low body resistance and they can become quite ill if their disease is not detected and quickly controlled in its early stages.

EQUIPMENT AND CLOTHING FOR THE NEWBORN

It is desirable that parents should arrange to procure and keep ready the various items which would be required for the care of the newborn baby well before the expected date of his arrival, so as to avoid unnecessary last minute hassles. You would require the following items for his day-to-day care: a baby cot with mattress; baby sheets; a waterproof sheet; soft baby blanket; small soft towels or napkins; bath towels; baby clothes; napkins and safety pins; plastic underwear; clean cotton wool; baby soap; baby powder; baby oil; a plastic bath tub; and a baby pram.

CLOTHES

The baby's clothes should be soft, comfortable, easy to put on and take off and comparatively loose. They should be cool in summer and warm in winter. The clothing should allow easy access to his nappy because it requires frequent changing. Clothes which are open at the back or down the front are easy to put on and take off. Vests, cardigans and top clothes with narrow necks can be extremely annoying for the baby. The underclothes should be made of cotton which is soft to the skin and absorbs sweat. There is no need to buy too many costly clothes because the rapidly growing baby will soon outgrow them. The clothing material for the top clothes should be soft, light in weight, non-irritating to delicate skin and non-inflammable. Avoid synthetic clothes as they can be very uncomfortable in hot weather.

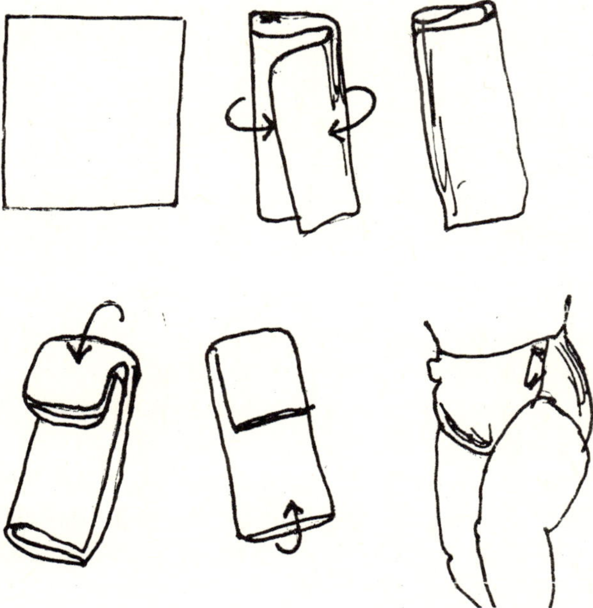

(Fig. 3.1)

The baby's nappies should be soft, absorbent and comfortable. He should have an adequate number of them as they would require frequent changing. Disposable napkins, though costly, are handy and convenient, particularly when travelling. While using a square napkin, you would need to place its double thickness in front for a baby boy and at the back for the baby girl. The positioning of pins on the sides would help to avoid hurting the baby's genitalia (Fig. 3.1). Special one-way liners are now available in India, these are useful since these allow urine to pass through to the towelling napkin outside leaving a dry layer next to the baby's skin.

BATHING AND SKIN CARE

It is not necessary to give a water bath to your newborn baby on the first day. You should just remove any blood and meconium from his head and face with clean cotton or a soft absorbent cloth soaked in clean warm water. Pat him dry with a soft towel. Do not try to rub and take off the white greasy material (vernix) as you might damage his delicate skin. The baby can have his bath on the second or third day. It can be further postponed if the baby is not well. You should, however, sponge clean his face, neck, hands and the diaper area daily with moist cotton wool using clean lukewarm water. Pat dry all areas carefully. Gently wipe around each eye, from the nose side outwards. Use a separate piece of cotton for each eye. Clean around the navel each day till the cord falls off.

You should choose to give bath to your baby during the day at a time which is convenient to you and when your baby is not hungry or sleepy. Make sure that the room temperature is comfortable and that there is no draught from outside or from the air conditioner. A plastic baby bathtub is very convenient to use. Water should be clean. In winter, it should be comfortably warm. You should check the water temperature before beginning to bathe your baby. Do not

(Fig. 3.2)

add hot water to the tub while your baby is in it, as he may get scalded. Wash your own hands well with soap and water before you begin to bathe your baby. First wash the baby's face and head. To wash his head, gently lower it over the tub and wash it with baby shampoo (or mild soap) and water and pat it dry quickly (Fig. 3.2). Next, apply soap all over the body while he is on your lap. Now immerse the lower part of his body into the water in the tub while keeping his head and shoulders clearly out of it.

Wash him well, taking particular care of the skin creases. After bathing, dry him gently and thoroughly with a soft towel with special attention to his armpits, groin and buttocks. You should avoid soaping and wetting of the navel area during the first 7-10 days till the umbilical cord falls off. Some mothers may find it easier to bathe their baby while holding him in their lap or across the legs and pouring water over him with a tumbler. It is not necessary to apply soap to baby's skin daily as it may make his skin too dry. The soap used must be quite mild. Gentle massaging of the baby with a baby oil helps the skin to retain its normal texture and your baby will enjoy it too. Liberal use of talcum powder should be avoided as it tends to collect in the skin creases and may cause skin irritation and rash. Care should also be taken to prevent talcum powder entering the baby's eyes and nose and avoid sprinkling over the navel area till the umbilical cord dries and falls off.

KEEPING THE BABY'S BOTTOM CLEAN

You must try to make sure that your baby's bottom is always clean. Do not allow his stool or urine-soiled nappy to remain in contact with his skin for long. He would then get an annoying skin rash in the diaper area and may develop bladder infection. It is also important that while cleaning the area, especially in a girl baby, the correct procedure is adopted, since doing it the wrong way would tend to spread the infection to both the vagina and the bladder.

THE CORRECT METHOD

1. After taking off the dirty nappy, wipe away the stool/urine from the baby's bottom with the unsoiled portion of the nappy or moistened cotton wool, soft cloth or tissue paper.
2. Now wash the bottom and genitals well with cotton wool and water. In boys, clean the whole area but do not pull back the foreskin over his penis. Do not try to separate the labia in a girl baby. While cleaning her, wipe from the vagina back towards the rectum to avoid spread of infection to the vagina or the urinary passage.

3. After washing, dry the bottom thoroughly. You may apply a skin cream as advised by your doctor, if he tends to develop a nappy rash. It is better to avoid using baby powder as it tends to choke the sweat glands.
4. Various types of nappies are now available, made of different fabrics and in different sizes. Fabric nappies work out to be cheaper in the long run as compared to disposable ones. These however, involve considerable labour as they need regular washing. Better choose a fabric which is easily washable, which does not irritate, is soft to the baby's skin and is also long lasting.
5. To prevent wet or dirty nappies soiling clothes, furniture or bedding, you may put on plastic pants over his fabric nappy. You must however, keep a regular check to make sure that the baby does not remain in his wet and soiled nappies beneath his dry outer covering.
6. Avoid the use of strong detergents and biological enzyme powder preparations for washing your baby's nappy as these will irritate his tender skin.
7. Wash the soiled plastic pants in warm water with a little washing-up liquid or soap. Too hot and too cold water would harden and spoil the plastic material. Leave them to dry before further use.

CARE OF EYES, NOSE AND EARS

When you wash your baby's face and eyes take care that no soapy water gets into his eyes. Clean the eyelids of his closed eyes gently, starting from the inner side close to the nose and moving outwards towards the ears. It is a common misconception among grandparents in most Indian families that putting *kajal* or *surma* with an applicator to a baby's eyes will make them bigger and thus more beautiful as well as improve his eyesight. This belief has no factual basis. On the contrary, the use of unhygienically made preparations may cause infection in his eyes. Besides, some *surma* powders have a high content of lead which can cause lead poisoning in the baby.

You need not worry much about the cleanliness of the inner portions of your baby's nose and ears. Nature has provided them with self-cleansing and self-protective mechanisms. Do not get influenced by the publicity campaigns of some cotton bud manufacturers. In your zeal to clean the wax out of your baby's ears you may introduce infection or damage his ear drum. Wax in the ear is a natural protective secretion of the skin lining the canal of the outer ear. Some babies produce wax more than others but this is normal and you should leave it alone. You should, however, gently clean the accessible portion of the outer ear with clean, moistened cotton or soft cloth and dry it.

The normal mild secretion and special cells in the inner lining of the baby's nose keep the inside of the nose clean and reasonably moist. They also prevent the passage of foreign matter and bacteria. Do not insert any cotton buds or wisps of cloth high up in the nose against nature's own protective mechanism.

ROOM TEMPERATURE AND CLOTHING

Your baby's living environment and clothing should be basically similar to those which would be comfortable for you. Small babies are not very good at controlling their body temperature. As their temperature can fall steeply in a cold environment, they should be adequately covered and protected but this should not be overdone. The baby may however be provided with one additional light layer of clothing or cover than for yourself. Avoid covering him with too many warm clothes or overheating the room in the winter. You can decide by touching the back of your baby's neck with your hands while he is sleeping. If you find the neck to be sweating, moist and warm, he is overclothed. If the neck feels cool, he needs extra warm clothing. Act accordingly. Do not decide just by feeling the baby's hands or feet. Be careful while using quilts and blankets so as to avoid blocking the baby's nose during sleep. Sleeping bags are good for older babies. They take away your worry about the baby throwing off his blanket at night. Never use a hot water bottle or an electric blanket directly in contact with the baby. His skin is very delicate and can get scalded easily. Unless very cold, keep your baby's head uncovered while he is sleeping indoors.

It is also important to see that the room temperature is comfortable for the baby in the summer. It should not be hot, but do not overchill his room. Avoid direct draughts of cold air. If the room is air-conditioned, provide him with light covers when he is in bed. His clothing during the hot weather should be soft, cool and airy.

BABY'S POSITION DURING SLEEP

You should always put your baby to sleep on his side or his back. Do not make him lie on his face in order to prevent him from getting choked. If your doctor has recommended a particular position for him to sleep in for some specific reason, you should follow the advice.

CLUES TO EARLY DETECTION OF ILLNESS

It is very important for you to know that sluggishness and lack of interest in taking feeds may be the only early manifestations of sickness in a baby during the first few weeks of his life. He may have no fever, cough, vomiting, loose motions or other commonly recognized symptoms of disease. If a baby, who has otherwise been active and taking his feeds well, suddenly becomes inactive, unusually quiet and ceases to take his normal feeds, he may be quite sick and you should promptly consult your paediatrician. Sometimes, a subtle change in his behaviour or looks may be the only early indication of his illness. Your own instinct and observation – finding him 'different' from his usual self – may be the best guide. If you think your baby is ill, even if you cannot make out what is wrong, better consult your doctor without any hesitation. You should not wait for fever or any other specific symptoms to develop.

You should also seek early medical advice if your baby shows any one of the following symptoms:

(i) if he is breathing fast or he has a catchy breathing;
(ii) if he looks unwell and his body and limbs are felt to be unusually floppy;
(iii) if he continues to cry persistently for long periods;
(iv) if he tends to choke on taking his first feed after birth.

A doctor should, of course, be consulted early if the baby develops fever, vomiting, loose motions, fits or any other commonly understood manifestations of disease. There is however no reason for you to worry unnecessarily. While you look after your baby with reasonable care and vigilance, you must remain calm and confident. Do not get perturbed by a sneeze, rash or any other minor problem in your baby. Despite their delicate frame and frail appearance, an overwhelming majority of newborn babies remain healthy and do not require any major medical assistance.

IMMUNIZATION

Most newborn babies would have received BCG vaccination and a dose of oral polio drops before discharge from the hospital. If not, these should be given at around 2 weeks of age and further immunization to be done later as per standard time schedule (see under section on Immunization).

VITAMINS AND IRON SUPPLEMENTS

The breast milk of a well-nourished mother contains sufficient vitamins to meet a baby's daily body requirement.

A healthy breast-fed baby does not therefore, need administration of multivitamin drops till his intake of breast milk diminishes at around 4-6 months of age.

Vitamin C is however present in insufficient quantity in cow's and buffalo's milk and it also gets destroyed when the milk is boiled. It is therefore recommended that babies wholly fed on cow's/buffalo's milk should be given vitamin C/multivitamin drops from the age of about six weeks onwards. On the other hand, if a baby is entirely fed on a commercial vitamin fortified infant milk preparation, your doctor would need to check its composition before advising you about the need, if any, for vitamin supplementation and its appropriate dosage.

To begin with, most multivitamin drops are advised to be given in a daily dose of 0.3 ml with subsequent increase to 0.6 ml.With the help of the graduated dropper provided by the manufacturer, the appropriate vitamin drops may be directly placed into the baby's mouth towards the inner side of one of the cheeks. Care should be taken to avoid squirting the back of the baby's throat as that might lead to choking. The baby is also liable to throw out drops if these are placed directly on his tongue.

Iron drops are generally prescribed for breast-fed babies from the age of 3-4 months onwards to prevent the development of iron deficiency anaemia. Iron drops may be started earlier when the baby is fed on cow's/buffalo's milk. A number of proprietory drugs with different iron formulations are available in the market. Your doctor will advise the correct dosage of a suitable preparation, taking into account your baby's body weight.

SPECIAL CARE OF PREMATURE BABIES AT HOME

ROOM TEMPERATURE AND CLOTHING

Premature and low birth-weight babies have a considerably reduced ability to maintain their body temperature. Their room temperature should be kept at a comparatively higher level, which may be rather uncomfortable for adult members of the family. In the winter, they must be well protected against the cold. The room may be kept warm with the help of a radiant heater. The baby's head must be kept covered with a woollen cap and his feet with woollen stockings. It would be helpful for the baby to sleep next to his mother, while taking care to avoid his being smothered. The mother acts as a good, comfortable, uniform source of heat for the baby. If the use of a hot water bottle becomes necessary, it should be wrapped up well in a towel to warm his bed, taking care to avoid leakage. As stated before, direct contact with the baby's delicate skin must be avoided.

FEEDING

Breast milk is best for a premature baby. If the baby is unable to suck at the breast, breast milk should be expressed and given to him through a bottle with an extra soft teat. The rubber teat should be boiled for some time to make it soft enough for the baby to suck. Alternatively, the expressed breast milk (or formula milk) can be given to the baby with a spoon or *paladai* (a traditional spoon with a long and narrow spout). Effort should be made to put the baby directly to the breast as soon as possible.

AVOIDING INFECTION

In view of their deficient immune system and high susceptibility to infections, premature and low birth-weight babies need extra protective measures. Their handling should be minimal. Your hands must be washed well with soap and water each time before touching or feeding the baby. The number of visitors must be severely restricted. Any relative or attendant who is suffering from throat or respiratory infection, fever or any other communicable disease should not be allowed to come in contact with the baby. He should be offered only boiled and cooled water to drink, when needed. Strict aseptic precautions should be taken while handling and feeding him.

VITAMIN AND IRON SUPPLEMENTS

Because of their early delivery, premature babies have poor body stores of vitamins and iron. The administration of vitamin E, some other vitamins and calcium to premature babies is usually commenced before their discharge from the hospital and this should be continued at home as per doctor's advice. They should be given iron supplements from the age of 6 weeks onward to prevent the development of anaemia. The appropriate dose of a suitable iron preparation would be recommended by your doctor on the basis of the baby's body weight.

IMMUNIZATION

A premature baby should receive all vaccines on time as per his age after birth (according to the standard immunization schedule), irrespective of the fact that he has not completed his full term in the mother's womb.

SPECIAL CARE: HOW LONG?

Premature and low birth-weight babies need special care only till they attain a weight of around 2.5 kg. Subsequently, they should be handled like normal babies. It is however desirable to monitor their development carefully and to watch out for any signs of abnormal behaviour. The baby should have regular periodic check-ups over the next few months to exclude the possibility of any physical or mental impairment.

4

FEEDING YOUR BABY

Appropriate feeding is essential for the maintenance of good health and for the proper growth and development of babies. Breast milk alone is the ideal food for a baby for the first four to six months of his life. Semisolid and solid foods should be gradually introduced in his diet later, while he continues to take breast feeds. If the mother has sufficient milk, breast-feeding of the baby can continue along with solid foods till he is well beyond one year of age.

EAST OR WEST — BREAST IS BEST

There is no doubt that breast milk is the best milk for your baby. Besides being good for your baby, it does a lot of good to you too.

ADVANTAGES OF BREAST-FEEDING FOR THE BABY

It is the ideal, complete food for the baby and made exactly right for him. Breast milk contains the best type of proteins, fats and carbohydrates as well as vitamins and minerals in the right proportions.

It is easily digested. The baby gets less stomach upsets due to wind and vomits less after feeds. He passes soft, less smelly stools and does not get constipated.

Breast milk contains antibodies, special white cells and other anti-infective factors which give your baby extra protection against infections. He suffers less from diarrhoea, pneumonia, colds and other infections. Cow's milk and commercial infant formula milk powders do not contain antibodies and other protective factors. The incidence of diarrhoea is about 15 times more and of respiratory infections 3 times more in non-breast-fed babies as compared to those who are breast-fed. Allergy (asthma, eczema and others) is less common among breast-fed babies.

Breast milk is especially good for premature babies.

It is sterile, safe, readily available and the baby always gets it at the right temperature

ADVANTAGES FOR THE MOTHER

It is very convenient. There is no bother of frequent washing and sterilizing bottles, preparing feeds, making sure of the temperature of milk, etc. Night feeding is especially easier. Above all, there are no problems of carrying the milk. Breast feeding costs practically nothing. Formula milk powders and even cow`s milk do involve significant expenditure. Breast-feeding helps you in regaining your figure quickly. The calories consumed by you in producing milk for your baby takes the extra fat off from your hips and waistline.

The oxytocin hormone released during breast-feeding encourages quicker contraction of the uterus and earlier stoppage of vaginal bleeding after delivery.

It offers some protection to the mother against cancers of the breast and ovaries.

When the baby is exclusively fed on breasts for the first 4 to 6 months it exercises a strong contraceptive effect.

EARLY MILK (COLOSTRUM) IS SPECIAL

During the first 2 to 4 days after delivery, the breasts produce a deep lemon-yellow coloured creamy secretion called the 'colostrum'. It is rich in proteins and minerals and contains some special anti-infective immunologic factors. Do not doubt its food value or usefulness. It is especially made to fulfill all your little baby's needs at this stage. It is particularly good if the baby is premature. Despite being secreted in small amounts, it does not need to be supplemented by additional milk, water or any other supplements.

HOW TO BREAST-FEED SUCCESSFULLY

PREPARE YOURSELF DURING PREGNANCY

During the later part of your pregnancy you should prepare yourself mentally to breast-feed your baby. If you perceive any problems about your breasts or nipples, consult your doctor. You should also get all your doubts about breast-feeding sorted out well before the birth of your baby.

BE CONFIDENT, START EARLY, DON'T GIVE UP

As a first-time mother, you may feel anxious and worry unduly about your ability to breast-feed your baby successfully. The secret lies in your being confident. Put your baby to the breast as soon as possible, preferably within one hour after his birth. He is most hungry during the first 2 to 3 hours. He may later just go on sleeping for the next 24 to 36 hours: do not get overanxious about it. You may also have some initial difficulties but these will pass. Offer milk to your baby as often as he wants. He will learn to suck milk from the breasts better at this early stage when the breasts are comparatively softer.

AVOID GIVING OTHER FLUIDS

Do not give him any other fluids, like glucose water, plain water, tea, cow's milk or powdered milk or honey, *ghutti*, gripe water, etc.

FOLLOW CORRECT TECHNIQUE

For successful feeding it is important that you make yourself comfortable in the right position and also hold your baby in the right position.

MOTHER'S POSITION

If you propose to sit and feed your baby, you should sit in a manner so as to be comfortable and be in an upright position. Ideally, you may choose a straight, arm-less, low chair. Otherwise you can sit in any chair, sofa, bed or even on the floor, well supported with cushions, so that you are comfortably sitting up supported with cushions, with your back straight. You can also feed your baby while lying down, tilted to one side, with pillows supporting your arm.

BABY'S POSITION

You should hold the baby in the crook of your arm and support him across the shoulder and the bottom part of his head. Turn the baby towards you with his head opposite your breast. Position his head slightly higher than his own stomach so as to make it easier for him to burp after his feeds. Hold him so that his mouth is at the same level as your nipple when he feeds. Do not bend over or pull yourself forwards to bring your breasts to the baby. What you need to do, is to bring your baby to your breasts.

BABY'S MOUTH

Now brush your nipple against your baby's cheek. He will instinctively turn his mouth towards it ('rooting reflex') and open his mouth. Make sure he takes a large mouthful of your breast, not just your nipple. Your baby's upper lip should be pressed against the breast, not pinching merely at the base of the nipple. Keep your breasts clear off his nose so that he can breathe while he is sucking (Fig.4.1).

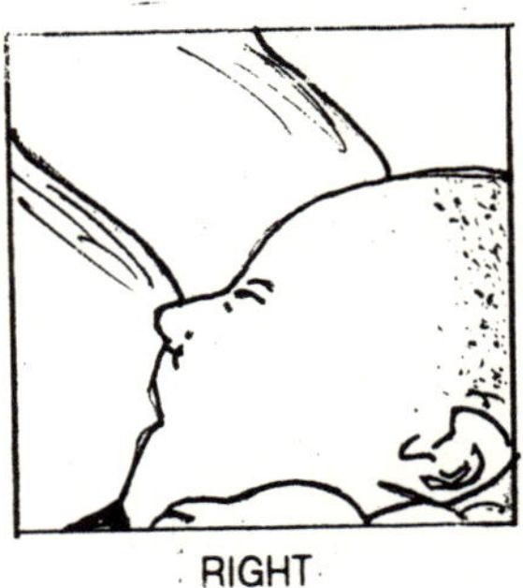

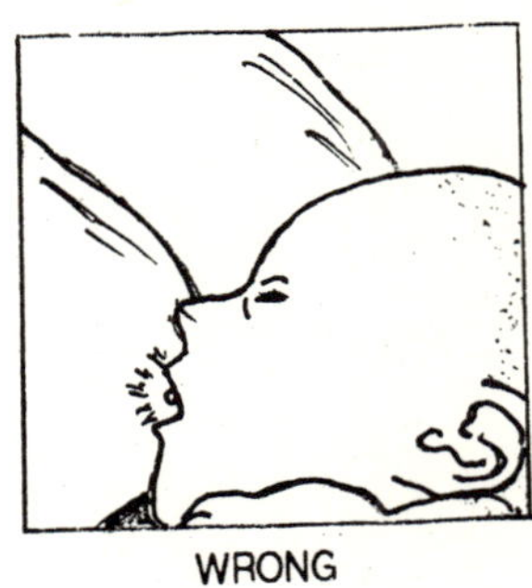

(Fig. 4.1)

OFFER BOTH BREASTS

Both breasts should be offered to your baby at each feed. If you start with your right breast, finish with the left. Next time begin the other way round, i.e., the left breast and end with the right. Follow this pattern of alternate breast feeding. It helps in emptying and stimulating both breasts to produce more milk.

BREAST-FEEDING: HOW OFTEN AND HOW LONG?

Offer your baby feeds as often as he demands it. To begin with he may demand 10 to 12 times or even more often in 24 hours. He will also insist on night feeds. You should feed him as he wants. Gradually, he will learn to take larger amounts of milk at each feed and fill his stomach better. He is then likely to settle into a more convenient 3 to 4-hourly feeding schedule with one night feed. You should, however, not try to prematurely force your baby a 3 to 4 hourly feeding schedule before he himself is ready for it. If he is denied a feed when he wants it, he will be fretful and hungry at his appointed feeding time later. It would then be quite difficult to feed him. He will just cry, refuse to get consoled and you may end up crying with him! Cooperation in the matter of feeding is a better policy than rigidity. Also remember that each baby is different; you need to be patient with yours.

Let your baby feed as long as he likes. To begin with he will suck the first part of breast milk – 'the fore-milk'. This contains a lot of water and helps quench his thirst. The latter part of the milk – 'the hind milk' – contains the energy (calories) which your baby needs. So let him first feed well on one breast before shifting to the other.

HOW TO STOP AT THE END OF THE FEED?

Don't pull him away before he has finished feeding, or else you will get sore nipples and a sore baby. Insert a clean finger into the corner of your baby's mouth to break the suction. He can then be separated quite easily.

AVOID WRONG FEEDING PRACTICES

DO NOT OFFER A BOTTLE INSTEAD OF BREAST

Your baby may feel hungry and demand feeds very frequently, almost every 2 hours. This may make you feel that you do not have enough breast milk and tempt you to offer a bottle feed instead of your breast. Do not do this because you would still have enough milk for him. If you feed him less often, your breasts will actually start producing less milk. However, if there is a problem, consult your doctor for advice before making use of bottle feeds.

AVOID OFFERING THE BOTTLE TOO SOON AFTER A BREAST FEED

For the same reason, avoid offering him the bottle soon after giving your own breast milk. The baby may start liking the easy feeding at the bottle and reduce his feeding at the breasts. Less stimulation would soon reduce the actual production of breast milk. The question as to whether you actually have enough breast milk for your baby or not is discussed later.

DO NOT OFFER PACIFIERS

You should not offer pacifiers ('dummies') or artificial teats while you are breast-feeding your baby. They can introduce infection into your child as well as diminish the baby's interest in feeding at the breast.

COMMON DOUBTS AND QUESTIONS ABOUT BREAST-FEEDING

IS MY MILK SUITABLE FOR THE BABY?

There is absolutely no reason for you to have any doubts about the suitability of your breast milk for your baby. There is no doubt that breast milk is perfect for him.

DO BREAST SIZE AND SHAPE OF NIPPLES MATTER?

Breast size does not matter. Breasts of all sizes and shapes are equally efficient in making milk. Milk is produced by milk glands which are the same in all of them, The sizes of breasts differ due to variation in the content of fatty tissue which plays no role in the production of milk. Most women with flat or inverted nipples are able to breast-feed successfully. Some with inverted nipples may need some help from the doctor.

WHAT REGULATES BREAST MILK SUPPLY?

The most important factor which determines the volume of milk production by the mother's breasts is the magnitude of her baby's demand for it. The mother's breasts produce as much milk as is sucked by her baby. The more milk your baby takes, the more milk your breasts will make. If he begins to take feeds at shorter intervals, the breasts will form the required milk faster to keep pace with his requirements. This happens due to the fact that when the breasts get emptied after feeding the baby, a physiological reflex is set up in your body. A hormone called prolactin gets released from the pituitary gland in your brain, which stimulates milk glands in the breasts to produce milk.

The key to producing more milk is, therefore, to offer your breasts to the baby whenever he feels hungry and demands it. This is especially important in the beginning. If you offer milk to the baby less often presuming that you do not have enough milk, you will actually start making less milk. Do not fall into such a self-defeating trap because of misconceived doubts about your own ability to produce enough breast milk.

HOW CAN I HAVE A GOOD MILK SUPPLY? WHAT SHOULD I EAT?

Rest and relaxation are important. You produce less milk if you are tired and tense. You should eat a well balanced diet with an extra helping more than your usual meals. It should contain sufficient proteins in the form of milk and milk products, pulses, legumes (and eggs and poultry, if you are a non-vegetarian). Ensure sufficient intake of green leafy vegetables, fruits and plenty of fluids. It is also advisable to take a proprietory drug preparation (containing appropriate amounts of vitamins and micronutrients) during this stage.

Do not drink too much tea, coffee and other caffeine-containing drinks like coca-cola. Excessive smoking and intake of alcohol should also be avoided. The use of contraceptive pills reduces milk supply. Choose alternative contraceptive methods for the first 5-6 months after the birth of your baby

Lastly and most important, continue to feed your baby as often as he likes. The more the stimulation, the greater the milk supply.

IS MY MILK ENOUGH?

There is no easy method of knowing how much milk your baby is taking. It also varies from one feed to the next; weighing the baby before and after his feed is not very helpful. You can be quite content about the adequacy of breast milk supply if:

your baby remains satisfied for a reasonable period time after being breast-fed and does not start crying almost immediately after being at your breast;

b) he has been gaining weight and continues to do so; the rate of weight gain can vary but it should be adequate on the whole and;

c) the baby passes urine 5 to 6 times a day.

CAN I BREAST-FEED AFTER A CAESAREAN DELIVERY?

Yes, but you need to be helped. Begin breast-feeding as soon as you are well enough after the operation even if you feel sleepy. You can rest when the baby sleeps.

IS MY BREAST MILK OKAY FOR MY PREMATURE BABY?

Mother's milk is especially good for premature babies and babies with low birth weight. If he is unable to suck, the milk should be expressed and given to him in a suitable manner. If he is too small it may need to be administered through a tube passed into his stomach. He can later have it with a spoon or *paladai* (a traditional spoon with a long spout). The bottle should be avoided and the baby be put on the breast as soon as possible. In the meantime, breast milk should be expressed regularly four to five times a day so that the breasts do not become engorged and stop secreting milk.

SHOULD I BREAST-FEED MY BABY WHEN I AM ILL?

You should not discontinue breast-feeding when you are suffering from a viral fever, cough, diarrhoea, a urinary tract infection, hepatitis or other common illnesses. Recent medical evidence suggests that a mother who is suffering from AIDS should better avoid breast-feeding her baby on account of the risk of transmission of HIV infection through breast milk. In case of any serious doubts, you may consult your doctor but do not stop breast-feeding on your own.

CAN I TAKE DRUGS WHILE I AM BREAST-FEEDING MY BABY?

While breast-feeding your baby, the use of drugs should be restricted as far as possible. Although most of the commonly used drugs may be safe, it is advisable for you to first consult your doctor. He will advise you a safer alternative drug, when medication becomes necessary. For example, the lactating mother should not take, on her own, ergot containing preparations (like cafergot) for a migraine headache. Safer alternative drugs are now available and are recommended for use while the mother is breast-feeding her baby. Only under very special circumstances, as when (i) the mother is receiving anti-cancer drugs, (ii) drugs for the treatment of thyrotoxicosis to curb thyroid gland overactivity (iii) gold salts (for joint disorders) and (iv) lithium (for depression), should breast-feeding be discontinued to avoid potential harm to the baby.

WHAT TO DO IF MY BABY TAKES FEEDS RESTLESSLY?

It may be that your baby is not holding the breast in his mouth properly. He may be sucking on only the nipple and therefore, not getting sufficient milk to satisfy his hunger. Once he is repositioned with his mouth fully around the areola, he will get his milk properly and stop being restless.

WHAT TO DO IF I HAVE TO GO TO WORK?

In such a case you need to combine the breast and bottle feeds. You can continue to breast-feed the baby while you are at home. The baby can be given your expressed milk while you are away at work. The expressed milk may, however, not be enough to meet all his needs while you are away and it may need to be supplemented with cow's milk or infant powder milk.

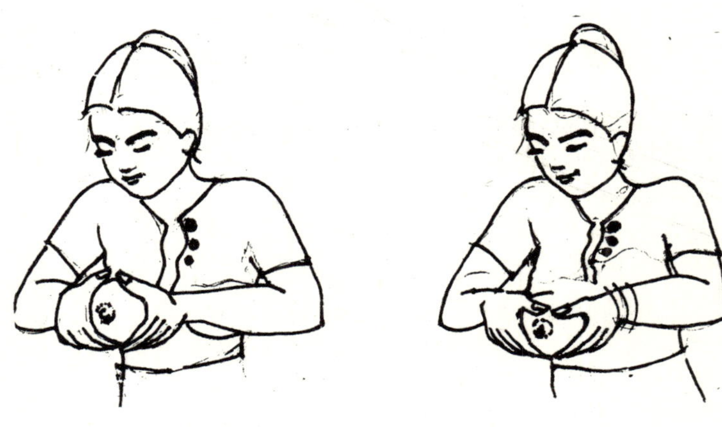

(Fig. 4.2)

HOW DO I EXPRESS MY MILK ?

Milk can be expressed from the breasts by hand or with a breast pump. Before you start, keep ready a bowl, a container and a funnel (all pre-sterilized by washing in boiled water or sterilizing solution). Wash your hands well. Hold the breast in both hands at its outer portion away from the areola (coloured portion around the nipple) as if you are holding a cup. Let your fingers hold from below and your thumb from above, as shown in the figure (Fig. 4.2).

Squeeze the outer part of your breast between your fingers and thumbs gently and firmly. Repeat this process about ten times at different points around the breast at the same level as before. Now repeat the squeezing action ten times around the breast at a level lower than before and nearer to your nipple. The squeezing action would thus have brought the milk down through the milk ducts into the milk reservoirs in the areola. Now, hold your breast in one hand and press at the edge of the areola with the thumb and forefinger of the other hand to express milk. Do not squeeze the nipple.

Another way to bring milk down into the areola is with

the help of the palm of one hand while holding the breast in the palm of the other. Final bringing out of milk is done in the same manner as explained above. You should stop expressing milk when it stops coming as a jet and starts coming in drops.

Different types of breast pumps are available for expressing milk. You should consult your doctor for detailed advice regarding their proper use, if you decide to use one to express your milk instead of doing it manually.

CAN I STORE THE EXPRESSED MILK?

It is best to use the expressed breast milk fresh. But if you need to store it, place it in the refrigerator immediately after collecting it, preferably in a plastic container. It can be refrigerated under proper hygienic conditions with uninterrupted electricity supply for up to 24 hours but it should not be allowed to get frozen.

SHOULD STORED BREAST MILK BE BOILED BEFORE USE?

Your own breast milk is sterile. It does not need boiling and should not be boiled so as not to lose its natural anti-infective properties. Some medical authorities also advise against the use of microwave oven for heating in case it has any harmful effect. Warm the bottle containing breast milk gradually by placing it in a bowl of hot water before feeding it to your baby.

BREAST PROBLEMS DURING FEEDING

ENGORGED BREASTS

When milk starts flowing freely into the breasts on the second or third day after birth the breasts may become swollen and somewhat tender and painful to the touch. This usually passes off after a few days. However, sometimes the breasts become swollen, tense and hurt a lot when the baby feeds. This is called 'engorgement ' of the breast. You can prevent this from getting worse by expressing a little milk before putting your baby to the breast. This makes the areola (the dark brown area around the nipples) less tense and your baby can take his feeds better. Feed your baby at shorter intervals, for shorter periods of time. Empty your breasts with your hands after each feed. If required, a breast pump may have to be used. The use of well-fitting, tight, breast support would reduce your discomfort. If the problem persists, seek your doctor's advice.

SORE AND CRACKED NIPPLES

This condition is generally caused by faulty attachment of the baby to the breast during feeding. When the baby is unable to draw milk while sucking only the nipple (and not the nipple and areola) he becomes restless, sucks vigorously and tends to bite at the nipple. This damages the delicate skin; the nipples develop cracks and become sore.

Besides ensuring proper breast attachment during feeding, you should take care to gently detatch the baby's mouth from the nipple at the end of feeding instead of forcefully pulling him off. Thereafter apply a small amount of your own expressed milk to the nipple and let it dry. This would help in early healing of soreness. Avoid frequent washing of nipple with soap and water. Wear loose clothes, avoid use of bra and plastic breast shields to allow proper aeration of nipples in between feeds. Some emollient cream may be applied over the nipples during this period.

You should however, continue to breastfeed your baby. It may be done more often and for shorter periods. Start on the less sore side and change sides once or twice during the feed.

LUMPY, TENDER BREASTS

Blocked milk ducts are usually responsible for this condition. To help, express some milk from the affected breast. If not too uncomfortable, let your baby feed on the sore breast. Stroke the lumpy area gently with your fingertips towards your nipple while the baby takes the feed from the affected breast. Consult your doctor too.

NIPPLE DISCHARGE

You may sometimes get a reddish, brown or chocolate-coloured discharge from your nipples during late pregnancy. Sometimes, it may discolour colostrum in the first days after childbirth. This normally subsides on its own. If it persists for three or four weeks, consult your doctor.

FLAT NIPPLES AND 'INVERTED' NIPPLES

There is considerable variation in the true nature and degree of apparently 'flat' or inverted nipples in different women. It is desirable that each case should be individually assessed by a doctor for proper advice. The management should begin during pregnancy and continue during the early stages of breast-feeding.

BREAST INFECTION (MASTITIS)

If you have breast infection your breasts will feel hot and tender and you may feel feverish and ill. If this occurs, consult your doctor at the earliest.

BOTTLE FEEDING

While breast-feeding is undoubtedly the best, it is possible that a mother may sometimes not be in a position to breast-feed her baby for some sound reasons. If bottle feeding is unavoidable, she should not feel guilty or unduly anxious about it. Bottle-fed babies also grow well. The mother can also develop as strong a bond of love with her baby as while breast-feeding.

WHICH MILK FOR BOTTLE FEEDING?

You may choose cow's milk, buffalo's milk or commercial infant milk preparations, as convenient, taking into account the cost and availability of reliable, good quality milk. When cow's or buffalo's milk is used, it should be given to the baby undiluted, after boiling. The buffalo's milk should however be boiled and cooled down and its cream taken off before giving it to the baby. (This is discussed at length later.) Do not use soya milk for routine feeding of your baby. If the doctor recommends soya milk under certain special circumstances, you should check with him as to when your baby can go back to cow's milk.

A number of commercial baby milk preparations in powder form are available in the market. Almost all of them are prepared basically from cow's milk, with some modifications to bring them as close to human milk as possible. There is not much to choose between the different commercial infant milk formulas marketed by the manufacturers. However, you might prefer to choose one which, when added to boiled water, dissolves quicker and does not leave many granules. Condensed milk preparations should not be used. These contain too much sugar, are poor in essential proteins and other nutrients and are unsuitable for your baby's needs. Skimmed milk powders are also not recommended for children below the age of five years because of their poor energy content.

WHAT ARE THE MATERIALS REQUIRED FOR PREPARING BOTTLE FEEDS?

It is desirable to have three or four bottles and four to six teats with teat covers so that at least one sterilized bottle with teat is always available for feeding your hungry baby. You would need a spare container (bottle, jar or jug with cover) for storing milk, a teaspoon for measuring sugar to add to the cow's milk, cleaning brush and detergent for cleaning bottles and teats, etc.

HOW TO STERILIZE BOTTLES, TEATS, ETC?

First wash the bottles, teats and other equipment thoroughly in hot water using washing powder or liquid. Use a bottle brush to clean the inside of the bottles and a small amount of salt to clean the teats. Rinse them thoroughly. Place the bottles, teats, caps, etc., in a container of water. Cover and boil for at least 20 minutes.

CAN ONE DO STERILIZATION WITH STERILIZING SOLUTION? IF SO HOW?

Yes. Some sterilizing solutions, mostly consisting of sodium hypochlorite (e.g., Steriliq) are now available in the market. First clean the bottles, etc., with hot water and detergent as explained above. Now prepare the sterilizing solution for actual use in the desired strength as recommended by the manufacturer and pour it into a container of adequate size. Place the bottles in the solution and you may use a plate to make sure that they remain fully immersed in it. Put the teats and caps upside-down, to prevent air getting inside the bottles. The bottles and other equipment should be kept submerged in the solution for the recommended period. Most manufacturers recommend this to be done for one or two hours to achieve sterilization. You can however continue to keep the materials in the solution for upto 24 hours after which the solution must be discarded and a fresh one prepared. There is no need to rinse off the sterilizing solution from the bottles, etc., before preparing milk feeds in them. However, if you want to do it, use previously boiled and cooled water to rinse and not tap water. If tap water is used, whatever was sterilized would again get contaminated.

HOW TO PREPARE BOTTLE FEEDS?

Before beginning to prepare milk feeds for your baby, you should first keep ready properly sterilized empty milk bottles, teats, a bowl and other equipment which you would need for preparing and storing milk for him. Wash your hands well with soap and water before handling milk and the sterilized equipment.

When cow's or buffalo's milk is used, it must first be sterilized by boiling it for 10 minutes. It should then be allowed to cool down to room temperature. In the case of buffalo's milk, the cream formed on its surface should be taken off. One level teaspoonful of sugar should be added for every 75 ml (2½ oz) of milk prior to giving it to the baby. Milk should not be diluted by adding water to it. Check the temperature of milk before giving it to your baby by letting a few drops of milk to fall on the inner side of your wrist. It should be lukewarm.

For preparing milk from commercial milk powder, put the required amount of boiled water into the bottle. Check it by holding the bottle at your eye level. Work out the amount of milk powder which is required to be added to it according to instructions of the manufacturer. Pick up the milk powder with the scoop provided in the milk formula packet and level it off at the top by removing the excess uniformly with a knife (Fig. 4.3). Do not compress the powder into the scoop.

You must avoid the temptation of putting more than the recommended amount of milk powder while preparing your baby's feeds. If you do so, the milk would become too rich and unsuitable for your baby. He may feel unduly thirsty and become restless on being fed unduly concentrated milk. Put the powder into the bottle containing the measured amount of water. Place the teat in reverse and tighten the cap on the bottle. Shake the bottle well until the powder is fully dissolved. Cool the bottle under running water. Check the temperature of milk by allowing a few

(Fig. 4.3)

drops to fall on the inner side of your wrist. It should be lukewarm when fed to the baby. If required, you may keep the made-up milk in the refrigerator but not for more than 24 hours. Before giving refrigerated milk it should be suitably warmed by keeping the bottle in a container of hot water for a few minutes (Fig 4.4).

(Fig. 4.4)

CORRECT TECHNIQUE OF BOTTLE FEEDING

Before beginning the feed, check that the hole in the teat is the proper size. When you hold the bottle upside down milk should fall steadily, drop by drop (Fig. 4.5). A continuous rapid flow of milk means that the teat hole is too big. During feeding the baby will have too much milk in his mouth and he will tend to choke. If the hole is too small, the milk drop will take several seconds to form and would not come out easily. In this situation the baby will suck a lot of air in an effort to obtain milk. The excess air in the stomach causes abdominal colic and vomiting after feeds. If the hole in the teat is too small, enlarge it with a red-hot needle. If too big, change the teat. As mentioned already, you should make sure that the milk in the bottle is lukewarm and not too hot.

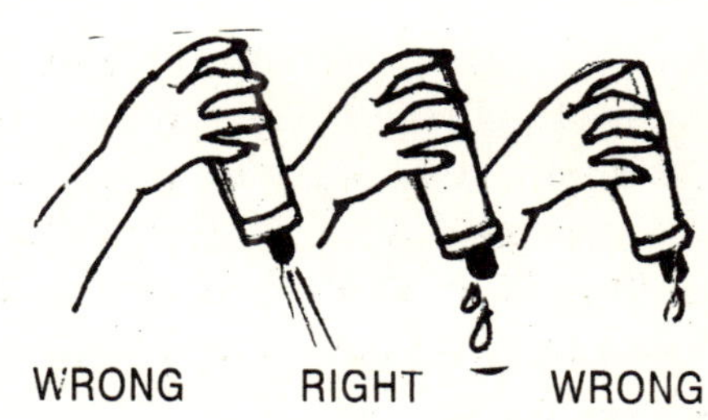

(Fig. 4.5)

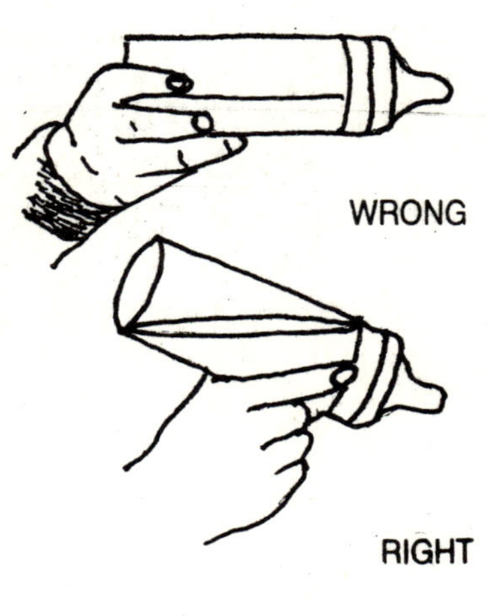

(Fig.4.6)

While you are seated comfortably, hold your baby in your lap, supported on your left arm with his head kept raised above his stomach level. As you feed keep the bottle tilted so that the teat is always full of milk (Fig. 4.6). This is important to prevent your baby from sucking in a lot of air during his feeds. If the teat becomes flat while the baby is taking his feed, pull gently on the bottle to release the vacuum.

FEEDING WITH A SPOON AND CUP

In view of the practical difficulties in ensuring suitable sterilization of milk bottles and other equipment needed for bottle-feeding, the use of a clean cup and spoon instead of bottle feeding is now being increasingly recommended. The baby is also less tempted to avoid the breast.

BURPING

Your baby may suck in a lot of air while at your breast, especially if he is very hungry or is eager to suck. This problem is also likely to arise when a baby frantically tries to draw milk from a bottle with a teat which has a very small hole. Besides, if during feeding the milk bottle is not kept properly tilted and the teat remains empty, the baby will suck air.

To help the baby bring up air, you should pick him up midway through his feed, and hold him upright on your shoulder and gently pat or rub his back for a while (Fig. 4.7). This procedure should be repeated after he completes his feed. After the feed, some babies may need to be kept against the shoulder for several minutes before they burp.

(Fig. 4.7)

MILK: HOW MUCH AND HOW OFTEN?

You should follow the same principles for bottle feeding as explained earlier for breast feeding. To begin with, give him his feeds whenever he feels hungry and demands it. He may demand it at short intervals and also two to three times at night. Gradually he will mature and fall into a three to four-hourly schedule and may subsequently not take night feeds.

HOW MUCH BOTTLE FEED SHOULD BE OFFERED?

Your baby will take milk according to his own needs. This may initially vary considerably. He is likely to take more after a longer interval. If he finishes the bottle at one feed, he should be offered a larger amount next time. The baby will take as much as he needs and leave the rest. Do not push him to finish the bottle or take more than he likes to. As he grows he will take larger amounts at each feed. Simultaneously, the intervals between feeds will get longer and the total number of feeds in a day will reduce. On an average, a baby takes about 150 ml of milk per kilogram of his body weight. The schedule below roughly indicates the general pattern of feeding by most babies at different ages.

SCHEDULE OF BOTTLE FEEDING

Age of Baby	Average Quantity of Each Milk Feed	No of Feeds in 24 Hours
Birth to 14 days	60 – 80 ml	6 – 8
14 days to 2 months	100 – 140 ml	5 – 7
2 months to 3 months	130 – 160 ml	5 – 6
3 months to 6 months	150 – 180 ml	4 – 5
6 months to 12 months	180 – 225 ml	3 – 4

BRINGING UP MILK

Many babies bring up some milk after their feeds. The quantity is generally small but it may seem quite a lot because of being mixed with saliva. This problem is more common among bottle feeders. It may also happen if the baby has had too much milk or if he takes it too quickly.

If your baby regurgitates too often, make sure about the following:

(i) the bottle is properly held and the teat always remains full of milk;

(ii) the hole in the teat is neither too small nor too large;

(iii) the baby is not moved about while feeding;

(iv) the patting or rubbing of the back to burp the baby is done gently and not too hard;
(v) the baby does not cry much before or during feeds;
(vi) he is not pushed too hard to take extra milk beyond his own inclination.

You should, however, consult your doctor if despite your having taken the above precautions, (i)regurgitation of milk persists; or (ii) it is unduly large or forceful or (iii) there is greenish bile or blood in the milk vomited by the baby.

POINTS TO REMEMBER

1. Do not force-feed your baby by insisting that he must finish the milk which he may have left in the bottle after finishing the feed on his own accord. Many babies would vomit out later the extra milk which they actually did not need to take in the first place. On the other hand, some babies may become excessively fat due to forced feeding.
2. The warm milk feed for the baby should be prepared a short while before giving it to the baby. As germs grow rapidly in warm milk, the prepared feed should not be kept standing at room temperature for more than one hour or so. The risk of infection is greater in summer months. For the same reason, do not keep hot milk in a vacuum flask for longer than one hour or so for use by the baby. If you have to store the prepared milk feed for some time, place it straightaway in the refrigerator or icebox. It should subsequently be lightly warmed immediately before giving it to the baby. If not used within 24 hours, the refrigerated milk feed should be discarded.
3. Throw away the milk remaining in the bottle after the baby has finished his feed; do not store it for later use.

D
C
B
A

5

INTRODUCTION OF SEMISOLID AND SOLID FOODS

WHEN TO START SEMISOLID FOODS AND WHY?

It is appropriate to begin giving semisolid foods to your baby when he is between four to six months of age. There is no advantage in starting them earlier. Prior to it the baby does not need these foods as the breast milk can fully provide him with the required nutrition. Besides, if started too soon, the baby's digestive system and kidneys may find it difficult to cope. It is however also desirable not to delay the introduction of semisolid foods in your baby's diet beyond six months of age. This is because he would soon need these foods to fulfil increasing nutritional needs as he gets older. There is a limit to the amount of milk a baby can drink and milk alone would fail to meet his requirements. It would need to be supplemented by additional nutrition in the form of energy-rich semisolid and solid foods to avoid growth retardation and malnutrition in the baby. The baby should also begin eating almost like the rest of the family by around one year of age and he needs some time to gradually adapt himself to taking new solid foods with different tastes and textures. As to the actual time of starting these foods, your own baby will help you in deciding it. You may notice that your baby now seems to be still hungry after finishing a good milk feed and that even the offer of more milk does not satisfy him. He demands more feeds at shorter intervals during the day and has even begun to once again insist on a night feed too. He also appears to be generally more restless than usual. In most babies these changes happen at around four months of age and are a signal for you to start giving him semisolid foods.

GENERAL GUIDELINES

(i) Once you know your baby is ready for semisolids, choose a time to give it when he is quite hungry but not restlessly so. His usual second feed time at about 10 A.M. or the subsequent noon feed time may be selected, keeping in mind your own convenience also. It can later become his breakfast or lunch. Give him the solid food first and then complete the feed with breast milk (or animal milk, if he is not being breast-fed). Some very hungry babies however, refuse to accept the teaspoon first and get agitated. They are willing to eat the solid food after their initial strong hunger has been satisfied with some milk. As the baby gets older, he may take enough solid food so as not need milk along with it at that particular feeding time.

(ii) Different babies vary in their fondness for semisolid and solid foods and the pace at which they take to them. Some are keener and faster, others take longer. Follow your own baby's pace and do not force-feed him.

(iii) Start with one new food at a time. Give it for two or three days to make sure that the baby has accepted it. If he does not like it, withdraw it. You can again try after several days. If the new food upsets him, you would know and you can avoid it for some time.

(iv) To begin with, each new food should be given in

small quantities. The amount of this food and the number of times it is given to the baby during a day, should be gradually increased over a period of several days.

WHICH SEMISOLID AND SOLID FOODS?

It is desirable that the complementary semisolid and solid foods for the baby should be prepared from the usual home food items. Home-made foods are economical, permit greater variety and allow scope for the mother to exercise her ingenuity. The infants also adjust to the common family food with greater ease.

AT 4 TO 6 MONTHS

You may begin with porridge prepared with *suji* and some milk (*suji kheer*) or one similarly prepared with wheat flour. The porridge can alternatively be prepared with ground rice (as *phirni*), *ragi*, millet, oats, etc. Commercial precooked cereal preparations (like Cerelac, Farex, Nestum) can also be used instead of the home-made preparation but with no distinct advantage other than convenience. When used, the commercial weaning foods should be prepared for consumption by the baby, by mixing a specified quantity of the precooked cereal with milk or boiled and cooled water, strictly in accordance with the recommendations of the manufacturers.

When offered to the baby, these semisolid foods should be lukewarm, smooth, creamy and free from lumps. On the very first day place just about ¼th of a teaspoon on the middle of his tongue and let him swallow it. Do not get anxious if you find him reluctant, or if he does not like it or even spits it out. He will slowly adjust to the new texture and taste of the semisolid foods. Starting with one or two teaspoonfuls gradually increase the quantity and frequency till the baby consumes about half a cup (50 g) of food in a day.

A week or so after the baby has got adjusted to the cereal preparation, he should be given some fruit at another time of the day. You may well begin with one to two teaspoonfuls of mashed ripe banana and gradually increase it to about one banana a day. He may alternatively be given ripe papaya, mango, *cheeku*, grapes or some other seasonal fruit. Their skin and seeds should be removed and the fruit mashed to a smooth, soft, non-lumpy consistency. It may be preferable to give more of papaya and prunes and less of banana to babies who tend to be constipated. Fruits like apple and pears can be stewed and a sieve or liquidizer used to prepare a puree. Sugar need not be added.

AT 6 TO 9 MONTHS

The baby can now have foods with a thicker consistency and a lumpier texture. He can have mashed dal, mashed vegetables and egg. De-husked *dals* like *moong*, *masur*, and *arhar* can be soft-cooked and mashed. Bland vegetables like peas, carrots, cauliflower, potato, beetroot and spinach can be given to the baby. These should be boiled or steamed and then mashed in the water in which they have been cooked. A little salt and a small quantity of butter may be added for improvement of taste and nutritional value. Use a sieve, mouli or liquidizer to form a puree.

You may start offering eggs to your baby when he is around 5 months. To begin with, give him a small portion of the yolk of a half-boiled or a full-boiled egg. Gradually increase it to the yolk of an egg. After the egg yolk has been accepted well by the baby, add gradually increasing amounts of the white of the egg till he receives a whole egg. Some children can be allergic to the proteins contained in the white of an egg. You should stop giving egg if your baby shows any symptoms of allergy such as a skin rash, itching, irritability, unexplained crying (due to abdominal pain) or vomiting. Consult your doctor for further advice. For the same reasons it is recommended that if the child is suffering from eczema or any other allergic disorder or there is a history of asthma or skin allergy in the family, giving an egg to the baby should be delayed beyond 8 to 9 months of age. Its quantity should also be increased more gradually while watching out for any symptoms of allergy.

The baby can further go on to have rice with *dal*, *khichri*, or a bit of *chapati* soaked and softened in *dal*, or gravy or *dahi* (yoghurt). He should have these complementary semisolid foods 3 to 4 times a day in addition to regular breast feeding (or bottle feeding, where breast-feeding has not been possible). For your convenience, recipes for the preparation of some weaning foods for babies at home are placed at Appendix 5.

Some older babies accept egg more easily when added to a vegetable, *dal*, cereal or milk preparation. You can use your ingenuity in presenting it to your baby in different forms and flavours. It may be given as boiled, fried, poached, as an omelette or as a dessert made up with milk and sugar.

When an infant is teething, he loves to bite and chew. During this stage, he may progressively be offered food items like a biscuit, rusk, a small piece of toast, a piece of *kheera* or a soft carrot to bite at and eat.

Give your baby a spoon to encourage him to feed himself. He may not be very successful but let him experiment and enjoy it. The actual feeding for him can be done by you with another spoon in your hand. If he likes to use his fingers and hand to take food to his mouth, let him do so. He would derive a great sense of satisfaction and accomplishment out of the mess he makes. Be suitably prepared by providing him a baby bib, spreading out a newspaper and arming yourself with a cleaning cloth and loads of patience.

AT 9 TO 12 MONTHS

The variety of foods offered to the child can now be widened. He can have *idli*, *dosa*, *pongal*, and *missi roti*. A 10 to 11-month-old baby can have minced cooked meat, fish and chicken. By the time babies are a year old, they can share practically all the non-fibrous family food cooked without much spices and excess fat. The food may however need to be chopped and mashed suitably. In view of the limited capacity of these babies to take substantial amounts of food at any given time, it is important they should be offered these foods at least 4 to 5 times a day at this stage.

A baby's daily diet at one year must include half a litre of milk and fresh fruits besides the usual family food as explained above. Extra consumption of cheese, lentils, peas and beans may be encouraged in vegetarian families where the baby is not offered egg, poultry, meat or fish preparations.

CONTINUING MILK: HOW IMPORTANT AND HOW MUCH?

Milk is a very important requirement for meeting a baby's nutritional needs. When he begins to increasingly take several spoons of cereal, vegetables or other solid foods his milk intake can be reduced. Between 9 to 12 months, about 500 ml to 750 ml (½ to ¾ litre) of milk is enough. He would continue to need about half a litre of milk till he is 5 years old. Children below 5 years must only be given whole milk and not skimmed or semi-skimmed milk, which are deficient in energy and essential fat soluble vitamins. Milk can be partly replaced by other calcium containing foods like cheese, yoghurt and other milk products.

FRUIT JUICES

Fruit juices contain vitamin C. You may begin giving orange or *mosambi* juice (after careful hygienic extraction and removal of seeds) to a breast-fed baby at around 4 months of age. He should initially be offered two teaspoons of juice diluted with equal amounts of boiled and cooled water. The amount of juice may be gradually increased to about 60 to 75 ml (2 to 2½ oz), diluted with equal amounts of water. Later, the child can have undiluted fruit juice. Contrary to widely held belief, fruit juice does not cause common cold, cough or fever in a child. You should not warm up the fruit juice before giving it to your baby as the heat would destroy vitamin C and thus nullify its nutritive value.

SOUPS, BROTHS AND *DAL KA PANI* (LENTIL WATER)

The widely publicized soups of different brands (including chicken soup) and the much glorified broths and lentil water (*dal ka pani*) have little nutritive value; these should not be given to babies. Their intake would lead to reduced intake of milk and other nutritious foods by the baby. Older children can, however, occasionally have soup as an appetiser as and when it is prepared for the family.

OTHER DRINKS

Breast-fed babies do not need to take water, glucose water, tea, fruit juices or any other fluids till the age of four months. The initial part of breast milk (fore-milk) contains plenty of water. During the hot summer months they can quench their thirst by sucking at the breast more frequently while the bottle-fed babies should be given cooled, boiled water to satisfy their thirst. Babies need to have more water as the solid part of their food increases. You should avoid the temptation of giving commercial fizzy drinks and squashes to your baby. They are poor in nutritional value and can adversely effect his intake of milk and other nutritious food. The stimulant effects of tea and coffee may keep a baby awake and restless and these should be avoided.

FEEDING SCHEDULE FOR A 9-MONTH-OLD BABY

The schedule indicated below is to give an idea of the timings and the kind of foods which may be given to a 9- month-old baby on a particular day. It is not meant to be strictly followed as such by every baby. Besides, your baby may like to vary his diet occasionally.

6.30 A.M.	Breast-milk feed
8.30 A.M.	Porridge (vermicelli + jaggery) A biscuit (to chew)
10.30 A.M.	Half of a boiled egg Juice of half an orange (simultaneously or later, depending on demand)
12.30 NOON	*Khichri* of rice, *dal* and spinach A piece of *Kheera* or boiled *ghia* to munch on
3.30 - 4 P.M.	Milk feed, mashed banana
6.30 P.M.	Boiled and mashed vegetables, potato, cabbage, peas, carrot, etc.
8.30 P.M.	*Aloo raita* (curd mashed with pieces of boiled potato)
10.30 P.M.	Breast-milk feed.

POINTS TO REMEMBER

1. You should continue to feed the baby during minor illnesses like a common cold, fever, cough and ordinary respiratory infections. Breast-feeding should continue during diarrhoea. To overcome the child's lack of appetite during illness, give him smaller feeds

at more frequent intervals. After recovery he should be encouraged to have more than his usual diet to help him recover the weight lost during illness.

2. Be very careful about hygiene while preparing supplementary foods for your baby. Wash your hands well with soap and water before handling and preparing the food. The cooking and serving utensils must be thoroughly clean. Lack of hygiene may cause contamination of baby's food with germs resulting in life-threatening diarrhoea.

3. Food for the baby should preferably be cooked shortly before serving it to him. In case of delay, it may be stored for a few hours in a refrigerator. Do not keep it for long at room temperature as disease causing germs can grow quite rapidly in warm food. The refrigerated food should be reheated thoroughly and then allowed to cool before serving it to the baby.

4. It is advisable not to store half-eaten food or milk for later use by the baby as germs may grow in it and its administration to him can be quite risky.

5. Do not add cereal or any other solid foods to the milk in the baby's bottle. These must always be kept in a bowl or cup for the baby to have.

6. The addition of extra sugar and salt to the baby's food should be restricted to the minimum. This dietary restriction is recommended because habits formed early in infancy tend to persist into adult life. The intake of excessive amounts of salt and sugar is detrimental to the health of an adult as they tend to induce high blood pressure and obesity with several resultant complications.

7. Use whole milk and not skimmed milk, at least till the child is five years old.

8. If an older baby feels hungry between meals, offer him fresh fruit, bread or savoury home-made preparations instead of sweets from the market, chocolates and sweet biscuits.

9. Do not leave your baby alone while he is feeding because of the risk of choking. For the same reason, it is advisable to avoid giving whole nuts to your baby till he is 5 years old. He may accidentally swallow it the wrong way and choke.

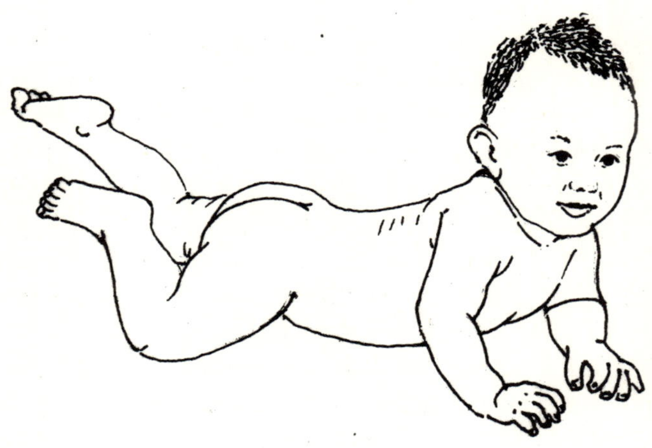

6

DIET FOR GOOD HEALTH

It is important that a child's diet should be both good in quality as well as adequate in quantity. The child needs it not only for maintaining his health and vitality but also for achieving good growth and development. If his diet is deficient in nutrients and energy it can adversely affect his weight gain and body growth. It may also cause various types of nutritional disorders, anaemia and deficiency diseases. Malnutrition causes lowering of a child's body resistance thereby making him prone to recurrent infections. Infections result in reduction of the child's appetite and intake of food which, in turn, contribute further to his malnutrition. A vicious cycle of malnutrition-infection-malnutrition is thus set up.

WHAT DOES THE CHILD NEED?

The child's diet should supply him with proteins, carbohydrates, fats, vitamins, minerals and other nutrients in adequate quantities. Each of these constituents serves an important function in the human body. Proteins are needed for body building, growth and for repair of body tissues. Carbohydrates are the main sources of energy. Fats contain energy in a concentrated form and are essential for the absorption of vitamins A, D, E and K. Various vitamins, iron and other minerals are required for the proper formation of blood, the laying down of bones, healing of wounds, maintenance of skin and for carrying out several other important body functions.

WHAT IS A BALANCED DIET?

A diet which contains all the nutrients (e.g., energy, proteins, fats, vitamins, minerals, etc.) required by a child for the proper maintenance of health and optimum growth is termed a 'balanced' diet. However, various foods vary widely in their nutritive value. For example, lentils (*dals*) and beans have high contents of proteins and a small amount of fat while bread is rich in carbohydrates but poor in proteins. An intelligent mother, therefore, needs to know certain basic facts about the different food items so that she can manage to provide a proper balanced diet in a palatable and acceptable form to her child.

CATEGORIZATION OF DIFFERENT FOODS

The various foodstuffs for a child's consumption can be categorized into four major and two minor groups on the basis of their composition. Broadly speaking, Group I includes *chapaties*, bread, rice, breakfast cereals, maize, potatoes, etc.; Group II, lentils, peas, beans, poultry and meats; Group III, milk, cheese, yoghurt, and other milk products; Group IV comprises various fruits and vegetables; Group V includes vegetable oils, ghee, butter and cream; and Group VI consists of sugar, sugary foods and drinks.

THE FOOD GROUPS: SOME IMPORTANT FACTS

GROUP-I

The main foods in this group are (a) *chapaties*, bread and other wheat containing food products; (b) rice and foods made with rice; (c) maize (corn), barley, oat products; and (d) potatoes and other starchy vegetables. These foods chiefly provide energy, starch and dietary fibre as well as some proteins, vitamins and minerals. Wheat and other cereals are also rich in Group B vitamins. The fibre in these foods prevents constipation.

GROUP-II

These are mainly protein containing foods such as lentils, peas, beans, eggs, fish, poultry, meats, nuts and are important for the child's growth and tissue repair. If your child does not eat meat, he can obtain the protein needed by him from the vegetarian foods in this group and from the cereals in his diet. Eggs, cheese and milk are also a good source of proteins. The food items in this group also contain some vitamins and minerals.

GROUP-III

Milk and milk products are the chief sources of calcium and phosphorus, essential for the formation of strong bones and teeth. They are also excellent sources of proteins, calories, vitamins A and B and several minerals.

GROUP-IV

This important group comprises all types of fresh fruits, fruit juice, vegetables and salad. They provide vitamins as well as fibre.

Oranges, *mosambi, malta*, lemon and other citrus fruits are rich sources of vitamin C. Red and orange coloured fruits and vegetables like mangoes, papaya, peaches, apricots, carrots and tomatoes are rich in vitamin A. Dark green leafy vegetables like spinach, cabbage and salads are excellent sources of iron and a number of vitamins, especially vitamin C.

GROUP-V

Vegetable oils, ghee (both *desi* and *vanaspati*), butter, margarine and cream make up most of the fats in our diet. Fats are important sources of energy as well as vitamins A,D,E, and K. You can make good use of them in improving the energy density of your child's food, especially if he is a small eater. However, if his food intake is generally adequate, it is advisable for him to consume food items rich in fat in moderation. As mentioned already, excessive intake of fat leads to obesity in a child who then goes on to become an obese adult. Obesity in adults carries high risks of heart disease and blood vessel disorders. In this context, you should know that your child derives the fats required by him not only from oils, butter and cream but also from sources like whole milk and milk products, egg, meat and fish.

GROUP-VI

This group includes sugar, sweets of all kinds, biscuits, cakes, chocolates, jam, sweet puddings and sugary drinks like fizzy colas, squashes and drinks. Although rich in calories and compellingly tasty and inviting, they hardly contain any other important nutrients. Their intake should be restricted so that the child can take an adequate quantity of foods from the more important first four major groups. However, they do add variety and no harm would be done by eating them occasionally.

HOW TO PROVIDE A BALANCED DIET

Your child would receive a proper, balanced diet if he eats a meal consisting of food items belonging to each of the first four major food groups. It is not necessary that he must strictly take one food from each group at every meal.

If he takes a mix of various kinds of foods from these groups during the space of a day or even during the space of a week, his requirements of different types of nutrients would be adequately met.

Since cooking oils and ghee (belonging to Group V) are fairly liberally used in the preparation of most Indian home foods and some fat is also present in foodstuffs in the four major food groups, the Indian mother does not usually need to pay special attention to foodstuffs of Group V in her child's diet. However, the rich energy fats assume special importance in the diet of children who are small eaters. The use of extra amounts of fats in the food of these children helps to enhance the energy content of their diet which is otherwise deficient in calories owing to the small size of its total intake.

Besides ensuring variety in the child's diet, it is also important for you to ensure that your child takes food in adequate quantity as a whole. Considering a child's inability to eat a lot at a time because of the small size of his stomach, it is advisable that his food should be comparatively rich in its nutritive value and that he should eat more often during the course of a day.

IRON AND VITAMINS

Iron is an important mineral for young children and its deficiency causes anaemia. Dark green vegetables and meat are rich in iron. It is also found in *chapaties,* bread, eggs, *dals*, nuts and beans. Different vitamins serve different useful functions in the human body. Vitamin A is useful for vision in dim light and for maintaining the health of skin and inner mucous linings of the body. Vitamin C promotes healing of wounds; helps in maintaining the lining of blood vessels and plays a role in the growth and development of bones. Vitamin D is necessary for the absorption of calcium and its deficiency causes rickets. Vitamin K is needed for normal clotting of blood. The vitamin B Complex group of vitamins comprise chiefly thiamine vitamin (B_1), riboflavin (B_2), niacin, pyridoxine (B_6) and vitamin (B_{12}). They serve varied functions in the human body. As a result of riboflavin deficiency, the tongue becomes red and sore, and develops cracks. Severe vitamin (B_1) deficiency may occasionally cause *beri-beri* in which the nervous system and the heart are adversely affected.

The various vitamins described above are present in varying amounts in a wide variety of food. What is important for you to know is that if your child eats a good varied diet, as explained earlier, he will have enough of the necessary vitamins and minerals. There is thus no need to give extra vitamin and iron supplements to a child who is eating a variety of solid foods as well as fruits and vegetables. However, if your child is too finicky and his intake of fruits and vegetables is very poor, you may need to give him vitamins and iron supplements. You must however, consult your doctor first.

PRACTICAL TIPS ON CHILD FEEDING

1. As advised earlier, let your child have a varied diet with food items derived from each of the four major food groups. It does not really matter if he insists on taking an almost fixed group of food preparations for a few days as long as he takes a balanced diet on the whole in sufficient quantity. With patient encouragement and his own changing tastes, he will gradually widen his choice.

2. Milk and milk products are important sources of energy, proteins, calcium and vitamin A. Besides other foods, a child must take about ½ litre (500 ml; 18 oz) of milk or milk products per day from the age of one year onwards. A child below five years should be given whole milk and not skimmed or semi-skimmed milk.

3. If your child is difficult and finicky about the common family diet you can help him by making more attractive and palatable food preparations. For example, milk may be given as a flavoured drink or as milk shake, or in the form of yoghurt, ice cream, milk pudding, *khoya*, etc.

4. Heavy snacks between meals should be discouraged as they spoil the child's appetite for his main meals. If need be, it is better to offer him fresh fruit (may be as fruit *chaat*), sandwiches with various fillings, salted *chana* (Bengal gram), peanuts and popcorn instead of sweets, cakes and chocolates. If he insists on having sweet snacks, it would be better to give him home-cooked preparations like rice milk pudding (*Kheer*), *sooji ka halwa, etc.*

5. Sugar is a major cause of tooth decay in children. You should cut down on sugary foods like sweets, chocolates, biscuits, cakes, fizzy colas and squashes. It is better to give fresh fruit juices instead of artificially sweetened and flavoured drinks. When the child takes chocolates, sweets or fizzy drinks, he should consume them quickly rather than nibble or sip them over long intervals. This reduces the sugar's contact with the child's teeth and the resultant damage.

6. Do not be overanxious about the probable inadequacy of your child's diet. If he is fit and healthy, growing and gaining weight and is full of energy, don't fuss about his eating. You can rest assured he is receiving adequate nutrition.

7. Mealtimes should be enjoyable, both for the child and for you. Talk about things other than food and avoid getting into a battle of will with him on the choice of food items at each meal.

8. If a child is a poor eater, try and get some other children of the same age who are good eaters to have meals along with him. A good example sometimes works. Some children eat better in the company of their grandparents or some other adult member of the family for whom they have some special liking.

9. If your child tends to be overweight, reduce the use of cooking oil and ghee while preparing your family food. Where feasible, grill or bake instead of frying his food. If you are a non-vegetarian, trim the visible fat off the red meat and skin off fish and poultry. It may also be preferable to use sunflower and corn oil to cook food for the whole family instead of saturated fats like ghee, especially if there is a strong family history of coronary heart disease.

7
IMMUNIZATION

The procedure of giving a vaccine to an individual to protect him from disease is called 'immunization'.

WHAT IS A VACCINE?

Some diseases like poliomyelitis and measles are caused by viruses and some others like whooping cough and diptheria are caused by bacteria. When a child suffers from one of these infections, his body produces antibodies against the causative germs. Those antibodies subsequently protect the child against another attack of the same disease. The basic principle underlying this human body response of producing protective antibodies against natural infections has been utilized by scientists to develop vaccines. Vaccines contain small amounts of weakened (or killed) viruses/ bacteria or their toxic chemicals. When a particular vaccine is given to a child, his body produces antibodies in response to the vaccine and the child develops protection against that specific disease. The organisms and toxic chemicals contained in the vaccine are however, too weak to cause any illness in the child.

WHY GIVE VACCINES?

Tuberculosis, poliomyelitis, diphtheria, whooping cough, tetanus, measles and mumps are serious diseases. They can cause grave illnesses in children involving the lungs, brain, heart and other vital organs. An affected child may get crippled with lifelong physical and mental disabilities like brain damage, deafness, paralysed limbs and heart disease, or he may die. Timely administration of vaccines protects children from these and some other serious illnesses.

COMMONLY USED VACCINES

The names of commonly used vaccines, the diseases against which they are effective and their routes of administration are given below:

Name of vaccine	Diseases prevented	Route of administration
1. BCG	Tuberculosis	Injection
2. Polio	Poliomyelitis	Drops by mouth (also available as injection)
3. Hepatitis B	Hepatitis B (a type of jaundice)	Injection
4. DPT (Triple antigen)	(i) Diphtheria (ii) Pertussis (whooping cough) (iii) Tetanus	Injection
5. Measles	Measles	Injection
6. MMR	(i) Measles (ii) Mumps (iii) Rubella	Injection
7. Tetanus Toxoid (TT)	Tetanus	Injection

Name of vaccine	Diseases prevented	Route of administration
8. Hib	H. influenzae type b infections	Injection
9. Typhoid	Typhoid fever	Injection
Optional Vaccines		
i. Varicella	Chicken Pox	Injection
ii. Hepatitis A	Hepatitis A (Common type of jaundice)	Injection
iii. Pneumococcal Vaccine	Pneumonia, Meningitis (casued by pneumococci)	Injection
Vaccines for special situations:		
i. Meningococcal	Meningococcal meningitis	Injection
ii. Rabies	Rabies	Injection
iii. Cholera	Cholera	Injection

IMMUNIZATION SCHEDULE

Some serious diseases like tuberculosis, poliomyelitis and whooping cough can affect babies very early in life, while others like typhoid fever occur later. Considering this and several other relevant factors, a timetable for giving different vaccines is formulated so as to provide timely and effective protection to children against various preventable diseases. The immunization schedule generally followed in India is placed below.

Age	Name of Vaccine	Dose
Birth to 2 Weeks	BCG Polio Hepatitis B	1 Dose 1st Dose 1st Dose

Age	Name of Vaccine	Dose
6 Weeks	Polio* DPT Hepatitis B Hib	2nd Dose 1st Dose 2nd Dose 1st Dose
10 Weeks	Polio DPT Hib	3rd Dose 2nd Dose 2nd Dose
14 Weeks	Polio DPT Hib	4th Dose 3rd Dose 3rd Dose
At 14 weeks or at 6 months	Hepatitis B	3rd Dose
9 Months	Measles	1 Dose
15-18 Months	Polio DPT Hib MMR	5th Dose 1st booster dose Booster Dose 1st Dose
2 Years	Typhoid	1 Dose
5 Years	Polio DPT Typhoid** MMR***	6th Dose 2nd booster booster booster
10 Years	Tetanus Toxoid (TT) or Td*	Booster (1)
16 Years	Tetanus Toxoid (TT) or Td*	Booster (2)
Pregnant Woman	Tetanus Toxoid (TT)	2 doses at 4 Weeks interval

* The polio vaccine should be given to the child on all national pulse polio immunisation days, besides those according to his own immunization schedule given above. Inactivated polio vaccine (given by intra muscular injection) is also now available. You may enquire about it from your doctor.

** Typhoid vaccination is recommended every 3 years to maintain continued protection.

*** A booster dose of MMR Vaccine is now recommended at 5 years of age (school entry). If missed, by 12 years, or so, especially in girls.

SCHEDULE FOR OPTIONAL VACCINES

Age	Vaccine	Number of Doses	Route of administration
At / above 15 month	Varicella (Chicken Pox)	(i) If age below 13 years: 1 dose (ii) If age 13 years or above: 2 doses at 4-8 weeks interval	Injection

Age	Vaccine	Number of Doses	Route of administration
At / above 18 month	Hepatitis A	2 doses at interval of 6-12 months	Injection
At 6, 10, 14 weeks + booster at 15 months	Pneumococcal (conjugate)	3 doses + booster (1)	Injection

WHY GIVE MULTIPLE DOSES OF A VACCINE?

In the case of some vaccines, a single dose does not produce sufficiently high level of antibodies so as to provide adequate protection. Further injections are necessary (e.g., a course of 3 injections in the case of DPT) for the development of adequate immunity. This immunity has, sometimes, to be reinforced later by giving 'booster' doses after an interval of 1 year or more in order to maintain continued protection to the child for a longer period.

WHAT MUST PARENTS KNOW ABOUT VACCINES?

BCG VACCINE

This vaccine provides protection to the child against tuberculosis. A single injection of this vaccine is given in the left shoulder region. It does not cause any immediate reaction, such as fever or pain at the site of the injection. A small nodule usually appears about 4 to 6 weeks later at the injection site. It may have a little watery or creamy discharge and vary in its size intermittently over the next 6 to 8 weeks. This is normal. The nodule usually subsides by about 12 weeks leaving behind a permanent thin, light-coloured scar.

If your baby shows no local reaction even 8 weeks after BCG vaccination, report it to your doctor. He may like to check whether the vaccine administration has been successful or not. It may, sometimes, need to be repeated.

If the child develops a swelling in his left armpit or in the neck, it may mean that a lymph gland in the area has become inflamed. Consult your doctor.

DPT (TRIPLE ANTIGEN)

This vaccine confers protection to the child against diphtheria, pertussis (whooping cough) and tetanus. The child may develop fever, irritability, pain and swelling over the site of injection which may last for one to two days. These symptoms can be easily relieved by giving the child a dose of paracetamol syrup as and when required.

You should consult your doctor if the swelling and pain at the site of the injection persist for more than three to four days. Very rarely, a baby may develop high fever (above 103°F or 39.5°C) or a persistent, shrill crying for more than four hours. If you notice these or any other unusual reaction (which are rare) seek advice from your doctor.

POLIO VACCINE

Your child must regularly receive oral doses of polio vaccine as per his immunization schedule to protect him from poliomyelitis. In addition, he should be given polio drops on all pulse polio immunization days. Polio vaccine does not cause diarrohea, fever or any other significant side effects. Besides oral, inactivated polio vaccine, which is given by intramuscular injection, is also available.

MEASLES VACCINE

The measles vaccine is generally recommended to be given to children in India at the age of 9 months. But if an epidemic of measles occurs in your area, the measles vaccine should be given to younger babies who are between 6 and 9 months of age. This should be followed by a dose of MMR vaccine (mealses, mumps, rubella) vaccine between 15 to 18 months of age in order to ensure that these babies develop adequate long-term protection aganinst measles.

There is no fever or any other significant rection soon after the administration of measles vaccine. The baby may, however, develop transient mild fever and rash over his face and body 5 to 7 days later, which subside on their own.

There is no upper age limit for giving the measles vaccine. If a child has not received measles or MMR vaccine, and if he has not already suffered from measles, the vaccine can be given to him at any age.

MMR (MEASLES, MUMPS, RUBELLA) VACCINE

The MMR vaccine confers protection against measles. mumps and rubella (German measles). Protection against rubella is particularly important for girls. If a pregnant woman develops rubella, especially during the first four months of pregnancy, her baby becomes highly liable to suffer from serious birth defects involving his heart, brain, eyes, and other vital organs. A dose of MMR vaccine is recommended at 15-18 months of age followed by a second dose at 5 years (school entry). It the second dose has not been given earlier, it should be given by about 12 years, especially in girls before child-bearing age.

TYPHOID VACCINE

Typhoid is a very common disease in India and many other developing countries. Children above 2 years of age are more at risk of developing this disease than younger children due to the greater chances of their exposure to contaminated food and water outside the home. It is, therefore, considered advisable to provide protection to over two year old children against typhoid fever with the aid of typhoid vaccine alongwith the observance of other preventive measures. (For details refer to Typhoid fever in the section on Common Diseases In Children.)

Three types of typhoid vaccine are now available, out of which two have to be given by injection, while the third is available in capsule form. There is no significant difference in the efficacy of the three types of vaccines.

(i) The older type of typhoid vaccine is inexpensive. Initially, two doses of this vaccine are given by injection at an interval of four weeks. Booster doses may be given at 3 years interval.

(ii) The new Vi typhoid vaccine is comparatively costly. A single injection is given to begin with and then repeat doses every three years. This vacine is recommended

for children at 2 years of age and above.
(iii) An oral typhoid vaccine has recently become available for children above 6 years of age. One capsule of this vaccine has to be swallowed as a whole on alternate days for three days (three capsules in all). Subsequently repeat doses are to be given every two to three years.

HEPATITIS B VACCINE

Hepatitis B virus infection, besides causing jaundice, can lead to chronic liver damage and liver cancer. Hepatitis B vaccine provides good protection against this infection. The first dose of this vaccine should be given within 2 weeks and preferably within 48 hours of the baby's birth (along with BCG and polio vaccine) followed by the second dose at 6 weeks of age (along with DPT and polio vaccine). The child should receive the third dose at 14 weeks or 6 months of age.

Although immunization with Hepatitis B vaccine should preferbly commence soon after birth, if missed, it can be started later in older children. The first dose of the vaccine is then followed by the second and the third dose after 1 month and 6 months of the first dose respectively.

If a pregnant monther during her routine antenatal checkup is found to be Hepatitis B positive, protective vaccination of her newborn baby must be started within 12 hours of his birth. In this situation, the baby also needs simultaneous administration of one dose of HBIG (Hepatitis B immunoglobulin) by intramuscular injection at a separate site along with the first dose of hepatitis B vaccine. The second dose of Hepatitis B vaccine is given 1 month later and the third dose 6 months after the first dose.

HIB VACCINE

Infecton by Hib (Haemophilus influenzae type b) organism is responsible for causing pneumonia, meningitis and several other illnesses in many children below 5 years of age. For protection against this infection, initially three doses of Hib vaccine are recommended, one dose each along with DPTand polio vaccine at 6, 10 and 14 weeks of age, followed by a booster dose at 15 months of age. When immunisation with this vaccine gets delayed and is started between 7 and 11 months of age, two doses are given 1 to 2 months apart followed by a booster at 15 months of age. Children from 12 to 14 months of age need one initial dose of this vaccine followed by booster at 15 months of age or older, but not less than 2 months after the previous dose. A single dose of Hib vaccine is given to children aged between 15 months and 5 years who have not received this vaccine earlier. It is not considered necessary to administer this vaccine to more than 5 year old children in view of the low incidence of Hib infection among them.

Hepatitis A vaccine: It provides immunity against jaundice casued by Hepatitis A varus infection. The vaccine is safe and effective. It is recommended for administration by injection in two doses at an interval of 6 months to 1 year to children from the age of 18 months onwards.

Chicken pox vaccine : This vaccine is useful but expensive. A single dose by injection is recommended for children from the age of 12 months up to 12 years of age. Children aged 13 years and above need two doses with an interval of 4 to 8 weeks.

Rabies vaccine: It should be administered as per doçtor's instructions in the case of bites by animals suspected to be suffering from rabies or unprovoked bites by stray and possibly rabid animals (dog, monkey, cat, mongoose and jackal).

MENINGOCOCCAL VACCINE (AGAINST ONE TYPE OF MENINGITIS)

Infection by a number of different bacteria and viruses can cause inflammation of the meninges, which is medically termed as 'meningitis'. Meninges are thin, sheet-like covering on the outer surface of the brain and spinal cord. Meningococci are one of the several organisms (bacteria and viruses) which can cause meningitis. The generally available meningococcal vaccine is effective only against infection and meningitis caused by meningococci (strains A and C only). It does not protect against all types of meningitis. There is no need for routine administration of this vaccine to all children. Strictly speaking, its use should be restricted to situations of an epidemic of meningococcal meningitis caused by meningococci in your area, under specific instructions of a paediatrician.

ANSWERS TO COMMON PROBLEMS

WHAT TO DO IF IMMUNIZATION GETS DELAYED?

It is advisable to begin immunization on schedule so that the child receives the protective vaccines in time. However, it is never too late. Do start straightaway in consultation with your doctor. He would arrange a suitable timetable for your child.

IMMUNIZATION STARTED BUT SUBSEQUENTLY MISSED

You do not have to start the whole immunization programme again. If your child had his first injection of a three dose schedule and he did not have his second dose on time (say, 4 months have passed while he was expected to have it after 1 month of the first dose), you can complete the course now by giving him the remaining two doses. There is no need to repeat the first dose of vaccine.

VACCINE IS DUE BUT MY CHILD IS ILL. WHAT SHOULD I DO?

If your child has a simple running nose, mild cough, a skin rash or some other mild illness without significant fever and the child is generally well, let him have his vaccine. There is no need to delay it. You should obtain your doctor's advice if the child has an acute infection with high fever, frequent loose motions, vomiting or some other serious illness. Immunization may sometimes need to be postponed for a while, but do remember to give it as soon as he gets well.

8

GROWING AND LEARNING

NORMAL PATTERN OF GROWTH

With age, children grow both in weight and height. Their rate of growth is however not uniform throughout the whole period of their childhood. Growth in the first few years of life is very rapid, it slows down later. Another spurt in growth takes place at adolescence. Most babies double their birth weight at 5 months and treble it at 1 year. While the average length of the baby at birth is about 50 cm (20 inches), it rises to 75 cm (30 inches) at 1 year, i.e, 1½ times than that at birth. It doubles to 100 cm (40 inches) by about 4 years. In later years, the child gains height at about 5 cm (2 inches) per year till the onset of puberty. There is a spurt in gain in height at puberty, which begins at around 10 years of age in girls and 12 years in boys. The expected average weight and height of Indian children at different ages is given below.

Boys

Age	Weight (kg)	Height (cm)
Birth	3.0	50.0
6 months	7.2	66.0
1 year	9.5	75.0
2 years	11.5	85.0
3 years	13.5	94.0
4 years	15.4	100.0
5 years	17.2	106.0

Girls

Age	Weight (kg)	Height (cm)
Birth	2.9	48.5
6 months	6.6	64.2
1 year	9.0	72.5
2 years	11.0	84.0
3 years	13.0	93.0
4 years	15.0	99.0
5 years	16.5	105.5

It must, however, be clearly understood that there is a lot of variation in the height and weight of children at different ages. There are also significant variations in the height and weight of children from different regions and communities in a vast and diverse country like India.

HOW TO ASSESS GROWTH?

A regular periodic check on the progress of a child's weight and height is a good method of assessing his health and progress. It is more appropriate than making a single recording of these parameters at any single point of time. It is recommended that the child should be weighed at monthly intervals during the first year, every 2 months during the second year and every 3 months thereafter up to the age of 5 years. The child's weight, height and some other important

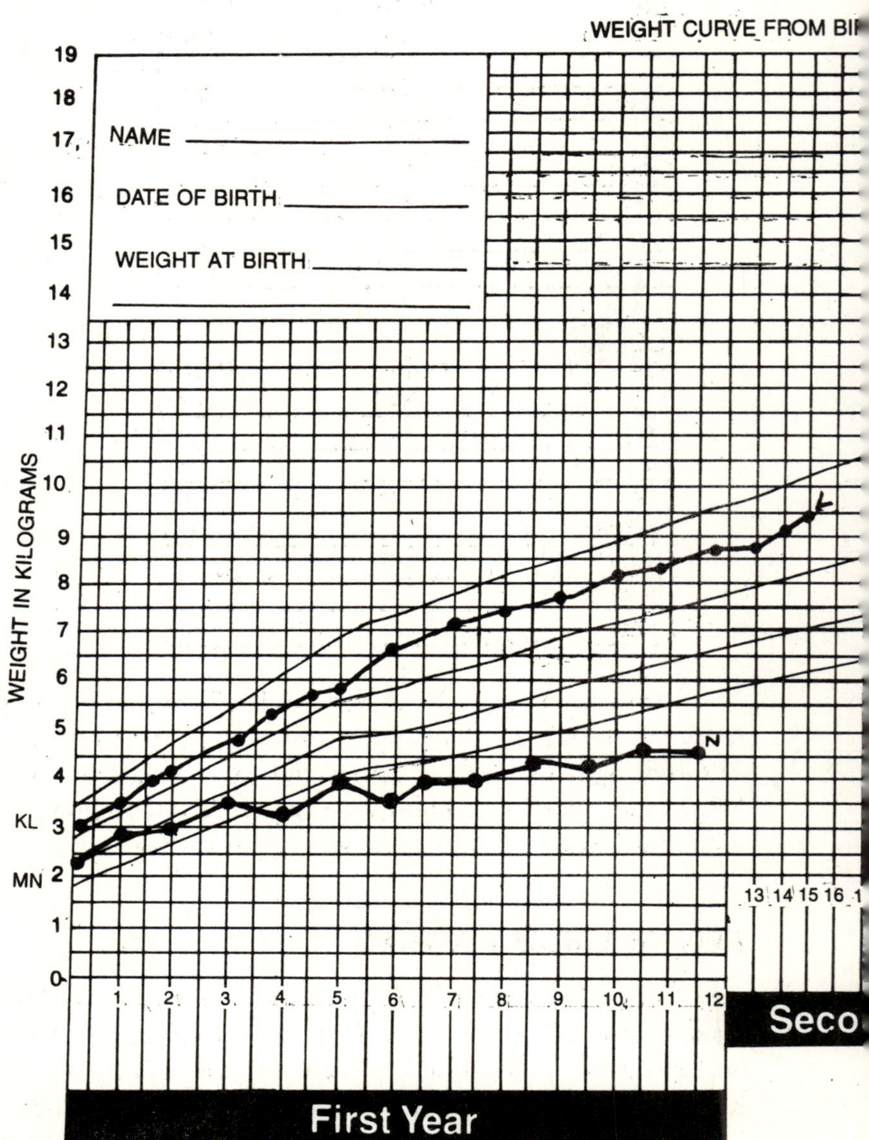
WEIGHT CURVE FROM BI
NAME
DATE OF BIRTH
WEIGHT AT BIRTH
WEIGHT IN KILOGRAMS
19
18
17
16
15
14
13
12
11
10
9
8
7
6
5
4
3
2
1
0
KL
MN
1 2 3 4 5 6 7 8 9 10 11 12
First Year
13 14 15 16
Seco

(Fig. 8.1)

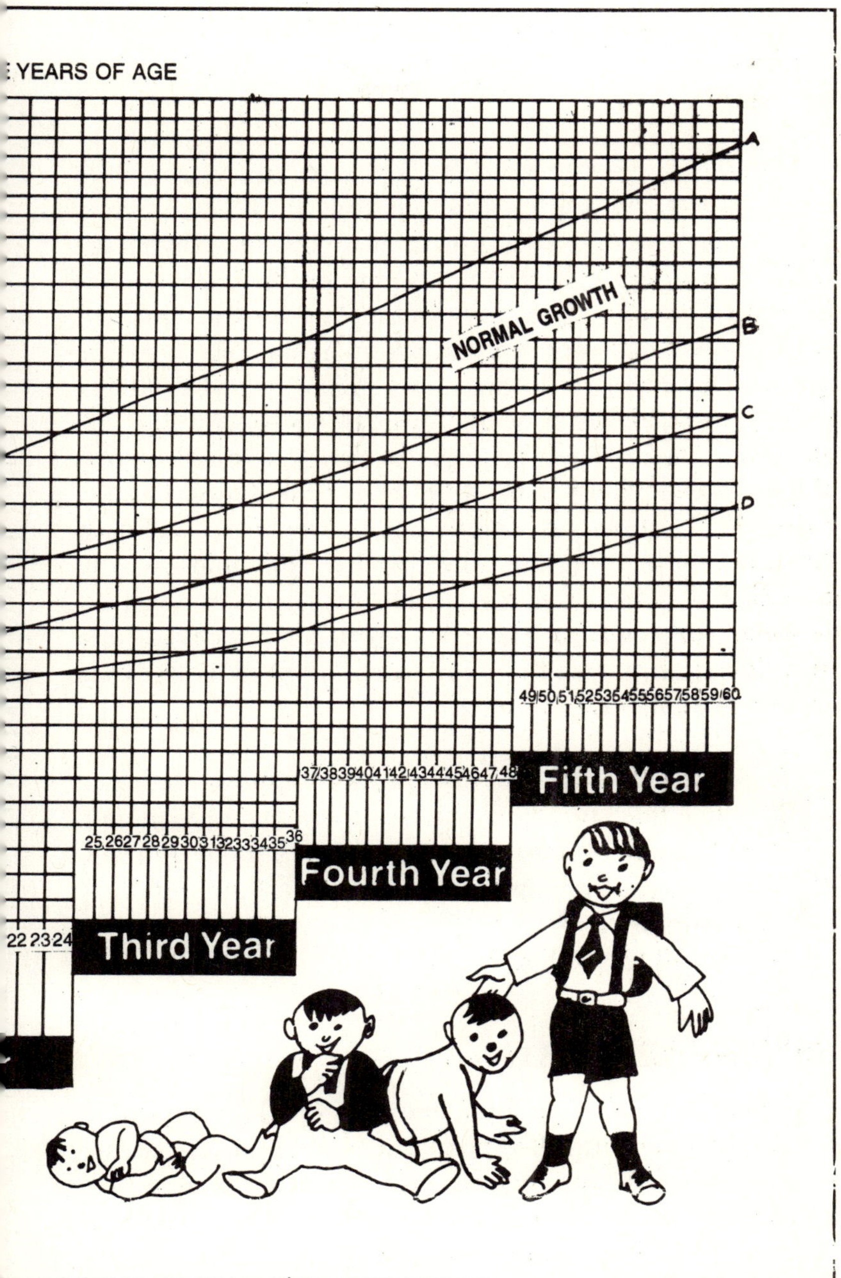
YEARS OF AGE
A
NORMAL GROWTH
B
C
D
49 50 51 52 53 54 55 56 57 58 59 60
Fifth Year
37 38 39 40 41 42 43 44 45 46 47 48
Fourth Year
25 26 27 28 29 30 31 32 33 34 35 36
Third Year
22 23 24

facts, like his immunization status, are recorded on a growth chart. Several types of growth charts are presently in use in India.

A growth chart commonly employed for assessment of growth and nutritional status of children in the community is shown in Fig. 8.1. This growth chart has the child's age on the horizontal axis, and the weight on the vertical axis. An individual child's weight is recorded on this chart by placing dots at the appropriate places against his age. The dots are later joined to draw the child's personal weight curve. If the child is growing normally, his weight line will run in the zone between the topmost curve 'A' and the curve 'B' lying immediately below it in a direction almost parallel to the 'A'/'B' curves. A healthy child's weight curve K-L is shown in Fig. 8.1. On the other hand, if the child's weight line falls below the 'B' curve, it indicates malnutrition (like the weight line M-N in Fig. 8.1). Further, if the height of a child does not progress properly or it stops altogether, he must be examined by a doctor.

It is useful to remember that a very important index of a child's health status are his levels of energy and activity, his appetite and his sense of wellbeing. A high spirited, exuberant, happy and playful child, who is eating well, may look rather thin, but that should not cause any worry to the parents regarding his health.

ACQUIRING NEW SKILLS

There is a wide variation among normal children with regard to the time at which they acquire different skills after birth, such as their ability to sit, stand or walk; speak words and sentences or handle objects. At the same time, a particular child may gain one skill earlier than the average group of children and master another later than the average.

WHY DO PARENTS NEED TO KNOW?

An understanding of a child's normal development enhances the pleasure of the parents in watching their child as he grows and acquires increasingly complex abilities. It also helps them in interacting with him suitably and devising play and other activities which would encourage the growth of such skills. An appreciation of the fact that one normal child may achieve a particular capacity (e.g., to begin to walk) later than another child of the same age, avoids unnecessary anxiety. At the same time, knowledge of the expected progress in a child's development helps the parents in early detection of any abnormal delays. In such cases, parents can seek expert medical opinion at an early stage. For example, it is generally the intelligent parents, who regularly watch their baby's daily activities and behaviour, that first pick up hearing defects in their babies. It is much more diffucult for a medical officer to do so during the rush of patients at the clinic, with the baby sometimes feeling sleepy or being uncooperative and cranky. And the earlier a problem, such as in his hearing, is detected less is the damage caused to the child and better would be the long-term results of his treatment.

MILESTONES OF DEVELOPMENT

BIRTH TO 6 MONTHS

As the baby grows older, he develops new abilities, so unique to his doting parents. He begins to watch his mother intently as she speaks to him at about 2 weeks and to smile at her at around 4 to 6 weeks. The mother should however take care not to misinterpret any inadvertent facial movement of her baby in sleep as a true smile. The baby must be seen to smile actively in response to gestures made to him. By about 6 to 8 weeks he can follow a bright coloured moving toy held at a distance of about 20 cm (8 inches). At around 3 months he recognizes his mother and starts to

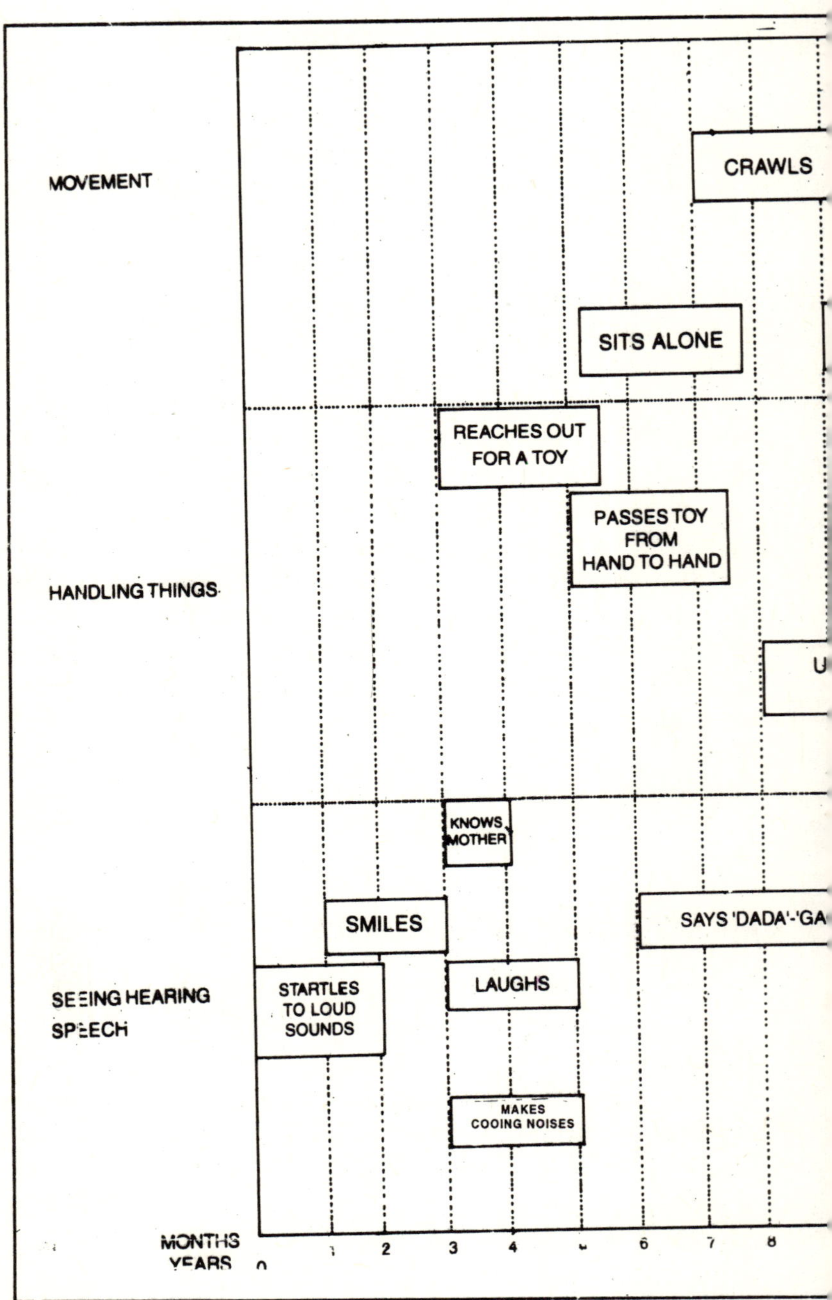
MOVEMENT
CRAWLS
SITS ALONE
HANDLING THINGS
REACHES OUT FOR A TOY
PASSES TOY FROM HAND TO HAND
SEEING HEARING SPEECH
KNOWS MOTHER
SMILES
SAYS 'DADA'-'GA
STARTLES TO LOUD SOUNDS
LAUGHS
MAKES COOING NOISES
MONTHS
YEARS
2
3
4
6
7
8

(Fig. 8.2)

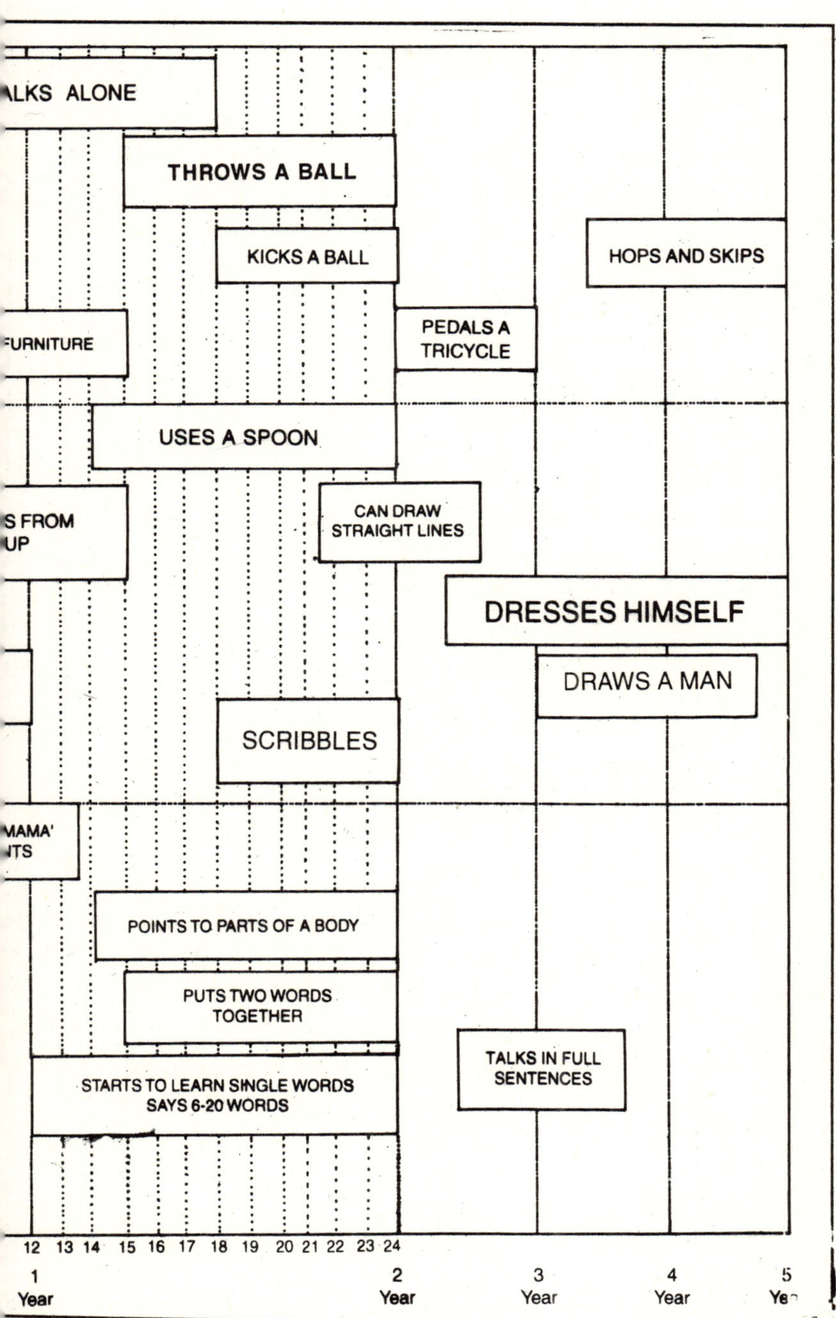
ALKS ALONE
THROWS A BALL
KICKS A BALL
HOPS AND SKIPS
FURNITURE
PEDALS A TRICYCLE
USES A SPOON
S FROM
UP
CAN DRAW STRAIGHT LINES
DRESSES HIMSELF
DRAWS A MAN
SCRIBBLES
MAMA'
ITS
POINTS TO PARTS OF A BODY
PUTS TWO WORDS TOGETHER
TALKS IN FULL SENTENCES
STARTS TO LEARN SINGLE WORDS SAYS 6-20 WORDS
12 13 14 15 16 17 18 19 20 21 22 23 24
1 Year
2 Year
3 Year
4 Year
5 Ye

chuckle, laugh and make cooing noises of his own. He is now able to hold a rattle in his hand and turns his head towards sounds made at his ear level. He reaches out for a toy when 3 months old and begins to transfer it from one hand to another in another 6 weeks' time. At about 6 months he can sit on the floor with hands held forward for support.

6 MONTHS TO 1 YEAR

At around 7 months he can sit without support for a few seconds and roll over from his lying position on his back on to his tummy. He tries to crawl at around 7 to 8 months. Some babies go backwards before they crawl forward and most finally succeed by about 9 months. At about the same time he learns to pull himself up to a standing position by holding on to the furniture. At around 10 months, while begining to wave with his hands he also starts to cruise around holding on to the furniture. Generally, by his first birthday, a baby can stand briefly without support, for about 10 seconds or so. Most of them are able to walk alone between 11 and 15 months. While there can be considerable variation between different children, you should consult your doctor if your baby is not walking by 18 months.

12 MONTHS TO 36 MONTHS

At around 15 months he starts crawling up the stairs and learns to feed himself albeit messily. He can now construct a tower of 2 cubes and progressively improves with effort, finally making one of 9 cubes by the age of 3 years. From about 18 months onwards he enjoys scribbling with a crayon. He can copy and draw a horizontal or vertical line at 2 years, a circle by 3 years and a plus sign by 4 years. He learns to draw the outline of a person (with something like a face and arms and legs) between 3 and 4 years. The parents can help the child in the early attainment of such manual skills by providing suitable materials, encouragement and practice. At around 2 years he begins to climb stairs placing both feet at each step. When 3 years old he can walk stairs with alternating feet but still uses two feet to a step while going downstairs. He learns to pedal a tricycle between 2 and 3 years of age.

AGE RANGE OF ACHIEVEMENT OF SKILLS

As has been emphasized above, there is an age range (and not a particular fixed age) during which most children gain different skills. The figure (Fig. 8.2) illustrates the time spans in which different abilities are acquired.

DETECTION OF ABNORMAL DELAY IN DEVELOPMENT

Although there are considerable variations in the time span during which children acquire different skills, a normal child is expected to definitely develop certain abilities by a particular age. If a mother notices that her child has not developed the following abilities by the age given against each, she must immediately consult a doctor for an urgent checkup of her baby. He may be in need of special help.

WARNING SIGNALS FOR PARENTS

AGE	MILESTONE OF DEVELOPMENT NOT ACHIEVED AS YET
1½ to 2 months	Baby not responding to voices or everyday sounds.
3-4 months	Not showing interest in persons and playthings.
4-5 months	Unable to hold up his head when held in a sitting position in the mother's lap or when pulled up by the hand from a lying to a sitting position.
9 months	Not able to sit on his own without support.
10 months	Not 'babbling' repetitively (i.e., saying 'dada' 'dada,' etc.) by himself and to others.

18 months	Unable to walk alone without support.
21 months	Not speaking single words (average 13- 15 months).
27 months	Not putting 2-3 words together in sentences (average 18-22 months).
4 years	Not using fully intelligible speech (average 3-3½ years).

ROUTINE DEVELOPMENT CHECKS BY YOUR DOCTOR

While parents should carefully observe the progress of a child's development as outlined earlier and seek medical advice in the event of his significantly lagging behind the average range, the child should be routinely taken to a child specialist for development checks (i) at 6 weeks, (ii) at 6 months, (iii) at 10 months, (iv) at 18 months, and (v) at 2½ to 3 years.

The aim is to allow early detection of developmental delays which may be occurring due to an otherwise unrecognized disease and which can be helped best by intervention at an early stage.

HEARING AND EYE CHECKUPS IN YOUNG BABIES

HEARING DEFECTS AND CHECKS

Adequate hearing is essential for the development of normal speech and to help the child understand the world around him. Hearing defect in a baby is often missed in the early stages and it is only when he is around 2½ to 3 years old, that he is wrongly suspected to be suffering from a speech defect or to be mentally subnormal. It is therefore, extremely important that parents begin to observe their baby early and watch his responses to sounds and noises around him when he is about 3 months old. At 4 months he should turn his head towards a rattle making noises at the level of his ears (but outside his line of vision). If he seems quite unaware of the sound, do consult your doctor. New hearing tests are now available which can help detect hearing defects in young babies.

VISION

Babies can see from birth, but they only begin to recognize their parents at a distance of about 20 cm (8 inches) from the age of about 2 weeks onward. They begin to smile in response to overtures at around 4 to 6 weeks. Blind babies tend to smile late. A baby's vision is tested by assessing his ability to follow a moving object with his eyes. An older child is asked to match shapes or letters with those on a chart placed at a distance.

INDICATIONS FOR EARLY CONSULTATION FOR EYES

You should seek early advice from an ophthalmologist if your baby shows any of the following features:

1. SQUINT

It must first be understood that many normal babies show alternating squint in both eyes in the first few weeks after birth. This is because initially each eye focuses on an object and forms a separate image. Later the baby slowly learns to fuse those two images into one. But a child who continues to squint, either constantly or intermittently, after 6 months or who develops a squint during early childhood, should be seen by an eye specialist.

2. DOUBTFUL VISUAL DIFFICULTY

If the baby is found showing little interest in people and objects close to him in his line of vision or does not follow a moving bright object held before him by 3 months of age, an eye specialist should be consulted.

3. ALTERNATING MOVEMENTS OF EYES

If at any stage, the baby shows rhythmical, simultaneous, repetitive or alternating movements of both eyeballs – sideways or up and down (nystagmus) – he should be shown early to an eye specialist.

9

TEETH AND EYECARE, AND TOILET TRAINING

TEETHING IN A BABY

Most Indian mothers are very conscious of teething in their young babies. They keep looking for it and have many wrong notions about its relationship with the baby's growth.

A child's first tooth usually appears when he is about 6 months old but this varies between 5 to 9 months of age. By the age of 1 year most children have 6 to 8 teeth. Occasionally, a normal 1-year-old baby may have only 2 to 3 teeth and yet have no growth problem. The first tooth to appear is usually the lower central incisor (in the middle of the lower jaw) followed by upper lateral incisor (the side one in the upper jaw). The child has his whole set of temporary teeth, 20 in number, by the age of 2½ to 3 years (Fig. 9.1). Shedding of the temporary teeth and their replacement by permanent ones begins around 6 years of age.

When a baby is teething, the gum over the erupting tooth may be swollen, red and sore. He may have excessive saliva formation and dribbling of saliva from the mouth, general irritability and a tendency to take his fingers and other objects into his mouth and to bite them.

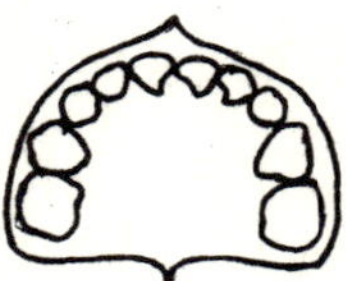

TEMPORARY TEETH

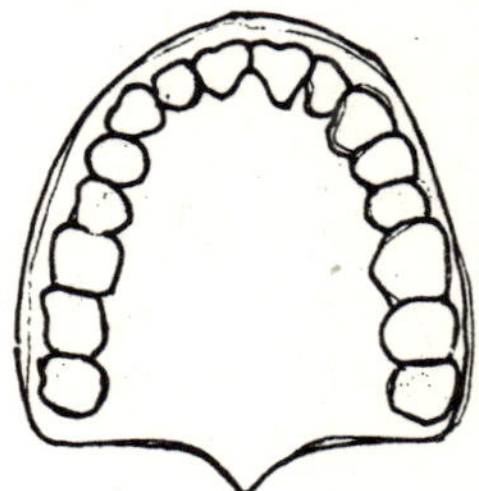

PERMANENT TEETH

(Fig. 9.1)

It must however, be clearly understood that teething does not by itself cause significant diarrhoea, vomiting, cough, or significant fever. Occurrence of any of these symptoms in your baby must not be just presumed to be due to teething and ignored. He must be shown to a doctor and treated for the underlying disease (which is usually an infection).

CARE OF THE TEETH

It is important to take care of your child's teeth and gums right from the start. Restricting the intake of sugar is the most important step besides regular cleaning of teeth, use of fluoride toothpastes and periodic visits to the dentist.

The most crucial factor in causing tooth decay (dental caries) is eating sugary food. Sugar gets broken down by bacteria on the tooth surface to form acid which attacks and damages the tooth enamel. The oftener sweet things are eaten, the worse it is for the teeth. Acid is thus produced over a longer period of time and is more harmful than eating a lot of sugary food at one time. Never give a sweetened dummy to your baby to suck and do not give sweetened drinks in a bottle or feeder. Older children must also avoid frequently eating and drinking sweet things. Avoid keeping biscuits, cakes, sweets, chocolates and sweet drinks in the house. Instead, let children have fruit, sandwiches, and savoury snacks between meals. Keep sweet things just for special treats. If used, let them be consumed quickly at one go rather than be spread over a long period. It is desirable to clean children's teeth thoroughly at least once a day, although twice a day after meals is preferable. The brushing of child's teeth should be started at an early age. A soft to medium-soft nylon tooth brush with a small head should be used. Every surface of every tooth should be well brushed – on both sides as well as the chewing surface. Help your child with brushing his teeth, at least until he is about 8 years old. Fluoride toothpastes help to prevent tooth decay.

Regular visits to the dentist, about every six months or so, are important. He can treat tooth decay if it appears at an early stage before it causes much damage.

HOW WELL CAN YOUR CHILD SEE?

One of your child's most valuable assets is sight. It is important for you to ensure that he has good vision and that he does not suffer from any other eye defects. The assessment of the child's eyesight must be done at an early age and you do not have to wait till your child starts school. A child of preschool age (3 to 6 years) may not be seeing properly or may be having a squint. Short-sightedness, if unrecognized, may seriously hamper a child's learning and his learning difficulties may be mistaken as mental subnormality. The eye testing of a child should be carried out regularly from nursery to school-leaving age.

WHEN TO CONSULT THE DOCTOR?

1. If you suspect that your child is having difficulty in seeing well. You may notice that the child turns or tilts his head, screws up his eyes or holds the book close to his face in order to see more clearly. A child at school may be having trouble reading the blackboard.

He should also have his eyes checked if he complains of headache or tiredness of eyes after reading for some time.

2. If you notice that the child has a squint.

3. If the eyes show redness or there is pus discharge or persistent itching.

VISION PROBLEMS

Short-Sight (Myopia)

In children with short sight (myopia) the near objects are clearly visible but the distant objects appear blurred. If your child holds the book close or if he always wants to sit very close to the TV screen, he may be short-sighted. At school a child with short sight is unable to see what is written on the blackboard, which may be the first sign of the child's visual difficulty.

Long-singh (Hypermetropia)

Long sight is also known as hypermetropia. A child with this problem can see distant objects well bout has difficulty in seeing near objects. It has, generally, a better outlook in the long run as compared to short-sight.

The basic problem is children with short right and long sight is that the image of objects seen by them does not get focussed properly on the retina. It falls either in front or behind the retina. The retina functions like a comera sereen and the image sensed and formed by it is transmitted by the optic nerve to the brain for final viewing by the child. Since the image in there cases is out of focus, objects appear blurred to the child.

To correct the afore said deficiency, appropriate type of lenses are prescribed for use in spectacles or as contact lenses. The lenses project the images properly on the retina and thereby correct the child's eyesight. The lenses may need change as the child (and his eyes) grow. Regular check-ups with an opthalmologist is recommended.

SQUINT

If a child shows evidence of squint after 6 months of age, he must be shown to an eye specialist. Squint is one of the common forms of eye defects in children. In this condition the two eyes are not functioning well together as a unit. This condition must be corrected at an early stage, as otherwise the vision in the squinting eye is liable to become worse and its subsequent correction may not be possible.

TOILET TRAINING

Many parents worry unnecessarily over their child not having gained control over his bowels or bladder while their neighbour's child, although younger has already achieved it. Parents need to know that different children master these functions at different ages and that it is best not to make these comparisons. Only 50 % of two-year-old children are able to control their urine during the day. It takes longer for them to be dry at night. Most do it by about 3 years of age, but some do not achieve this till they are 5 years old. Children are generally, able to control passage of stools earlier than their urination.

WHEN TO START BOWEL AND BLADDER TRAINING?

It is important that parents are not in an undue hurry. A baby can first be made to sit on a baby potty at around 1 year of age. However, true training can only be started later when the child is likely to be physically mature and ready for it. Until about 15 months of age a child passes stools and urine automatically without realising it, both before and after doing so. It is usually between 18 months and 2 years that most children know when they are performing these acts. Soon thereafter they begin to recognize when they are about to pass stools or urine and are able to tell their parents in advance. The child may stand still, clutch himself, go red in his face or otherwise signal impending motion or urination. These indicate that the child is now physically ready for toilet training and it can be started with his willing cooperation.

BOWEL TRAINING

Approach the problem of bowel training in a relaxed manner; do not try to rush the child into it. Initially, let him become familiar with his 'chair potty' as an item of furniture to sit on for himself and his teddy bear. Slowly explain to him the purpose of his special potty as being similar to that of the lavatory seat used by elders in the family. Tell him that he is now growing up. Encourage him to sit on the potty two to three times a day and do not worry if he does not deliver any stool to begin with. Praise him gently for each successful effort and gradually build on it. Ignore his failures, which are bound to happen initially. A small child is usually quite afraid of sitting over an adult lavatory seat with a large hole. A chair potty is useful, easy for the child, portable, and easy to clean.

BLADDER TRAINING

In the beginning, the time interval between the child feeling a full bladder and his passing urine is very small and he therefore often fails to control it before reaching the potty. Gradually, around 2 years of age he learns to delay the flow for several minutes and to make use of the potty. This learning process is a slow one with intermittent failures. Compliment him for his achievement and quietly disregard it when he fails. As he gains control, you should gradually take off his nappies during daytime. He should however, continue to have them on during his naps and outdoor travel and at night for some more time. Encourage him to become independent. Let him pull his pants down, get his pot or go and use the pot himself in the toilet or bathroom. Finally, he can use the big seat with a baby seat fitted on to it. The problem of persistent bed-wetting in some children has been discussed in the section on Behaviour Problems.

10

CLOTHES, SHOES AND FOOTCARE

CLOTHES: CHOOSING THE RIGHT ONES

A large variety of children's clothes of different materials are now available in the market. Most fond parents are tempted to purchase the ones which are more costly and good to look at without regard to their suitability for their child. It is important to remember that his clothes must essentially be cool in summer, warm in winter and comfortable to wear. These should be easy to put on and take off, comparatively loose, without any constricting bands and be easy to wash, dry and iron. Cardigans, vests and top clothes with narrow necks can be extremely disturbing and annoying to small children and must be avoided. There is no need to buy too many costly clothes because the rapidly growing baby will soon outgrow them. At the same time, the temptation to buy large sized ones should also be avoided. The child looks clumsy to begin with and the clothing later become shabby, following repeated washing. It is better to have fewer, comparatively simple, good quality clothes of appropriate size. The clothing material should be soft, light in weight, porous to allow the sweat to dry, non-irritating to delicate skin, non-inflammable and easy to wash. The under clothes should be made of cotton, which is soft to the skin and absorbs sweat. Parents may be surprised to realize that even a small 2- to 3-year-old child may have strong preferences about his clothes. They should give due respect to his feelings to avoid unnecessary battles of will. When buying clothes for a small baby, buy clothing which would allow easy access to his nappy, as it will require frequent changing.

Clothes with wide necks or which open down the front are easy to put on and take off. Terry towelling suits, with poppers in the crotch area or right down the front and leg are very practical. Elastic waisted shorts and pants are easy to take off.

It is better not to use zip flies to avoid the risk of the penis getting caught in them. Avoid pure man-made synthetic fibre clothing as they can be very uncomfortable in hot weather. In the winter, mini track suits, dungarees and all-in-one stretch suits are appropriate for small babies. Cardigans are more sensible than matinee jackets as they button up the front and keep the infant warm. Beware of fancy patterns as they can so easily trap the baby's fingers. He should not be over dressed with several sweaters and jackets to protect him from catching cold. If kept too hot, he will just sweat, be very uncomfortable and may even become ill. He should be given just one extra layer of clothing as compared to adults to provide him with adequate warmth. While going out, cover your baby's head and feet with a woollen cap and booties and take them off on returning indoors.

Sleeping bags are vary useful to ensure all night protection in cold weather. They also ease the mother's constant worry about her child's habit of kicking off his blanket and getting exposed at night.

Terry towel napkins are absorbent, durable and comfortable. Special one-way liners are now available; these are useful since these allow urine to pass through to the towelling napkin outside leaving a dry layer next to the baby's skin. Disposable napkins are quick and convenient, particularly when travelling.

FOOT CARE

Most people's feet are good at birth but about 75% adults have some kind of foot problem, chiefly due to poor foot care during childhood. The bones of a child's feet grow particularly fast in the first few years of life and during puberty. If the feet are cramped due to ill fitting shoes and socks during this period, the bones and joints can get distorted.

SOCKS

Babies feet should be left as free as possible. The normally curly toes of their feet are not able to straighten out if they are made to wear tight bootees and socks or all-in-one suits. Make sure bootees, socks, etc., leave enough room for the toes both in length and width. When standing, there should be at least 1/3rd cm spare material of the socks beyond the longest toe. If the feet of a stretch suit become too small, cut them off, hem the edges, and use socks instead. It is better to avoid pure stretch nylon or acrylic socks because they can damage soft and pliable feet. Use cotton or a mixture of natural and man-made fibre socks in summer and woollen ones in winter.

SHOES

Whenever it is safe and convenient let your child go barefoot. This helps to strengthen his muscles which are not so well exercised inside shoes. Do not make your baby wear shoes until he can walk unaided.

You should make sure while buying shoes for the baby that these are adequate in length and width and do not cramp his feet. They should be 2 cm in length beyond the longest toe and wide enough for all the toes to lie flat. Choose shoes with laces, straps or velcro fastening to hold the heel in position so as to prevent the foot from sliding down and cramp the toes. Leather shoes are preferable to those made of synthetic materials: they are flexible, mould to the shape of the feet, absorb sweat and thus allow the feet to 'breathe'. It is advisable to have the size of his shoes checked every 3 months or so since the feet can grow quite rapidly.

CARE OF FEET

Wash your child's feet every day with soap and water. Dry the feet thoroughly, especially between the toes to avoid fungus infection. Let him wear new clean socks every day. Trim the nails regularly but not too close to the skin and do not leave any sharp corners.

11

THE IMPORTANCE OF PLAY

PLAY IS VALUABLE AND ESSENTIAL

While play provides much needed enjoyment to a child, it is also a very important source of learning for him. Parents' anxiety about academic achievements by their children notwithstanding, the time spent by them during play must not be considered as a waste. Play is, in fact, essential for the appropriate physical, emotional, mental and social development of a child. Through play, children learn how to use their muscles; to coordinate what they see with what they do; and they gain mastery over their body. They learn many fine motor and other skills which are useful to them later in life. Games involving vigorous physical activities promote the development of strong muscles and bones and a good stamina for hard work.

Activities like drawing, painting and an imaginative use of modelling clay and building blocks encourage creativity. Playing with puzzles and other problem solving games promotes the development of a child's ability to analyse complex situations, make rational deductions and act logically. The child also cultivates the important ability of applying his mind and keeping it focussed on the task at hand. A small child looking at picture books with explanations provided by an elder and listening to stories told with meaningful gestures by a family member promote his quicker understanding of word meanings, faster language development and acquisition of valuable new knowledge about the world around him. The child develops an interest in books and is stimulated to later read on his own.

Through the medium of artistic play, children find an acceptable way of expressing some of their strong but otherwise socially disapproved emotions, such as those of aggression, anger and envy. An aggressive child is likely to identify himself with an angry lion and draw its picture and a quiet child with a meek mouse. Parents can learn a lot about their child's emotional attitudes as the drawings made by him are reflections of his perceptions of what is happening around him.

Group-play with peers exercises a very positive role in fostering healthy social and emotional development of a child. He learns to follow rules, take turns, respect what belongs to others, share his own things with others and be a good loser as well as a happy winner. Facing unfavourable situations during competitive games help him to slowly gain control over his feelings of disappointment, anger, and jealousy – an ability which will subsequently stand him in good stead. Thus play in its various forms helps a child to gradually grow into a healthy, well-rounded personality.

PATTERNS OF PLAY

A child begins to show an interest in play as early as around three months of age. He is amused by a bright moving object suspended above his cot and enjoys sounds made by a rattle. A month later, he likes to hold the rattle and shake it. A small infant engages in 'exploratory play' as he explores his toy (a rattle or cloth ball) by sucking, chewing, kissing, shaking, or throwing it. Subsequently when he begins to crawl and walk around, he embarks on a potentially risky 'hunt and check' exploration all around the house. Toys, crockery, utensils, ashtrays, decoration pieces, books, anything and everything he can lay his hands on are picked up and examined inside out, tested for their taste and smell and even whether they can be pulled apart or thrown around. Medicines meant for elders may be swallowed and little fingers poked into electrical sockets. At this stage, you have to be extremely careful and protect your child against possible accidents while allowing him reasonable opportunities to explore and learn.

Infants around 7 to 8 months of age begin to engage in 'imitation play'. They imitate gestures and actions (shaking the head, picking the nose, clapping, etc.), sounds (grunting and shrieking) and other behaviours that they can see and hear. Such imitation increases in frequency and complexity between 1 and 3 years of age. At this stage, they try to do everything they see their parents doing, like sweeping the floor, dusting, cooking, shaving, telephoning, reading the newspaper or putting on their father's coat and shoes. Through imitation play they learn to perform new actions.

Another kind of play is 'pretend' play in which a child assumes the role of another person such as a father, mother or doctor. Some psychologists believe that pretend play reflects a child's attempt to cope with anxiety and conflict. In the 'dramatic' form of active play a child may assign a lifelike role to his toy soldier or a doll. He may also himself enact various types of make-believe scenes of dramatic action with his peers or family members.

In the 'amusement' type of play, the child derives enjoyment from watching or listening to something entertaining like watching animals in a zoo, looking at pictures and television or listening to stories and music. While watching a parent fix a leaking water tap or doing some other repair work is essentially a passive activity, it often arouses an active interest in the child to later take up practical, useful activities on his own. Most children like indoor games such as hide and seek, musical chairs and snakes and ladders. Children vary in their liking for different outdoor games like running races, swimming, football, cricket and tennis.

HOW PLAY ACTIVITIES EVOLVE WITH AGE?

It is interesting to observe changes in the pattern of play indulged in by children as they grow from infancy to adolescence. These occur as a result of changes in their physical and intellectual capabilities, emotional makeup and environmental influences. In the beginning, a child engages in 'onlooker' play. A 8-month-old infant just laughs while he watches two children engaged in a mock fight. At around 1 year of age, the child is interested in solitary, independent play. He plays alone with his own toys, different from those of others and makes no effort to get close to other children. Between 2 to 3½ years, a child tends to engage in 'parallel' play. Two children play with similar toys or have the same activity like playing in the sand-pit but they do so independently of each other. They may exchange comments but do not try to influence each other. Around the age of 4 years, children have 'associative' play as different children now begin to associate with each other. They converse between themselves about the common activity and freely borrow and lend play material. Their play is, however, not an organized one. There is no common goal and no division of labour. Each child acts as he wishes. His interest is more in association than in completion of the task. When he is about 5 years old, a child begins to take part in organized supplementary play. Competitive groups are formed, different roles are assigned to each member and one or two children take up the role of leaders. This is the precursor of organized games in future with well-defined rules.

HOW CAN PARENTS HELP?

You should allow your child sufficient time, arrange adequate space and provide proper play equipment for his play activities. Create some space for your child's play in the backyard of your house. Alternatively, find some open space for him to play in a nearby park or school ground. Your child may also need your assistance in having some suitable playmates, preferably of his own age-group, to play with. Besides, you should arrange your work schedule in a manner so as to be able to spend some time with him in the evening. You may participate in his play or read him stories at bed-time. Your close interaction with your child will foster strong bonds of affection and understanding, besides helping him in his physical, emotional and intellectual development. He will be happy to have your help in learning and mastering new and complex games. You must, however, avoid the mistake of getting carried away in your enthusiasm. Avoid taking over the game, leaving him a mere spectator. Do not also try to show off your sports skills as this will make him feel inferior. He will lose confidence in himself and feel disinclined to continue with the game because of his self-perceived incompetence and fear of failure.

You should help your child in dividing his time suitably between his studies and play activities. There should also be a proper balance between his 'active' and 'amusement' play, between outdoor and indoor activities and between individual and group play. To begin with, you may encourage the child to involve himself in a wide variety of activities such as reading, music, drama and dance besides the indoor and outdoor games. After trying his hand at different activities, he will find some of them of particular interest to him. He will then try to concentrate and excel at them.

Generally speaking, you should allow your child total freedom during his play. However, it is advisable to exercise a measured supervision in the event of a serious group clash. Your child is inevitably going to become dirty and get a few cuts and bruises. You should not criticize him for soiling his clothes, for instance. Let him enjoy himself thoroughly without any inhibitions and fear of reprimand on account of his getting dirty, which is beyond his control. Minor mishaps during play should not make you deter your child from engaging in vigorous outdoor activities which are so essential for his physical and social development. You should, of course see to any cuts and wounds which he may get while playing. (This has been explained elsewhere in this book in the chapter on Dealing With Medical Emergencies at Home.)

CHOOSING THE RIGHT PLAY EQUIPMENT

Choose the play equipment for your child wisely. The latest mechanized toy with an impressive price tag is unlikely to be the right choice for your child.

First and foremost, the play equipment must be appropriate for your child's age. It should meet the child's needs, interests and abilities at that time. For example, a complicated puzzle game or a tricycle would be of no benefit or practical use for a 2-year-old child.

A child generally finds much pleasure in playing with simple rugged toys which he can carry, play, eat, and sleep with and mess around without any interference by elders. Cuddly toys, rag dolls, bunny rabbits and other simple toys purchased from the market or made at home by the mother are favourites with most small children. Toys for them should be colourful and appealing in their looks as well as the sounds made by them. As far as possible, they should be soft, washable and sturdy enough to withstand rough handling. Most small children like spoons, pots and pans, ashtrays, telephone, etc., as toys to play with in preference to costly sophisticated toys purchased from the shop. You need to exercise your own judgement before choosing a toy for your child, taking into account its suitability, safety and affordability. You can have an idea of the child's interest by taking him with you to the toy shop. Remember, a highly sophisticated mechanized toy may impress you but your child may find little interest in it after a short while because of his own inability to do much with it.

Do not buy too many toys of the same type. For example, one or two good stuffed toys which can be used roughly are enough and there is no need to accumulate a dozen of them. On the other hand, there should be variety in the type of his play materials which would satisfy and stimulate his diverse interests and faculties. While push and pull toys, tricycles, skates, swings, see-saws and slides are useful for a child's physical development and for fostering large muscle coordination; crayons, pens, modelling clay, pencils and scissors promote small muscle coordination and creativity. The judicious use of picture books, comics and puzzles help language and intellectual development. Building blocks, with which a child builds houses, bridges, towers, etc., and toys like a wooden toy engine with some open bogies, which can be made into different types of toy trains and other imaginary articles encourage constructive and dramatic play.

Last, but not the least, it is important for you to ensure that the child's toys and other play equipment are entirely safe for him to play with. Some poor quality toys may have lead in their coating of paint which may come off while a small child tries to suck or chew them. This can cause lead poisoning in a child with serious harmful effects. The toys should also have no sharp corners or cutting edges which might hurt a child. You should not allow your child to play with dangerous toys like bows and arrows, pellet firing pistols, swords and daggers, as these may cause serious injuries to him or to other children. Also make sure that the toy does not have any loose or detachable parts like buttons, rings, springs, screws, etc., which may be pulled out by a small child and swallowed.

A brief list of play equipment appropriate for children of different age groups is given on the following page.

SELECTING THE RIGHT PLAY EQUIPMENT

PURPOSE AND FUNCTION OF TOY	TOYS SUGGESTED
First 3 months	
Bright objects to look at.	Colourful toys to be hung across baby's cot.
3 to 6 months	
Sound-making toys. Toys to hold, suck and chew.	Plastic rattle, music producing toys. Small, soft, washable toys made of rubber or rag material, such as small animals, balls, dolls and teething rings.
7 to 15 months	
Toys and other articles to handle roughly, make noise with, bang, drop. Toys to pull apart, join, put things into and take out. Toys to build small towers.	Squeaking toys, drums, household pots and pans, piano, rubber and rag material. Sets of plastic glasses of different sizes, ring sets; empty cardboard containers and ping pong balls. Simple building boxes.
Toys to push along.	Big wheeled truck, bus and other such toys.
Toys to call his own.	Baby crockery set, baby telephone, picture book etc.

15 months to 3 years	
Toys to push and pull; toys to ride in.	Push cart with big wheels. A wooden animal toy on wheels with string to pull or ride on (like a wooden horse).
Toys to carry for company.	Teddy bear/other big soft toys.
Toys to take apart and fit together.	Simple take apart toys, and toys with detachable and refittable parts.

3 years to 6 years	
Toys and play materials to encourage manual skills, body control, constructive play and creative activities.	Blunt scissors and old newspaper. Building blocks, lego sets, jig-saw puzzles. Crayons, pencils, paint material, drawing and paint books. Plasticine and modelling clay, sand pit.
Play equipment to promote physical development.	Tricycle, outdoor play equipment like see-saw, slides, swings, climbing frames.

12
PRESCHOOL EDUCATION

WHY IS IT REQUIRED?

In general, children go to a regular school in India at around five years of age while in the West, they do so when they are six years old. There exists a vast difference between a child's home environment and the one which he will encounter on his entry to a regular school. The school has a regimented and disciplined life-style where he has to deal with a large number of strangers, both children and adults. He is also required to perform at formal studies. At the time of his school entry, he needs to be socially adequate, capable and confident of interacting with several other children and adults. It is, therefore, essential that the child should go through an adequate preschool preparation prior to his entry into a regular school.

A reasonable period of learning in a good nursery or kindergarten school provides a child with the desired type of preschool preparation. In India, children begin at a nursery school at around 2½ to 3 years of age and go on to kindergarten at the age of 4 to 4½ years. In most Western countries, children attend nursery school between 3 and 5 years and a kindergarten school between 5 and 6 years of age.

HOW DOES IT HELP?

A nursery school offers a child many advantages which are difficult to obtain elsewhere. It provides him with carefully planned activities which are tailored to his interests and abilities. As he experiences success in performing the given activities, his confidence grows and his self-image blossoms. Through play with other children, he learns to cooperate towards common goals and develops his sense of understanding the other's point of view. And when cooperation turns into conflict, he learns how to deal with the frustration, anger and hurt feelings. These preschool experiences are valuable in preparing him for tougher situations in the regular school. Nursery school is also good for him because for the first time he learns to be under the supervision of someone other than his parents. It also provides him a routine of loosely patterned, purposeful activities in contrast to the unplanned, spontaneous activities that prevail at his home and in his neighbourhood. This pattern of play slowly changes under the watchful supervision of his nursery school teachers – from playing alone to gradually increasing social interactions with his peers. He learns here a new way of life that he has never known before. A good nursery school also provides space and equipment suitable for his needs as well as for his physique. The nursery school is also a great relief to the mother who can have a few hours of freedom from the constant demands of her child. Young mothers are sometimes prone to nervous breakdowns after spending 24 hours a day with a small child, seven days a week. The child's entry into a nursery school provides her with some much needed respite.

SELECTING A NURSERY SCHOOL

Nursery schools vary in quality from the very good to the very poor. It is wise to visit 3 or 4 of them in your neighbourhood before you choose one for your child. You should select one which provides the right type of preschool training and not mere formal academic teaching and has a suitable teacher pupil ratio. It should have adequate equipment and space for children to engage in enjoyable and creative activities as part of both individual and group play.

APPROPRIATE PRESCHOOL EDUCATION

A good nursery school helps a child express himself creatively. Children are provided with practical materials such as paper, crayons, pencils and brushes and are encouraged to paint or draw whatever they like. A child may just make a few marks here and there and later go on to form some circles and dots. The child may name some of his creations even though they may bear no resemblance to any particular thing. As a wise parent you should accept your young child's creative efforts even though they may be primitive. Encourage him by praising his work gently and quietly. Do not commit the mistake of correcting his efforts, criticizing him or laughing at him. You should let your child have a free play with his crayons and paper instead of trying to restrict him by asking him to follow a rigid pattern.

A good nursery school teacher does not insist on every child commencing formal lessons at the same age. The right age of beginning lessons varies greatly and it should not be imposed upon a child if he is not ready for it. The child should be prepared gradually to learn the three 'R's reading, writing, and arithmetic. The pace of teaching must, however, be tailored to the abilities of each individual child. If you try to teach him too soon, he would simply get demoralized and that would harm his personality.

You should also take due care to speak to your preschool child distinctly and clearly at all times. If his speech is particularly poor or if he stammers, take advice from a speech therapist.

13
WORKING MOTHERS

MOTHER-CHILD BONDING

The first two to three years of a child's life are particularly important for his optimal development and growth. A close and affectionate bonding between the mother and her child during this period plays a crucial role in this vital process.

Over the years, the number of working mothers in India and many other developing and developed countries has grown considerably. Progressive industrialization and a higher level of education and awareness about their rights have contributed towards this significant change. Many mothers take up jobs to supplement the husband's income in order to meet rising living costs. Professionally qualified mothers want to work to satisfy their intellectual needs and for emotional and social reasons. A few of them such as doctors, engineers, architects and managers may have spent many long years in highly competitive study and training to acquire specialized professional skills and subsequently are keen to derive a sense of fulfilment through the practice of their professions. On the other hand, a few divorced, widowed or otherwise single mothers have to work to bring up their children.

COMBINING MOTHERHOOD WITH A CAREER

While you, as a working mother, are engaged in the pursuit of a career, you need to strike a proper balance between the pressing and essential needs of your child and the demands of your job. This task becomes comparatively easier if you live in a joint family and there is the child's grandmother, an aunt or some other relative available to look after the child while you are at work. Alternatively, this job can done by a good *ayah* (nursemaid) though it is becoming increasingly hard to find and afford one.

TRAINING THE CHILD MINDER

The *ayah* should be adequately trained by you so that in your absence she can look after the child intelligently, with understanding, affection and ready responsiveness to his needs. You should instruct her regarding the preparation of baby feeds, his schedule of feeding, toilet care and strict adherence to hygiene. Where necessary, you may put down the instructions in writing. At the time of recruitment you should get the *ayah* medically examined, including her chest X-ray and stool examination, to exclude the possibility of chest, intestinal or other infections. A small baby is extremely prone to catch such infections because of his low body resistance. You may sometimes need to exercise a lot of patience and good communication skills in order to bring around the child's grandmother or an old, so-called 'experienced' *ayah* to your point of view.

UTILIZING HOME-TIME WISELY

While you have to spend your time at work away from your child, you should utilize the rest of your time wisely in the best interest of your child. You should breast-feed the child while you are at home and you may leave expressed breast milk for him before leaving for work. The correct procedure for expressing and storing breast milk has been explained earlier in the section on Feeding Your Baby. The expressed breast milk may suffice for only one feed and you should leave clear instructions for the remaining feeds. You may also like to sterilize the bottles and keep other articles ready for your baby's feeding, as far as feasible, before leaving for work. You need not feel guilty about not being able to give whole-time care and attention to your child. Millions of working mothers have successfully combined the twin tasks of pursuing their careers and bringing up their children. What matters in the final analysis is the quality of care and not its quantity. Many non-working mothers while away their time at home neglecting the care of their children. In fact, many studies in the West have shown that a mother's employment can have a positive effect on both her and her children, especially girls. Employed mothers are often better pleased with themselves than mothers who stay at home. They enjoy time spent with their child more because they are not with him the whole day. Children of working mothers have been found to be more independent and have less stereotyped ideas about sex roles. Working mothers serve as successful models, especially for their daughters whom they tend to orient towards careers that are not traditionally feminine. In any case, as a working mother you must not spoil your child to compensate for any perceived guilt to make up for your failure to spend the entire day with him.

FATHER'S ROLE

You can do justice to both your work and taking care of your child with thoughtful planning and the support of your husband and other family members (and sometimes the help of a professional child-minder like an *ayah*.) The child's father should appreciate the difficulties of his working wife and the fatigue she experiences and should readily share her burden. The mother would not only get much needed relief but would also feel comforted and happier to carry out her own arduous tasks.

MAKING ADJUSTMENTS

Both parents should try to arrange their work schedule in a way that one of them can stay with the child. This may, however, not be always feasible due to fixed office hours of most government and other establishments. The mother may then like to choose a lighter job or a part-time job in the initial years of her motherhood, or if possible, take long leave in order to be able to stay with her child longer. Alternatively, she may choose to place her child in a good day-care centre (creche) during her own working hours.

14
SPEECH PROBLEMS

All parents eagerly look forward to hearing their baby speak for the first time and the first word spoken by him is remembered and frequently recalled years thereafter. On the other hand, they become extremely anxious if the baby's speech is delayed beyond what they assume to be the right time, particularly if another baby, who is younger, has already begun to speak. It must, however, be understood that there is no single fixed time for the onset of speech for every baby and that it varies considerably within a broad range. In an overwhelming majority of cases parental anxiety about this is premature and uncalled for as most children begin to speak quite soon.

However, some children may have a truly delayed speech development. The parents should, therefore, have some basic knowledge about the normal process of speech development in children in order to enable them to quickly recognize any abnormal delays. In actual cases of delayed speech development, it is also extremely important to diagnose the underlying cause and to take suitable corrective measures at the earliest in order to secure the best possible results.

DEVELOPMENT OF SPEECH AND COMMUNICATION

A baby begins to communicate as early as at about 6 weeks by making gurgling sounds. At three months he makes cooing noises. By six months he is making repetitive sounds like 'gagaga' and 'dadada' to anyone and enjoys making variations. He starts to use particular sounds, like 'mama' for his mother between 10-13 months. Beginning with two to three words at around 15 months, he can speak between 6 and 20 recognizable single words at 18 months. However, sometimes an otherwise normal child (with timely attainment of other milestones of development, such as, sitting , standing, walking, expressing properly by actions) may not begin speaking even as late as at 1½ year of age. He may just be a late talker. Remain patient. He may soon begin speaking. By two years, most are using two-word phrases but it is normal for a two-year-old to pronounce words wrongly. During the second year a child's vocabulary is small and he uses 'overextensions', for example, all animals may be called 'doggie'. During the third year his vocabulary increases markedly. Most children are now able to talk well in proper sentences but a few of them may still be difficult to understand.

Girls tend to learn to talk earlier than boys. Children's ability to use language, however, depends a great deal on how much they are talked to. This accounts for differences between children in the time they learn to talk and in their vocabulary.

DETECTION OF ABNORMAL DELAY

In spite of the variations in the time span during which children begin to speak, a normal child is expected to develop certain abilities by a particular age. The following should alert a watchful mother:

WARNING SIGNALS FOR PARENTS

Age	Speech Capabilities
10 months	**Not babbling repetitively (i.e., saying 'dadada' 'dada', etc.) to himself and others**
21 months	**Not speaking a single word (average 13 to 15 months)**
27 months	**Not putting two to three words together in a sentence (average 18-22 months)**
4 years	**Not using fully intelligible speech (average 3-3½ years)**

The delay in speech beyond the limits indicated above must not be mistakenly attributed to the so-called 'tongue tie' in a child and therefore neglected. This condition (described in chapter 2) does not actually prevent a child from speaking. Further, as the tongue grows with age, it does so in its front portion; the cord on the under surface also gets elongated, and the tongue begins to look normal. It is only rarely that the short cord may need to be surgically cut in a child to improve the quality of his speech.

DELAY IN SPEECH DEVELOPMENT; ITS CAUSES AND MANAGEMENT

There may be several reasons for an abnormal delay in speech development in a child. These include defective hearing, mental retardation, brain damage, birth defects like cleft palate, lack of adequate stimulation for the child to speak, and emotional difficulties.

A child with delayed speech should undergo complete physical and neurological examination and developmental screening by a paediatrician. His hearing should be thoroughly checked (including detailed audiometry testing) by an ENT specialist. A child with a high frequency hearing defect may respond to loud sounds like that of a loud radio or falling crockery but be unable to hear normal human speech in a distinct manner. He is therefore, unable to reproduce speech on his own. Deafness may be present in a child at birth or it may develop later due to middle ear infection or other diseases. Several children with delayed speech development due to hearing defects can now be helped immensely through the use of appropriate hearing aids and some specialized apparatus, like the radio transmission aid along with intensive speech training.

Slow speech and language development may occur in some children due to mental retardation or brain damage. An overwhelming majority of these children are also slow in acquiring motor skills (e.g., holding the head, walking), recognizing mother and family members, smiling and laughing, handling objects and attaining other developmental milestones. Such children require a thorough checkup and investigation to ascertain the basic underlying disease responsible for such delayed development (including thyroid hormone deficiency) which can then be appropriately treated.

HOW TO STIMULATE LANGUAGE DEVELOPMENT?

You should arrange to provide your baby a playful environment with lots of sounds and speech around him, especially in the first year of life. You should often talk to him face to face as you would to an older child. Sing to him or hum some soothing tunes so that he learns to listen and find pleasure in listening. Let him also listen to a variety of different sounds like that of rattles, toys, noises and music.

When your child is about a year old help him learn to understand conversational speech, such as, by explaining and telling him the names of clothes, his body parts, home food items, family members, etc. It is important that you help him learn which word goes with an object as you would with other children. If he initially does not try to repeat it after you, do not worry. He is still learning the meaning of words. If he tries to say the word, praise him for repeating after you.

STUTTERING SPEECH (STAMMERING)

Some children find it hard to speak fluently and tend to repeat syllables and parts of words. For example, the child who stutters, would speak the word 'good' as 'g-g-good'. Occasionally he may find his speech blocked and not be able to speak at all. The maximum difficulty is usually experienced at the start of a sentence or over a long word.

This problem begins mostly between the age of 2 to 3½ years, when a child is learning to speak and then between 4½ to 6 years of age as he begins to attend school. The problem is three times more common among boys as compared to girls. In some cases, this speech difficulty is triggered by anxiety and stress, such as, due to the child's being in a new school, the birth of a sibling or parental conflicts at home. Many children with this problem feel very embarrassed and inhibited as they fear ridicule by their classmates and suffer from a sense of deficiency. Although a majority of children grow out of this problem before they become adults it must not be ignored. The parents need to handle this problem calmly, with patience and understanding. At home and at school, the child should be encouraged to talk without being under any stress. He should be allowed all the time he needs to complete his talk without being hurried.

He should be listened to with interest and attention for what he says and not for the way he says it. The teachers should encourage him to recite in class as often as his classmates. They should not accept written work from him as a substitute for his speaking tasks. He should also be inspired to take part in extracurricular activities and praised for his participation without commenting on his stuttering.

The child should not be made to feel overconscious about his speech problem by frequently telling him to talk very slowly, to take a deep breath, to think before he speaks or to repeat again when he has difficulty. When he develops blocks during his speech, do not supply the missing word for him. Let him try to break his own blocks.

Parents and teachers should help him to feel that he is as much loved and respected as his other siblings and treated like his other classmates at school. His home environment should be calm, happy and free from any stress. Discrete praise at home as well as in school helps to build self-confidence, which a stutterer so desperately needs. He must not be made a target for fun and no sibling should be allowed to undermine his confidence by uncalled-for mimicry of his speech. He must never be embarrassed or reprimanded for his speech difficulty. Do not force him to speak in front of strangers. While you provide confidence and emotional security to your child, you should not overdo it by being over-protective. You should not wait long if the problem persists and within a few weeks of its onset the expert assistance of a trained speech therapist should be obtained through your paediatrician.

15
LEARNING DIFFICULTIES

DIFFERENT TYPES AND THEIR CAUSES

In today's environment of intense competition in all walks of life, most parents are victims of over-anxiety about the scholastic abilities of their children. Some of them find it hard to accept that their child is anything short of extraordinarily brilliant. It, however, needs to be realized by all parents that children vary in their learning ability and that this skill is not dependent on the level of intelligence alone. As many as one in eight children experience some degree of difficulty in learning at school. Some children do not do well because of lack of self-confidence. In some cases parents and teachers have unrealistic expectations, with the result that the child's performance is always considered poor even though he may be doing reasonably well. This puts the child under constant pressure and he may react by becoming apathetic or aggressive. On the other hand, an exceptionally intelligent child may find his school to be too simple and boring and thus lose interest in studies. Such a child may be wrongly labelled as a poor learner by an inexperienced teacher. A child with mild deafness or defective vision may not be able to fully grasp what is being taught, resulting in poor performance. A few perform poorly due to lack of continuity in their studies, either because of ill health or on account of frequent changes of school. Domestic problems and parental disharmony may also adversely affect a child's school performance.

A very small number (5%) of school children suffer from a deficient functioning of the nervous system. These functional disorders are responsible for causing certain specific learning difficulties in different children. They are often associated with scholastic under-achievement, behaviour difficulties and problems of social adjustment.

Attention disorders constitute a major problem among this group of children. Children with attention deficit disorder are unable to concentrate on any subject and get easily distracted. They are generally restless, overactive, talkative, and often complain of being bored. They are also often very impulsive and can be disturbingly aggressive and disruptive at school and at home.

Some children may have problems with their memory, a few with their ability to recognize shapes of written letters or words while others may find difficulty in understanding or expressing their feelings. A few may be lacking in sophisticated thinking and problem solving skills. A combination of these deficiencies results in a child having difficulty in reading, spelling, writing and mathematics. Older children may experience particular problems in the study of sciences or learning foreign languages. A very few children are able to read and spell much less well than their general level of ability would suggest. This specific reading difficulty is known as 'dyslexia'. In rare cases a child may have true subnormal intelligence due to improper brain development or malfunctioning of a part of the brain.

WHAT SHOULD PARENTS DO?

If your child is having some learning difficulties at school, you should first discuss it with his teacher. An intelligent, perceptive teacher will tell you about your child's real weaknesses and strengths. Your sharing with him your own assessment, doubts and fears as well as your domestic problems, if any, would be of great help. It is desirable to make sure that the child is not suffering from unrecognized mild deafness or defective vision. If the learning problem in your child persists, he would need careful assessment. After the initial examination by a paediatrician, his problems would require to be evaluated in detail by a team of experts, including the paediatrician, an educational psychologist and a clinical psychologist. The facilities for such a group evaluation are available at Child Guidance Centres and at some schools. The child would go through a physical and neurological examination as well as detailed development screening with the help of specially prepared questionnaires and test kits. Such evaluations generally include tests for his level of intelligence (IQ).

The educational psychologist would assess how a child learns as well as his level of ability. He will determine the range of skills of which a child is capable, his response to a challenge, differences between his verbal and non-verbal abilities and the child's mental attitude.

After the basic problems in the child have been identified, steps are taken to help him through a combination of different strategies. The first and most important step is for the child, the parents and the school teachers to accept and recognize the existence and nature of the child's problems, so that these can be handled in an appropriate manner with a positive attitude. The team of professionals helping him to overcome his difficulties may subsequently also include a speech therapist, an occupational therapist, a neurologist and a social worker.

ASSESSMENT OF INTELLIGENCE: INTELLIGENCE QUOTIENT

General intelligence includes a child's ability to reason, his speed of learning, memory and perception of similarities and differences. Intelligence is, however, not a stationary, innate function but is deeply influenced by environment, psychosocial factors and the child's ability to properly receive and interpret stimuli from the environment.

Several intelligence tests (like Stanford-Binet, Wechsler, NCERT) have been devised to measure a wide range of abilities, including language development, drawing, special concepts, number, verbal and non-verbal reasoning, memory, hand skills, etc. On the basis of the standardized intelligence scale, the test conducted on a particular child enables the examiner to establish his mental age. The mental age of a child, when compared with his chronological age (actual age in years) and expressed as a percentage gives his intelligence quotient (IQ).

$$IQ = \frac{\text{Mental Age x 100}}{\text{Chronological Age}}$$

If a child is of average ability, his IQ will fall between 85 and 115. One should, however, be very careful in attaching too much significance to an IQ finding. For example, since language ability plays a very important part in all IQ tests, a mildly deaf child or a child from a linguistically poor background may not score well. He may thus be wrongly designated as a child with a low IQ. Despite such limitations, including the difficulties of designing appropriate tests for children with widely different environmental backgrounds, the IQ test is a fairly reasonable screening test. However, it is necessary to use tests which are appropriate for a child's age and environmental background and to repeat them at suitable intervals.

MENTAL RETARDATION

Children with mental retardation suffer an impairment in their intelligence and a limited ability to adapt and deal with changing situations. The degree of mental retardation may be mild (intelligence quotient between 50 and 70) or it may be severe with an IQ of below 50. About 90 % cases of mental retardation are of a mild degree.

Mental retardation may occur due to a wide variety of causes. There may be abnormalities in the structure of the brain. The child's brain may suffer damage due to various factors: while in the mother's womb, at birth or later during childhood. During pregnancy, the developing brain of the unborn baby may suffer damage due to certain infections occurring in the mother, the mother's exposure to excessive amounts of x-rays, or her heavy consumption of alcohol. In some cases, brain damage occurs due to lack of oxygen supply or injury to the baby's brain during or soon after delivery. Occasionally, deficient functioing of the thyroid gland may cause mental deficiency. In a few cases, mental retardation may be due to chromosomal abnormalities (for example, Mongolism) or genetic abnormalities. In later childhood, meningitis, encephalitis and severe head injury may be responsible for causing brain damage and mental retardation.

Children with mental retardation are late in acquiring muscle control and movement, recognition, speech, language and learning. The normal range of milestones of development has been described earlier in this section. Some of the mentally retarded children may additionally suffer from fits, stiffness of body, visual difficulties and other behaviour disorders. Mentally retarded children require careful examination and detailed assessment. It may be necessary in certain cases to carry out chromosomal, genetic and metabolic studies. The management of a child with mental retardation is many-sided in nature. It has to be tailored to meet the specific needs of each individual child. Children with mild mental retardation (IQ between 50 and 70) are often educable upto the 5th grade reading levels, although they may need to be placed in special classes. As regards children with moderate mental retardation (IQ 35 to 50), efforts should primarily be directed at helping them gain maximum capacity to look after themselves. They are generally unable to go beyond the 2nd grade and need some supervision in their daily activities. While a very small number of cases (like that of thyroid gland deficiency) can be helped by specific drugs, no specific treatment is available for the majority of cases.

It is important that the parents of a mentally retarded child keep their anxiety and stress under control. During the child's training it is better to lay stress on the areas in which the child has less difficulty so that he be seen to be making progress. The child's problems need to be addressed with a positive approach with the help of trained professionals. While a mentally retarded child may need help from professionals such as a general practitioner, child specialist, physiotherapist, speech therapist and occupational therapist, the best therapists are the child's mother and father. However, the parents need to be realistic in their expectations while managing their child.

In the early years, efforts should primarily be made to help the child to develop his abilities to look after himself and then to gradually master some reading, writing and other academic skills. As the child approaches adolescence, greater stress should be placed on vocational training and community living. Simultaneously, his other medical problems like fits, hearing and vision difficulties should be attended to. Parents should seek help from their doctor in finding out about special institutions for the mentally retarded near their areas of residence. Some government institutions and voluntary organizations make available special informative literature and training manuals for the guidance of parents of the mentally retarded. The names and addresses of a few such organizations are placed for reference at appendix 6.

DYSLEXIA

Dyslexia is a condition in which the child has great difficulty in learning to read and write despite having normal abilities and adequate teaching. It is a complex problem and requires expert handling. Dyslexia should be suspected if the child has the following difficulties:

(i) He is slow in learning, reading and spelling skills, while he appears to be just as able as his classmates in other skills such as oral class work, puzzles or games.

(ii) He is unable to follow and perform actions in a sequential order, such as describing days of the week.

(iii) He is confused over right and left directions and confuses letters of alphabet which appear as mirror images of each other, such as 'b', 'd' and 'p', 'q'.

If you suspect such a learning difficulty, you should seek an early assessment by an educational psychologist.

16

BEHAVIOUR PROBLEMS

Almost all parents, at some time or other, feel lost and upset when their child suddenly starts behaving in an unacceptable or even anti-social manner, such as using bad language, being aggressive towards other children, indulging in masturbation or stealing. They get worried when their child acts that way and think they have failed as parents. If you are one of them, there is no cause for you to feel guilty.

WHY DO THEY OCCUR?

You must understand that almost all children display some behaviour problem at some stage of their childhood. This is because children face a variety of emotions as they grow – anxiety, frustration, anger, jealousy, and other feelings. Unable to cope appropriately with such strong feelings, they exhibit various forms of difficult behaviour. Children also react to family upsets and to the moods of people close to them. Their behaviour is also affected when they are tired, hungry, overexcited or bored.

Behaviour problems vary with children's age because of the differences in the stage of their emotional development and the nature of demands placed on them by their environment. For example, as babies become more independent at around 18 months to 2 years, they try to assert their control over their environment and their parents. When such a child encounters resistance he gets angry, and he throws tantrums, cries, and even develops breath holding spasms. Around this age, he is also passing through the 'anal' phase of his development and may start playing with his excreta to the great embarrassment of his parents. Between the age of 3 and 4 years boys become particularly interested in the penis and the girls in the clitoris area (the 'phallic phase'), often leading to masturbation. These are normal occurrences; they do not indicate sexual perversion and they pass over with age. But it is essential that parents are aware of such events happening during a child's development so that they may handle the problem in a realistic manner. As the child grows older he interacts more with his parents, siblings, other children and adults in and out of home. This may produce elements of anxiety, hostility or aggression in the child's behaviour, thoughts or fantasies. These anxieties may be expressed as nightmares or as fears of separation or death. The arrival of a new baby, for instance, can be extremely stressful to a small child. He may feel neglected, jealous and resort to disturbed behaviour. Children who had some problems of adjustment in the past like thumb sucking or bed wetting may start having them again. Some may develop fresh ones, like stuttering or have difficulties in learning.

HOW TO PREVENT AND HANDLE THEM

Behaviour problems are usually an expression of distress. You must try to understand the reality and extent of the child's problems and the possible reasons for it. Besides love and good intentions you would also need to develop some skills for handling them adequately and preventing them. The following broad principles will help you deal with your child:

Give your child lots of love and encouragement and be always positive. Praise him for his strengths and good deeds. There is no better tonic for his soul.

Parents must avoid the mistake of making unfavourable comparison of a child's performance at school or his behaviour with a classmate or even his brother or sister. Every child needs appreciation and encouragement as a distinct individual. Unhealthy criticism and adverse comparisons breed resentment and feelings of defiance in a child towards his parents.

You should be realistic in your expectation of the child. He should not be nagged for accomplishing the extraordinary as that puts him under undue pressure. He starts suffering from a sense of failure due to his inability to come up to your own expectations. He may then react by turning indifferent to his studies, getting defiant or by developing some other behaviour disorder.

Listen to him and give due respect to his thoughts, young though he may be. Explain reasons for your decision when you disagree. This will give him a sense of self-respect and self-confidence which would help him later in adult life.

There should not be too many rules hampering a child's freedom of action. He may then become too dependent on authority and stop thinking for himself.

While discipline is a must for every child, you do not have to be absolutely rigid. Be flexible.

Both parents and other elders at home must follow the same set of rules for the child. They must also be consistent in applying these rules. The child should not be punished for some behaviour disorder one day and then encouraged to do the same for public amusement the next day.

Do not be overprotective, or your child may never learn to take responsibility, assess the potential dangers of a situation or learn from his own experience.

Never strike your child even when he has been violent. Control your anger. You have to maintain self-discipline and good conduct before you can expect your child to do so.

Your child's behaviour may be bad and unacceptable but the child is not. Do not use the word 'bad' for him. Let him have no doubts about your love and his freedom to come to you for help under all circumstances.

Keep your own sense of humour. It will help you immensely in handling your child's problems. Be calm, self-confident and retain a sense of balance. And take care of yourself, your family and your home. Your child will do well only in a truly happy, harmonious and balanced home environment.

The cause, features and appropriate ways of handling some common behaviour problems and difficulties seen among children are discussed below.

TANTRUMS

Outbursts of temper are an extremely unpleasant experience, both for the child and the parents. They usually occur between the age of 18 months and 4 years. More than half of all 2-year-old children have tantrums at least once a day. They tend to be more common among lively and intelligent children. When a child at this young age is denied something he wants or he is stopped from doing something undesirable or dangerous, he feels extremely frustrated and his anger gets out of control. He may rush around the room, wild and screaming and throw anything which comes his way. If you do not protect him he may bang his head against the furniture or walls. He may throw himself on the floor, rolling, kicking and screaming.

You should try to prevent tantrums by keeping your toddler's frustration within limits. When you have to stop him from doing something he enjoys, do it as tactfully as you can. Avoid being too rigid in dealing with him.

Tantrums tend to occur more often when children are tired or hungry. Besides frustration, jealousy can also lead to tantrums. Try to work out and tackle the causes. More time, attention and love will help. Even if you cannot be sure of the reason, understand and accept the anger your child is feeling.

WHAT TO DO

At the start of a tantrum, try to divert your child's attention. Show him something out of the window – a bird, cat or anything. Making rhythmic noises may help on some occasions. During tantrums prevent the child from getting hurt, or hurting anyone or damaging anything. You may hold him gently but firmly, until the tantrum passes. Some toddlers get angrier if held. Don't insist on overpowering him. Remove anything which he is likely to break and just make sure he does not physically hurt himself.

Try sitting the tantrum out. Don't lose your temper or shout back. Stay calm. If it happens in a public place, take him away into a safe, secluded place.

Do not give in to his tantrum. If you have said no, stick to it. If you submit to his demands now, he will get the wrong message. He will feel encouraged to repeat his tantrum to get what he wants in future.

Do not offer a reward in return for his stopping his tantrums. At the same time do not punish him for his tantrum. With proper handling, things get better with the passage of time. As he gets bigger and stronger he becomes more competent in handling frustrations and controlling his anger.

However, if tantrums occur at the slightest provocation in an older child, for example in a child aged 6 years, it should not be ignored and expert help should be obtained.

BREATH-HOLDING SPELLS

A few toddlers, when in a temper, hold their breath for a long time after a shrill cry. Due to the temporary lack of breathing and exchange of oxygen in the lungs, they turn blue and may become unconscious and develop fits due to lack of oxygen supply to the brain. This becomes extremely alarming for the parents. However, this apparently dangerous condition passes off on its own due to natural adjustments made by the body. Automatic breathing soon resumes, the child regains colour and recovers. He may, however, remain drowsy for some time or sleep it off.

It is important that the parents should recognize the basically innocent nature of this condition and not resort to heroic measures to deal with this problem. Never pour water in the child's mouth at this stage; he may choke to death in his drowsy condition. Splashing cold water on the face, turning him upside down, slapping him, etc., are not required and do not help. Just make him lie down in your lap, with his head lowered to a level slightly below that of the rest of his body and with his face turned to the side. He will be all right in a short while.

Such episodes are uncommon in babies below six months and children over five years of age. If a child gets repeated attacks or if his age is outside the above-mentioned limits, a doctor should be consulted. Otherwise, he should be managed for his tantrums as discussed earlier.

AGGRESSION

Almost all normal children between the ages of one and four years, sometime or the other engage in some form of aggressive activity. They may bite, hit, kick, throw objects, shout or call names and abuse. It is their way of expressing anger or getting what they want. Aggression is a problem, however, when it becomes destructive or a threat to others' safety. A child who repeatedly fails to correct himself despite the advice of his parents, teachers and peers also needs to be properly taken care of. Children between the ages of 1½ and 6½ years consider aggression to be the means to get what they want. They do not have patience. An 18-month-old cannot express his wants so he goes for action. Some children, particularly boys, may be more assertive by nature. Such children may possibly be encouraged by violence on television. A child is, however, most influenced by the behaviour of his parents and older siblings at home. If they engage in heated arguments or fight, so would the young one.

Kindergarten schools provide a good training ground for teaching proper, non-violent forms of social behaviour. Aggression again becomes pronounced in the behaviour of children around the ages of 11 and 12 years. They may even associate with rowdy groups and form children's gangs.

WHAT TO DO

The child should be taught to control his impulses and to express feelings verbally instead of physically. Tell him that is the way he will have more friends. Bullying others will only isolate him.

A toddler can best be handled by distraction. If he still pushes or grabs, firmly say no and take him away from his playmate.

You may sometimes be tempted to hit the child to teach him a lesson. Don't do it. It would only strengthen his feelings that physical assault on others is after all, okay.

Talk to your child in a calm manner and try to find the cause. It may be he has been feeling insecure; your love will calm him down. Situations involving group aggression by older children would require careful assessment, intimate discussion with them and gentle, intelligent handling.

DEFIANCE

Defiance of parents and elders and saying no to them is most common among children around the age of two to three years and later at adolescence. A small child does this to assert his independence and so does the adolescent. The 2 to 3-year-old is beginning to establish his own identity. He does not want to be ordered to have dinner when he is playing. He wants to choose his own clothes and may refuse to go to bed just because it is convenient for his mother.

To handle such small children, it is good to let them have some reasonable freedom of choice. For example, you can offer your child two or more choices of dresses appropriate for the season. Be flexible. However, you do have to set limits, like a firm no to your small child wanting to cross busy streets all on his own. Both parents must also be united in their views and consistent in setting down sensible limits.

Negative attitudes and defiance of elders' suggestions commonly occur in children at adolescence. They may feel proud of their new knowledge and ideas and find the knowledge of their peers to be superior to yours. This is a very delicate period in a child's life and you need to handle it calmly with a lot of patience and understanding.

STEALING

Society considers stealing as bad and deserving of punishment. Parents feel horrified and find it difficult to comprehend and condone it if they find their own child stealing.

The seriousness of stealing by a small child, however, needs to be assessed according to his age. Before the age of 6, children do not know the meaning of taking something from a store without paying for it. They do not yet understand the system of paying for goods taken. They just reach out and take what fancies them. Older children know better. They may, however, steal something they would love to have and that their parents won't give them. A child who does not feel loved by his parents may also steal to attract their attention.

A 10 to 12-year-old child lacking in self-confidence may begin to shoplift when 'dared' to do so by his playmates to impress them.

WHAT TO DO

When you come to know of your child having stolen for the first time, remain calm. Assess the situation and the possible reasons for your child's stealing. When your young child who did not know that helping himself to the chocolate bar in the shop was wrong, gently and in simple terms, explain to him the purchase principle. Quietly take him back to the store to apologize and pay for the stolen item. Explain that stealing is an unacceptable behaviour. He will gradually learn.

The problem is more difficult if it occurs in an older child. He may be asked the reasons for stealing. Help him by being his friend and by explaining. Besides, you are the role model for him. Make sure you are absolutely honest in your own dealings. If the stealing persists despite your best efforts to stop it, seek expert help.

OVERACTIVE CHILDREN

Some children can have extremely high levels of energy. They can be extremely active, restless and difficult to manage. They may not sit still at meals or behave well in the market. If your child is overactive, try not expecting him to become docile quickly. Avoid difficult situations outside the home. Start by asking your child to be still or controlled or to concentrate for very short periods. Gradually build up. Keep to a routine as far as possible.

Help him by taking him out every day for some time outside the home to a garden, or a playground where he can really run wild; he needs to burn off his extra energy. Very rarely, a child's uncontrollable hyperactivity and inability to concentrate may be the result of brain damage or developmental delay. If you find the problem to be persistent and unmanageable, seek medical advice.

THUMB SUCKING

Most children around six months of age suck their thumbs. They find pleasure in placing everything they can lay their hands on into their mouth. This oral phase of their emotional development is normal and lasts for a few months. Most babies stop doing it when they become toddlers.

However, some particularly shy children continue to suck their thumb. Some resort to thumb sucking when they feel insecure, for example, when going to bed or feeling frightened. They find it soothing, as with holding tight their stuffed teddy bear or the bed sheet. A few children who had earlier given up thumb sucking resume it when faced with a new insecure situation like the birth of a sibling, going to a new kindergarten school or the arrival of unfamiliar guests in the house.

Thumb sucking by a child upto 6 years (the stage of temporary teeth) is not serious. If the habit persists after that age the alignment of permanent teeth can be affected resulting in their permanent deformity. Such deformities would need specialized and prolonged orthodontic treatment.

WHAT TO DO

Thumb sucking by your child largely signifies a sense of insecurity felt by him. Be patient. You would need to persist with your efforts to slowly wean him off this habit. Do not try to punish him. Avoid scolding him or making fun of him by calling him a 'little baby' in front of others. Be prepared for some setbacks in his progress. Stress the positive and praise him when he stops sucking for a while. You should first aim for free intervals during the day. Thumb sucking at night or when alone may pass off over a longer period.

BED-WETTING

The involuntary passage of urine and soiling of clothes by an older child can be extremely distressing for his self-esteem and socially embarrassing both for him and his parents. This problem is however, not very uncommon. One out of 12 boys aged 5 years, and about one out of 25 boys aged 10 years wet their beds at night. The prevalence of this condition among girls is about half that in boys. As is evident from these figures, most children tend to grow out of this problem with age.

Generally, children develop control over the passage of urine during the day between the age of 2½ and 3½ years and take some more time to acquire this ability at night. Some children however, do not acquire this capability and continue to wet the bed at night. This may be the result of inappropriate toilet training in early childhood or chronic psychological stress. On the other hand, sometimes children who had earlier gained control and were dry at night, subsequently start bed-wetting. This is generally due to emotional stress induced by events like the child's new school, anxiety about school performance, birth of another sibling or conflict between parents at home. Occasionally this may occur due to a urinary tract infection, diabetes and other disorders.

Your doctor would examine your child and have his urine examined to exclude any organic cause for his bed-wetting, although these are uncommon. He would want to do a more detailed assessment, including psycho-social evaluation of children who continue to dribble urine all the time or are unable to control it even during the day.

The following general principles of management will help in tackling this annoying problem:

The parents should not be unduly disturbed about this problem and understand that given time, most children get out of it. The child should be encouraged and praised for dry nights, even if they are few to begin with. He may be awarded a 'star' as a prize for his positive achievement and the child may maintain a 'star chart' as a source of confidence and inspiration to do better.

He must not be scolded, punished or made to feel ashamed on days when he wets. Let it be quietly ignored. Only the positive aspects must be emphasized.

Do not give any liquids to him after dinner. If he is used to milk at bedtime, give it to him in the evening instead. The evening meal may also be re-scheduled so as to be taken early, well before he goes to sleep.

Most children tend to wet their beds at almost the same time, every night. You can find out by observing him for a few nights. You should wake him about half hour prior to the expected time and make him pass urine. This helps him to develop bladder control and finding a dry bed next morning helps build his self-confidence. Children who tend to wet during the day should be made to go to the toilet at frequent intervals for the same reason.

Some drugs are said to help by enhancing the control of urinary bladder and through a positive influence on the child's emotional state. The doctor may like to use them in certain situations. Some children with persistent bed-wetting, who fail to respond to other measures may be advised to use an electronic buzzer in their bed at night. When the child begins to wet his bed during sleep at night, the first few drops of urine trigger the alarm and the child wakes up. After a month or so, the child gradually becomes conditioned to wake up on his own, when he senses his bladder to be full. The use of this system must however, be continued for 4 months for proper results.

MASTURBATION

Most infants and toddlers enjoy touching and playing with their genitalia. Some appear to derive pleasure by rubbing the thighs against each other or by rhythmic swaying movements. The small child is not a sex pervert. However, if the child does it excessively, he should be got examined and any cause for local skin irritation, if present, be treated. Masturbation is less common during middle childhood. At adolescence masturbation is probably universal among boys and somewhat less common among girls. Children who masturbate excessively may require help.

NIGHTMARES

Nightmares are bad dreams that awaken a child and stay in his memory. These generally start around the age of 3 or 4 years. These dreams are just as genuine to children as day-time reality. For them monsters, witches and dragons can and do exist. Don't dismiss a child's fears as silly by calling it just a dream. Instead, hug and gently reassure him that there are no monsters in his room, or if there were, you would make them go away. Leave a night light on, so that the child can himself see and feel reassured. Restrict the child's viewing of horror TV shows and films and reading scary books.

NIGHT TERRORS

Night terrors occur less frequently but they are more serious if they persist. Children are less likely to remember the event, even if you wake them up. Usually they scream suddenly and sometimes break out in a cold sweat. They seem awake but are actually in a state of semi-consciousness, perhaps staring into space. The child can become even more agitated if you try to comfort him. Stand behind his bed without touching him until the episode passes. It can be alarming but try to be calm and reassuring, if he does wake up. This is because part of the child's brain is still working. Typically, children outgrow them as they mature neurologically. But if your child has night terrors that persist or if he also sleepwalks or has body tremors during the episode, consult your paediatrician.

17
HANDICAPS IN CHILDREN

A child is considered to be handicapped if a disability of his body or mind interferes with his ability to lead a normal life or to benefit from a normal education. Although exact figures are not available, the global population of such handicapped children is estimated to be around 150 million with the developing countries accounting for more than 80 % of them. According to some surveys conducted in India about 7 to 10 % of persons (of all ages) in a given area were found to be suffering from some form of disability.

TYPES OF HANDICAPS AND CAUSES

A child may have one or more handicaps:

1. Partial or total blindness.
2. Partial or total deafness.
3. Bone, joint or muscle disorders. (For example, inborn defects of spine, after-effects of major bone fractures and joint infections, muscular wasting disorders.)
4. Nervous system disorders, like mental retardation, cerebral palsy, spinal cord defects, after-effects of poliomyelitis, etc.
5. Long-standing heart, lung, kidney and other organ diseases.

The handicap may occur in a child due to some disease or disorder affecting him during his life in the mother's womb, during the process of birth or later during his childhood. In some cases, like muscular dystrophy, the handicap occurs as a result of an inherited disorder.

HOW TO PREVENT THEM

The problem of handicaps in children, their prevention, early detection and appropriate management are matters of vital importance and pose a great challenge to parents as well as the whole community. Careful pre-pregnancy planning, regular medical checkup and care of the pregnant mother and supervised delivery of the baby are important steps towards prevention of several handicapping disorders. Timely immunization against poliomyelitis, diphtheria and other preventable diseases and early treatment of the affected child help to prevent many lifelong disabilities.

EARLY DETECTION IS IMPORTANT

It is important that the handicap in a child is detected as early as possible. Timely intervention helps to correct or limit disability and permits optimum results of rehabilitation therapy. While some defects are obvious, some abnormalities in small babies like mental retardation and visual and hearing defects may remain unrecognized by parents for quite some time. Parents should therefore have some basic knowledge of the normal process of a baby's development so that they can perceive early any abnormal developmental delays or deviations in their child and seek medical advice at an early stage. They should also get the child routinely examined by a paediatrician for his developmental status at the age of 6 weeks, 6 months, 10 months, 18 months and 2½ years. The child should also be routinely assessed for his hearing and vision in early infancy. (For details, refer to chapter on Growth and Development.)

HANDLING A HANDICAPPED CHILD

If you happen to be the parent of a handicapped child, you should get the child carefully examined and thoroughly assessed in respect to his physical and mental status. You should discuss the child's problem at length with the paediatrician and understand

(a) the exact nature of your child's difficulties and his abilities;

(b) the underlying cause of his problem and its genetic implications;

(c) its likely outcome in the long run; and

(d) the outline of his proposed management.

While some defects may be improved, corrected or cured by early diagnosis and treatment, a few may be more difficult to manage. It is extremely important that while, in general, you remain positive and optimistic in your approach, you should be pragmatic and realistic in accepting the existence, nature and severity of the handicap.

You should not harbour any sense of trauma, guilt or shame in association with the handicap. This mental approach will enable you to look after him properly and assist him in growing and developing to his highest possible potential. You must avoid feeling embarrassed in public in the company of your disabled child. He should be given reasonable opportunities for free interaction with relatives, family friends and other children.

Like any child, the handicapped child needs consideration and respect. Concerted efforts should be made to ensure that he retains his sense of self-esteem despite his disability and faces his difficulties with confidence.

He requires love and security but you must not be overprotective. You should exercise appropriate discipline and control over him without harbouring any irrational fears that such control might aggravate the child's illness. For example, disciplinary restrictions will not cause worsening of fits in an epileptic child. He should be allowed to learn from his own experiences and disappointments.

TREATMENT AND REHABILITATION

Handicapped children require different kinds of treatment and rehabilitation measures, depending upon the nature and severity of the disability. It may involve management by a physiotherapist, occupational therapist, speech therapist, psychologist, nurses and social workers. Some may require expert assistance of an ENT surgeon, eye specialist, orthopaedic surgeon, rehabilitation expert or a medical geneticist. Having understood the course of management and rehabilitation outlined for your child, you should participate in it as an active partner along with the paediatrician and other members of his therapy team.

The aim of the rehabilitation programme is to help the handicapped children to achieve the maximum possible physical, educational, emotional, vocational and social capabilities within the limits of their disability. Where feasible, all efforts should be made to provide them education in normal schools and give them adequate vocational training so that they can live a near normal, independent life of their own.

You should seek information from your doctor if any specialized facilities for the management of your child are available in your town or nearby. Besides the government, some non-governmental organizations and groups of parents of affected children are also engaged in providing information and occasional material support to families of children with certain handicaps. Your doctor will guide and help you in securing the assistance of such groups and societies. Addresses of a few organizations engaged in the care of the handicapped in India are given in Appendix 6. You may write to them and seek information about branches of these organizations and their arrangements for specialized care for your child near your place of residence.

The first-hand information of parents' group in dealing with day-to-day problems involved in the long-term care of handicapped children, including procurement of special medicines, equipment and other facilities, is often extremely useful. Besides, such groups provide invaluable moral and emotional support to parents. You can also obtain from these societies some very useful informative literature about your child's disease, its essential principles of management as well as some packages for providing practical training for your handicapped child at home.

Some children with severe mental or physical disabilities like mental retardation, learning disorders and blindness, require education in special schools. You should obtain your doctor's guidance and help in this regard.

When your child's handicap is considered to be due to a genetic disorder, you should seek the expert advice of a geneticist with regard to having further children. You must, however, ensure that any one parent is not blamed for your child's disability as this may lead to serious marital discord.

18

ACCIDENTS

It is extremely important for parents to protect their children against accidents, both at home as well as outdoors. Every year, accidents cause a very large number of serious injuries to children and many tragic deaths. Children are inquisitive by nature and they love to explore, play and experiment with almost anything and everything within their reach. In the process, they may sustain burns, cuts and wounds, ingest poisonous substances, fall from heights, suffer injuries, get an electric shock or be drowned. Yet most accidents can be prevented by parents through simple precautions, thinking ahead and teaching children the right habits. They should never merely rely on their child's good behaviour or common sense. Constant vigil and adherence to basic safety precautions are essential.

DANGERS AND PRECAUTIONS

The normal dangers to which a child is exposed at home and outside and the safety precautions useful in protecting him are given below.

BURNS AND SCALDS

Keep anything hot, like tea-pots, tea mugs and cups out of children's reach. Watch out for the table cloth hanging at the edges which, if pulled, can bring a hot drink or tea-pot down on a small child.

Do not drink anything hot with the child on your lap. Before use, always test the temperature of the hot water meant for his bath and that of his hot drinks before offering them to him.

Use a proper guard around a hot stove or electric heater kept on the floor to prevent your child's access to it.

Keep matches, cigarette lighters and gas lighters out of your child's reach.

The cooker, the saucepan handle and the hanging wire of the electric kettle must not project beyond the edge of the kitchen shelf because these may be pulled at by a child bringing hot food, boiling milk or water on him.

FALLS, CUTS AND GRAZES

AT HOME

Never leave a baby in a high chair or on a table unattended. Once a baby is crawling, use a stair gate to seal off the stairs, preferably at both the top and bottom of stairs.

Make sure an older child cannot get on top of the banisters or balconies by climbing over horizontal rails. The upright poles supporting it should be close enough together to prevent a small child from squeezing through. The landing above a stairwell should be properly fenced off.

The upstairs windows must be properly barred or fitted with safety latches to prevent the child from falling out.

Baby-walkers can be dangerous. They can trip over steps, go down the stairs, or get caught against a radiator.

Low-level glass panels in doors and windows are also dangerous, especially for the crawling baby.

Do not let a child walk around holding anything made of glass or a sharp metallic object. Discourage him from placing a pencil or similar object in his mouth or ears.

OUT OF DOORS

Children enjoy climbing trees, walls and other high places. A fall may result in head injuries, bone fractures, cuts and wounds. Do not stop him from climbing altogether but allow the child to do so only as far as his capabilities permit.

Do not allow a child up to 5 years of age to cross the road by himself. Young children are unable to gauge distances properly and the speed of vehicles. They can be gradually trained and may become competent to cross quiet roads by 7 to 9 years of age.

When travelling by car, it is desirable that small children be kept properly restrained and held secure by adults. It is safer for them to travel on the back seat. Standing on the back seat, or in the gap between the two front seats is very dangerous. Where feasible, a safety belt or special baby seat may be fitted in the car.

DANGER OF POISONING

AT HOME

Babies tend to put things in their mouth automatically. Toddlers and children may eat or drink something out of curiosity or because they mistake it for something else. A large number of children accidentally drink kerosene oil, kept negligently in the kitchen in plain bottles, thinking it is water.

Many land into serious trouble after swallowing aspirin, paracetamol, sleeping pills, tablets for high blood pressure and other medicines meant for adults. Keep all medicines locked away in a cupboard. Do not keep them loose in drawers and handbags.

The medicine bottles must carry appropriate labels for correct identification and proper use. This would avoid medicines meant for local application from being accidently administered to the child by mouth.

Don't put dangerous liquids like kerosene oil or acid in any bottle or jar that might make them look like a drink, and keep them well away from the reach of children.

Domestic fluids and powders meant for washing, cleaning, disinfecting and polishing, caustic soda, chemicals, weed killer tablets for preserving wheat, naphthalene balls for fighting moths in clothes, etc., are highly dangerous; these must be stored away safely.

Tell your child never to pick and eat any berries, seed, or other parts of plants or fungi growing in the wild. Many children develop serious *dhatura* and other plant poisonings in this way.

DANGER FROM ELECTRICITY

Young children are unable to understand the serious risks of exposure to electricity currents. Their curiosity can result in electric shocks, even instantaneous death.

Make sure that all unused sockets are protected from the inquisitive fingers of your child by blank plastic plugs or by placing heavy furniture in front of them.

Electrical appliances should have no bare or broken wires and all plugs must be properly earthed. Main appliances like portable electric heater or kettle should never be used in the bathroom or near water. Shocks can kill, especially when the skin is wet.

DANGER OF CHOKING AND SUFFOCATION

Keep small objects like coins, beads, safety-pins, buttons, etc., away from babies and small children who might put them in their mouth and choke.

Do not give whole peanuts to children under five years of age for the same reason.

All polythene bags should be kept away. A small child may try them on as a helmet and may get suffocated as a result of the bag slipping down around his face. Similarly, do not allow him to play with strings without supervision. He may wrap one round his neck and get strangled.

DANGER OF DROWNING

Never leave a baby or a young child alone in the bathtub, even for a brief period. A small amount of water is enough to drown him, if he slips into it.

Always watch and stay near children playing in or near water – a pond, a swimming pool, lake, river or sea. Teach your child to swim as soon as possible.

COPING WITH ACCIDENTS

Parents sometimes have to cope with accidents to their young child at home. Most of the accidents are minor. The prompt management of an occasional major one may, however, make a difference between a child escaping with some minor temporary disorder and his incurring severe damage to some of his vital organs or even between life and death. The essential steps to be taken by parents in handling such emergency situations before any expert medical aid is available are described in the next section.

19

DEALING WITH MEDICAL EMERGENCIES AT HOME

WHY MUST PARENTS KNOW?

Children are by temperament curious to know about and eager to experiment with all new things. They often do so without much concern for the possible dangers involved and may suddenly land themselves into serious trouble like a bad accident, body burn, choking or swallowing a dangerous poison.

These emergency situations may arise at any time of the day or night. The child's life then will depend upon the quality of emergency aid given to him within a very short period and often much before a doctor can be reached. It is, therefore, very important that you should know some essential life-saving emergency first aid measures. This would help you to remain calm and deal properly with a life-threatening situation, if and when it actually arises with your child.

BASIC PRINCIPLES OF HANDLING EMERGENCIES

1. Be calm and confident.
2. Assess the problem at hand quickly and carefully. Act logically, gently but firmly.
3. Reassure your child that everything will be alright. He will then cooperate better.
4. First check whether the child is conscious and breathing. If he is not breathing, start mouth-to-mouth breathing immediately. (Resuscitation procedures have been described later in this section.)
5. Assess the nature and severity of the problem.
6. Get expert medical help while you handle the immediate problem.

MANAGEMENT OF BLEEDING SKIN WOUNDS

While playing, children often sustain injuries to different parts of their body which result in bleeding. Take the following steps:

1. Make the child sit or lie down, as he may feel faint.
2. Apply direct pressure on the wound with your thumb or both thumb and fingers to stop bleeding. Preferably, place a clean pad or dressing on the wound and then put pressure over it. If regular sterile dressing is not available, a clean handkerchief may be used. Continue to maintain pressure for about 15 minutes to stop the bleeding and prevent its recurrence. You may need to do this for even longer.
3. Raise and support the injured part of the arm or leg above the chest level (heart level). This reduces the blood flow to the injured part and bleeding from the wound.
4. If the wound is significantly big, place a broad sterile dressing over the wound. Cover with a pad of cotton and bandage firmly in position.
5. If the bleeding restarts after dressing the wound, do

not remove the dressing. Firmly add one more on top of the previous one.

6. Take the child to your doctor or to the casualty department of the nearest hospital.

BLEEDING SKIN WOUND WITH EMBEDDED FOREIGN BODY

1. If a piece of glass, metal or some foreign body is embedded in the wound, do not attempt to remove it.

(Fig. 19.1)

2. Control the bleeding by pressing the area immediately above and below the foreign body and not directly over it.
3. Place pads of cotton wool or sterile dressing around the object till these are as high or higher than the object. Now cover and bandage (Fig.19.1).
4. Raise the injured part above the chest level.

BLEEDING NOSE

Picking the nose is one of the commonest causes of nose bleeds in children. Some may have it in the summer season. It may also be caused by hard nose blowing or sneezing when the child is suffering from a common cold, an injury to the nose, a foreign body in the nose, nasal polyps or sinusitis. Some blood disorders can also lead to nose-bleeds, besides bleeding from other parts of the body.

WHAT TO DO

1. The nose bleed in a child may seem disproportionately serious as compared to the actual amount of blood loss. Do not get frightened; handle your child calmly.

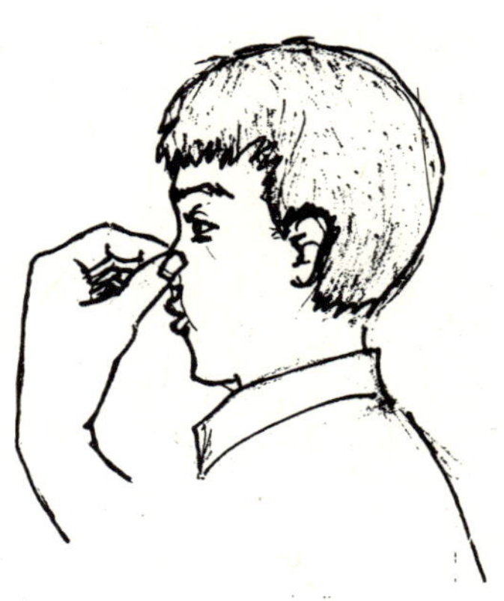

(Fig. 19.2)

2. Ask him to sit down with his head bent forward over a basin or a sink. Grip his nose between your thumb and fingers over the soft part of his nose just below where the bone ends and apply firm pressure to both nostrils to stop bleeding. Continue to press the nostrils for 10-20 minutes or till the bleeding stops (Fig.19.2).

3. Ask your child not to put his head back during the nose bleed because blood is then likely to drip down his throat to his stomach which may cause him to vomit later.

4. Ask him not to touch his nose or blow it hard for some hours or else blood clot may get disturbed and bleeding may recur.

5. If the bleeding does not stop, consult your doctor. He should also be consulted if (i) your child has repeated nose-bleeds; (ii) he has bleeding from the mouth, skin or anywhere else besides the nose; and (iii) if he looks pale or ill.

Nose-bleed in a child who has had a head injury requires urgent attention and investigation by your doctor.

BURNS

A child may get accidentally burnt due to exposure to fire, hot metal, boiling water, milk or oil or contact with faulty electrical appliances or exposed electric wires. Firecrackers during Diwali and on other festive occasions are also responsible for causing serious burn injuries to a large number of children every year.

WHAT TO DO

1. Move the child away from the source of injury. If his clothes have caught fire, make him lie down on the floor and pour water over him to put out the flames. If water is not immediately available, smother the flames by wrapping a blanket, rug or coat around him.
2. The burnt area should be cooled down quickly to reduce further damage by heat. Hands, arms, legs and feet affected by burns can be immersed in a bucket of cold water or placed under running cold water. Ice cubes in a plastic bag can be applied locally to cool a small area of burn on the face, neck or elsewhere over his body. The cooling should be continued for 10-15 minutes or as long as the child can tolerate it. It would be better to do it for a longer period so that the skin and the deeper tissues get cooled down sufficiently to escape damage by heat. Avoid cooling with ice-cold water over a wide area as it may harm the small child by lowering his body temperature too much.
3. Do not try to take off his clothes or anything else which may be sticking to the wound.
4. If the child has got burnt by some boiling fluid or chemical, you should carefuly remove or cut away the soiled clothing.

5. Cover the burnt area with a sterile non-fluffy dressing or a clean handkerchief or sheet to prevent infection. Do not use ordinary absorbent cotton as it may get stuck to the burn area.
6. Do not apply oil, butter, ink, mustard oil, cream or ointment.
7. Do not prick the blisters. The wound is then more likely to get infected.
8. You may give your child a dose of paracetamol syrup or tablet as recommended for his age to relieve the pain.
9. If the burn is more than a small, superficial burn consult your doctor. Always consult the doctor for electrical burns and for burns on the face, even if these appear to be small and superficial.

ACCIDENTAL POISONING

Toddlers and young children are very liable to swallow poisonous substances because of their restlessness, their intense curiosity, a desire to put everything into their mouth and a strong urge to imitate adults. Parents contribute to the danger by neglecting to provide proper storage of potentially harmful household substances, like kerosene oil or napthalene balls and medicines meant for adults.

COMMON POISONS INGESTED

The common poisons and harmful substances which are accidentally swallowed by children include:

(i) Kerosene oil. The child generally drinks it mistaking it for water;
(ii) Weed-killer tablets and pesticides;
(iii) Corrosives like sulfuric acid used for cleaning floors;
(iv) Napthalene balls;
(v) Sleeping pills and other medicines; and

(vi) Poisonous berries or other plants, e.g., *dhatura*, opium, or wild mushroom.

Corrosives like sulfuric acid and caustic soda cause a burning sensation, severe pain and blisters in the child's mouth and the food pipe immediately after being swallowed. On the other hand, a child may not have any immediate symptoms on swallowing some pills or other poisonous substances, like napthalene balls, but these can be very dangerous for him over a longer period.

WHAT TO DO

1. Try to quickly locate the suspected poisonous substance the child has actually taken. Pick up and preserve carefully any remaining portion of the swallowed substance for identification and for informing the doctor. Get an idea of the probable amount of substance swallowed by the child.
2. It is best to take the child to the casualty department of the nearest hospital as soon as you can.
3. Do not waste much time in trying to make the child vomit. Do not give him too much salt and water to induce vomiting. Large amounts of salt can harm him.
4. NEVER try to produce vomiting in a child who has taken kerosene oil, a strong acid or alkali like sulfuric acid and caustic soda. It can cause serious damage to his lungs and the linings of his stomach and food pipe.
5. If he has a burning sensation and pain in the mouth due to the strong acid or alkali, give him sips of cold milk and water to drink. It will reduce the pain.
6. Most important, get the child to hospital quickly.

DOG AND OTHER ANIMAL BITES

A child may sometimes be bitten by a dog, monkey, cat or some other animal. The major worry in these cases is that the animal could be rabid and the child may develop rabies as a result of the bite, which is almost always fatal.

Stray, infected dogs are a major cause of rabies among human beings. Cats, monkeys, mongoose, jackals and cattle may also be occasionally responsible for rabies in this country. Bats, foxes, wolves and skunks are known to transmit rabies in USA and Latin America but not in India. Rat bites do not cause rabies.

WHAT TO DO

1. First and foremost, the wound caused by a dog or other rabid animal bite should be immediately and thoroughly cleaned with soap and water.
2. After removal of all traces of soap from the wound, apply locally povidone-iodine (Betadine or Wokadine) 1% lotion, or tincture of iodine, or 70% alcohol. In an emergency any alcoholic liquor of 86-proof or higher may be used.
3. Remember that thorough flushing and cleaning of the wound with plenty of water and soap is the most essential and really important first line of treatment. The subsequent application of antiseptics is of secondary importance.
4. Take the child to your doctor quickly. He will attend to the wound appropriately. He may also like to remove dead tissues at the site of the wound.
5. You must take steps to trace, identify and keep track of the offending dog or animal for 10 days after your child has been bitten. If the animal lives that long, one can safely exclude rabies. But if the animal is found to be showing abnormal behaviour suggestive of rabies, it should be immediately reported to your doctor. If the animal is untraced, it is presumed to be rabid. If the animal dies, arrangements must be made for taking the dead animal to a suitable laboratory for examination of its brain and confirmation of the diagnosis of rabies.
6. Taking into account the status of the animal, the site and severity of the wound and other relevant factors the doctor will decide on the administration of

anti-rabies vaccine to your child. Three kinds of anti-rabies vaccines are now available in India. Your doctor will explain to you their respective advantages, cost, doses, etc. You must strictly follow his instruction regarding vaccine administration to your child.

7. Your child may also need protection against tetanus depending upon his earlier immunization status.

IMMUNIZATION OF PET DOGS AND CATS

Pet domestic dogs and cats must always be properly and regularly immunized against rabies under advice from a trained veterinary surgeon. The immunization should begin when the animal is 3 months old.

WASP AND BEE STINGS

Wasp and bee stings usually cause severe pain, itching and local swelling at the site of the sting. Occasionally, a child may develop a severe reaction due to hypersensitivity. He may have a rash or a wheal formation over his skin, difficulty in breathing and he may become markedly pale with a steep fall in his blood pressure.

WHAT TO DO

1. If the wasp or bee sting is visible, remove it carefully without allowing it to break inside the child's skin. This may be done with the help of a forceps or tweezer.
2. Local application of an ice pack, a soothing lotion like calamine lotion or an anaesthetic cream, like Xylocaine or Gesicane Topical cream would help reduce the pain and the irritation. He may also be given paracetamol tablet or syrup and an anti-allergic drug like Phenargan syrup for the relief of pain and swelling.
3. In the rare event of severe hypersensitivity reaction,

the child should be rushed to the nearest hospital for emergency management.

SNAKE BITE

Snake bite is still encountered as an important medical emergency in many parts of India, especially in the rural areas. In India, 52 out of 216 species of snakes are poisonous.

WHAT TO DO

1. Calm the child and put him to rest. A child may die simply due to fear and shock even when the snake is non-poisonous. It is therefore important to reassure and comfort the child.

2. Do not allow the child to run around. The leg or arm which has been bitten by the snake should be tied down with a splint and not moved about. Lack of movement will reduce the absorption of poison into his body.

3. Do not try to suck out poison from the snake bite wound, it is of no use. Making a cut in the wound or putting into it any drug or chemical, such as, potassium parmaganate is potentially harmful. You should not tie any bandage or tourniquet above the wound site as it can cause increased bleeding and other complications.

4. Try to know wheter the attacking snake is dangerous. Knowledge of the types of snakes in your area and what the snake looked like would help. If the snake is killed, it should be taken to the hospital for identification.

5. Rush the child to the nearest hospital or medical centre.

6. In case the child is bitten by a poisonous snake, he will need urgent treatment and hospitalization.

FOREIGN BODIES

FOREIGN BODY IN THE EYE

A dust particle or a loose eyelash may enter the child's eye and cause him considerable irritation and discomfort. The eyes may water a lot and the child may be reluctant to open them.

WHAT TO DO

If you see something loose over the white part of the eye, you can try removing it. Do not try to do this if the foreign body is lying on the black part of the eye or if it is firmly fixed to the eye.

1. Advise the child not to rub the eye.
2. Ask him to sit down in a chair facing a good light, lean back his head slightly and look up. Stand beside him, and while supporting his chin with one hand gently pull the lower lid down (Fig.19.3).
3. If you can see the foreign particle on the eyelid or the white part of the eye, take it off with a moistened wisp of cotton or the corner of a clean handkerchief.
4. If you do not find it on the lower eyelid, check beneath the upper eyelid. This is a bit more difficult. Ask him to look down. Hold the upper eyelid by the

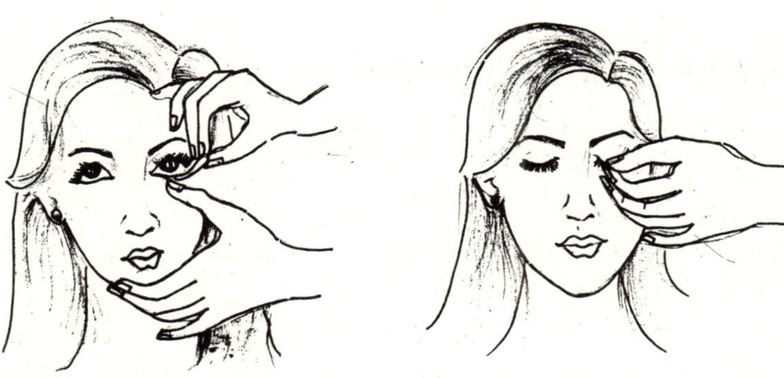

(Fig. 19.3) *(Fig. 19.4)*

eyelashes with your thumb and finger. Then pull it slightly down and turn it over. If noticed over the eyelid or the white part of the eye take off the foreign body as explained above (Fig.19.4).

5. If you do not succeed, ask him to put his eye under clean water in a bowl and ask him to blink. The particle might well float off.

Do not try any heroic steps to remove the object. If unsuccessful, take your child to the doctor. In any case, never try to remove an object if it is embedded firmly in the eye, or if it is resting on the black part of the eye.

FOREIGN BODY IN THE NOSE

Small children like to 'explore' and may push up a variety of objects into their noses. Parents may come to know only when they notice the child having difficulty in breathing or breathing noisily through the nose. His nose may become swollen. Sometimes, the child may have a smelly (infected) or bloodstained discharge from the nose as long as two to three days after the actual entry of the foreign body.

1. DO NOT ATTEMPT to remove the foreign body yourself.
2. Keep your child quiet, ask him to breathe through the mouth.
3. Take him to the nearest hospital casualty department.

FOREIGN BODY IN THE EAR

Children may also sometimes push in a small bead or other foreign body in your child's ear. Occasionally an insect may fly or crawl into the ear and get trapped there.

1. Calm the child. Ask him not to get alarmed by the buzzing sensation, if it is an insect.
2. Ask your child to sit down. Let him tilt his head to one side so that the ear with the foreign body is facing upwards, towards you.

(Fig. 19.5)

3. Gently flood the ear with mildly warm water so that the insect or foreign body floats out (Fig.19.5).
4. If this does not work take him to the hospital. Do not try any extreme measures such as removing it with a pointed implement.

SWALLOWED FOREIGN BODY

As mentioned before, toddlers and young children often tend to put anything which they can lay their hands on into their mouth. Sometimes small objects such as coins, buttons or pins get accidentally swallowed.

WHAT TO DO

Do not give your child anything to eat or drink. Do not try to make him bring up the swallowed object. What you need to do is to arrange a quick consultation with a doctor or preferably take him to a hospital casualty as soon you can.

INHALED FOREIGN BODY

Sometimes the foreign body taken by your child may accidentally slip into the respiratory passage instead of going into the food pipe and stomach. The child may then choke and need urgent management for choking. Sometimes he may have no immediate symptoms after inhaling the foreign body but may subsequently develop cough and other symptoms of lung disease. These occur due to late effects of blockage of a respiratory passage by the inhaled foreign body and superimposed infection.

WHAT TO DO

If you suspect that your child has swallowed or inhaled a foreign body, and even if he seems to be alright after a while, do take him to your doctor or a hospital for proper assessment. You should also watch him carefully over the next few days and weeks.

CHOKING

A foreign object, like a coin, button, pin, etc., which is put by a toddler or a young child in his mouth, may suddenly slip into the back of his throat. This may either block the throat or cause acute contraction of muscles around it, leading to a very uncomfortable sense of choking. He may find it hard to speak and breathe. His skin may turn blue and he may look terrified, gasping for breath.

WHAT TO DO

STEP 1

You must act immediately. If he is a baby or a small child, hold him firmly by his legs with one hand and turn him upside down. He will now be hanging with his feet up, with his head facing the ground. Now with your free hand slap his back firmly between his shoulder blades. This should release the inhaled object. If it does not, repeat this upto five times (Fig.19.6). To carry out the same procedure in an older child, he should be made to bend over the back of a settee or the arm of a chair so as to assume practically an

(Fig. 19.6)

upside down position. In case of a young child you should first sit in an armless chair. Make the child lie on his tummy across your thighs and to assume a head down feet up position. In either case, give the child upto five good thumps between his shoulder blades with moderate force.

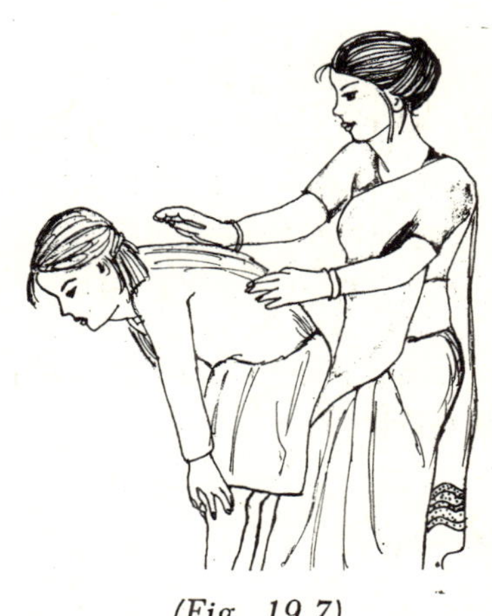

(Fig. 19.7)

If step 1 (slapping the child's back between the shoulder blades with him upside down) does not succeed (Fig. 19.7), carry out step 2 (abdominal thrust) in which sudden pressure is exerted on the child's stomach to expel the foreign body.

STEP 2

Make the older child stand. Now stand behind the child, put your arms around his body and interlock your hands below his rib cage. Sharply pull your locked hands up and

(Fig. 19.8)

into the child's body. The resultant sudden increase in pressure inside the chest will make the foreign body stuck in the respiratory passage come out (Fig. 19.8).

These manoeuvres must be conducted quickly to save life. If breathing stops or the child becomes unconscious begin resuscitation without delay. The resuscitation procedure has been explained at the end of this chapter. Ask your relative or neighbour to dial 102 for an emergency ambulance.

DROWNING

Children may accidentally drown in a swimming pool, tank, an open *nullah*, sewer, canal, river or sea. An unattended baby may drown in a bathtub or a bucket. Immediate first aid is of utmost importance in saving the life of a child who has drowned.

The air passage should be cleared immediately with a finger or a handkerchief and mouth-to-mouth breathing started without delay. Do not waste precious time in trying to remove water or froth which may be pouring out from his mouth. Do heart massage by compressing his chest along with mouth-to-mouth breathing if he is found to be pale and his pulse is not felt at his wrist. Mouth-to-mouth breathing and heart massage must be continued till the child reaches the nearest hospital.

ELECTRIC SHOCK

You need to be prompt but careful in handling a problem of electric shock. Switch off the current immediately. Separate the child at once from the electric current with the help of a dry wooden stick or rubber gloves. Do not try to pull or push him directly with your hands as this may give you a severe electric shock as well. After the child has been separated from the source of electric current, make an immediate check about the status of his breathing.

If he is not breathing, start mouth-to-mouth breathing immediately. If he is pale and you cannot feel his pulse at the wrist carry out heart massage by compressing his chest along with mouth-to-mouth breathing immediately. Rush him to the hospital for further management. The management of burns caused by electric current has been described in the section on Burns.

FRACTURES (BROKEN BONES)

A child with suspected fracture following an injury should be handled gently in the position in which you find him. You should initially steady and support the injured bone by placing one hand above and the other below the site of injury and then call for an ambulance. If the child has to be moved, it should be done very gently. If a leg is broken, tie this leg gently but firmly to the uninjured leg with some padding placed between the legs. In case of injury to the arm, it should be placed in a sling before moving him. However, do not move the child if you suspect that his neck or spine may be injured. It is necessary that such a child is only handled by trained paramedical personnel. You should not give the injured child anything to eat or drink after the accident till he has been examined by a doctor. Administration of fluids or food to the child would delay correction of his fracture if it has to be done under anesthesia.

HEAD INJURY

Children often get knocked about and hit on the head during play activities. Most of these injuries are of a minor nature and very soon these children resume their normal activities. Occasionally they may sustain scalp wounds with some bleeding which would need local cleaning, dressing and sometimes stitching.

You have to be careful if the child develops any of the

following symptoms:

(i) unconsciousness or cloudiness of sensorium, even for a short period;

(ii) dizziness;

(iii) headaches which persist and tend to increase in severity;

(iv) vomiting;

(v) drowsiness or irritability;

(vi) leaking of blood or light yellowish fluid from the nose or ears.

WHAT TO DO

Sometimes, a child with fairly severe internal injury has practically no significant symptoms in the beginning. But over the next few hours he may develop headache, drowsiness, irritability or vomiting. The delay in symptoms is usually due to an injured leaking blood vessel causing gradual accumulation of blood inside the child's head or on account of slowly increasing swelling of the injured brain. If the process is allowed to continue unchecked the child may get worse. He may lapse into unconsciousness, suffer from serious brain damage and may even die. It is therefore, important to closely watch the child for his level of alertness and of any of the above symptoms over the next 12-24 hours.

If the child has a discharge of blood or blood-stained fluid from the nose or ears after a head injury, it may mean that he has sustained a fracture of his skull bones at its base. This is a bad sign and the child must be taken quickly to the hospital for X-rays/CT scan/M.R.I. of his head, and for observation and proper management.

FITS (CONVULSIONS OR SEIZURES)

FEBRILE CONVULSIONS

A child may suddenly develop a fit or convulsion for several reasons. The commonest cause of fits in children between the age of 3 months and 6 years is a sudden rise of temperature which is most often caused by a viral infection. The child suddenly becomes unconscious, his body goes rigid and soon thereafter he starts vigorous jerking of his upper and lower limbs. The jerking and unconsciousness may continue for several minutes. He then recovers slowly, looks confused and drowsy and may go off to sleep. The fit caused by the sudden rise of temperature in this age-group is called 'febrile convulsion' and is generally benign in nature. It may run in some families and recur during episodes of fever.

The mother should remain calm during her child's febrile convulsion. She should not pour water or try to force any liquid into the child's mouth during the fit or while he is drowsy afterwards. No effort should be made to forcibly open his clenched teeth. He may be held lightly to avoid injury to his limbs. After the jerking stops, the child should be turned on his side so that he does not inhale his saliva or get choked on his tongue.

Tepid sponging should be commenced to bring down the temperature and paracetamol given when he is fully conscious. In a child with past history of fever associated fits, these measures should be taken promptly to prevent development of high fever. In addition, to prevent fits, the doctor may advise you to administer him diazepam (a drug), by mouth or as rectal suppository, at the onset and during the duration of fever.

EPILEPSY AND FITS DUE TO OTHER CAUSES

Recurrent convulsions in children may also be due to epilepsy. This condition requires proper investigation and regular administration of drugs under the supervision of a doctor. The immediate management of an epileptic fit in a child is done on the same general lines as described above for febrile fits. The problem of epilepsy has been discussed at length in the section on Common Diseases in Children.

If the fits persist for longer than 15 minutes, other more serious causes of fits like infection of the brain (encephalitis) and its membranous covering (meningitis), and others need to be identified. The child should be quickly taken to a hospital for proper management.

UNCONSCIOUSNESS

A child may suddenly become unconscious following an injury to his head, due to fits associated with fever, epileptic fits, an overdose of insulin or excessive rise of blood sugar in a diabetic child or some other condition affecting the functioning of the child's brain.

WHAT TO DO

1. Do not let the child lie on his back. Turn him halfway over onto his front. Let his head and face also rest sideways so that the nose is clear from the ground (Fig. 19. 9).

(Fig. 19.9)

2. Do not give him anything to eat or drink. Stay close to him and watch him carefully all the time.
3. Gently shake him by the shoulders or pinch his ear lobes. If he responds, watch him further. If he does not, check if he is breathing.

4. If the child is not breathing, begin mouth-to-mouth breathing immediately (as explained below under 'Resuscitaion').
5. You may further need to simultaneously do chest compression, if you cannot feel his pulse. Continue these measures until the child begins to breathe on his own or medical help becomes available.

RESUSCITATION

WHAT IS IT AND WHY DO IT?

In order to survive all of us need a constant supply of oxygen. The brain of a child may get permanently damaged or he may die if he does not get oxygen supply for as short a time as three minutes. This may occur due to the child being unconscious for some reason and not breathing or if there is complete obstruction to his breathing passages.

In order to revive the child three essential things are needed:

(1) The throat and lower passages through which air travels into the lungs must remain open. If there is any obstruction in them (for example, due to an inhaled foreign body) steps have to be taken to clear the obstruction.

(2) The child is made to breathe or we have to breathe for him and thus supply oxygen to his blood and brain. This is done by giving 'artificial ventilation'. One simple, readily available way is to do mouth-to-mouth breathing. We blow our own expelled air into the child's lungs.

(3) If the child's heart stops, we physically 'compress the chest' to squeeze blood through the heart and around the body in order to supply life sustaining oxygen to the child's brain and other vital organs. Many times we have to do both artificial ventilation and chest compression, (heart massage) after ensuring that air passages are open.

MOUTH-TO-MOUTH BREATHING

1. Make the child lie on his back on the floor or some hard surface.

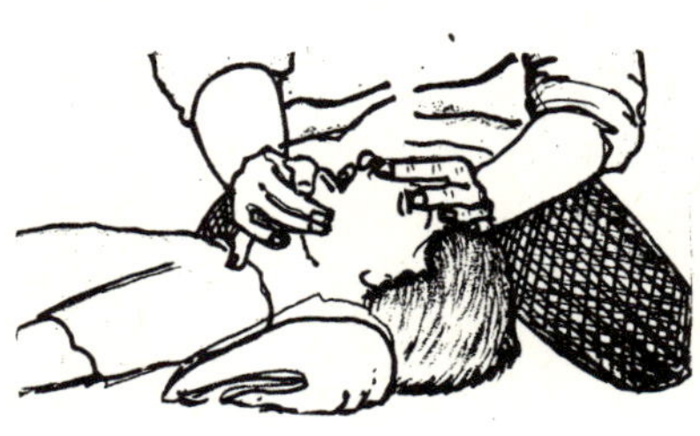

(Fig. 19.10)

2. Use your finger to clear his mouth of any foreign body, dirt, vomit or blood. Don't apply unnecessary force.

3. Bend the child's head back with one hand and lift up the chin (lower jaw) with the other. This is done to lift the tongue so as to clear the air passage at the back of the throat.

4. Keep his head tilted backwards with his mouth open and his jaw supported with one hand. Squeeze and close off both the nostrils of his nose with fingers of the other hand (Fig.19.10).

5. Now begin the actual procedure of mouth-to-mouth breathing. Take a deep breath and hold it. Open your mouth and make a tight seal with your lip around the child's mouth.

(Fig. 19.11)

6. Breathe out into the child's mouth with sufficient force from your lungs until you see his chest rise (Fig.19.11).

7. Take your mouth away and let the child's chest fall.

8. Continue giving breaths at a rate of 15 to 20 breaths, per minute till he starts breathing on his own or medical help arrives and takes over.

9. After the child resumes breathing place him in the 'recovery' position.

MOUTH-TO-MOUTH AND NOSE BREATHING

(FOR BABIES AND SMALL CHILDREN)

1. The nose and mouth are very close to each other in babies and small children less than 2 years old. It is therefore, easier and more practical to breathe into their mouth and nose together. You should also push in comparatively smaller amounts of air with less force when breathing into them.

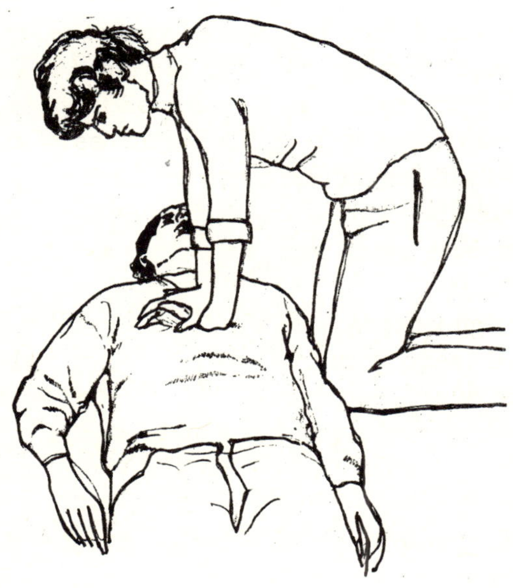

(Fig. 19.12)

HEART MASSAGE

When a child is unconscious and not breathing and continues to look pale or blue-faced in spite of your mouth-to-mouth breathing, it means that his heart may also have stopped beating. If so, you must start massage along with mouth-to-mouth breathing (Fig. 19.12).

1. Lay down the child on the back on the floor or a hard surface.
2. Kneel beside him facing his chest.
3. Place the heel of one hand over the lower half of the child's breast bone. The breast bone lies in the mid-line on the front of his chest. It extends from mid-point between the two collar bones at the base of the neck to the pit of the stomach.
4. Move yourself forwards over the child's body so that your shoulders are directly over his breast bone.
5. Keeping your arm straight and without bending at the elbow, press down on the breast bone.
6. Repeat the chest compression at a rate of about 80-100 per minute.
7. After every five chest compressions, stop and give him one mouth-to-mouth breathing.
8. Continue the cycle of these two combined procedures, i.e., five chest compressions followed by one mouth-to-mouth breathing.
9. If another pair of hands is available, you can do the heart massage and he can do mouth-to-mouth breathing in the above manner. You should temporarily stop doing chest compression when your help does the mouth-to-mouth breathing.
10. Once the heart has started beating, keep on the mouth-to-mouth breathing till the child himself starts breathing.
11. Place the child in 'recovery' position and watch him carefully.

HEART MASSAGE FOR BABIES LESS THAN TWO YEARS OLD

The basic procedure for doing heart massage is the same as for older children but with the following differences:

1. The pressure to the baby's chest is applied with two

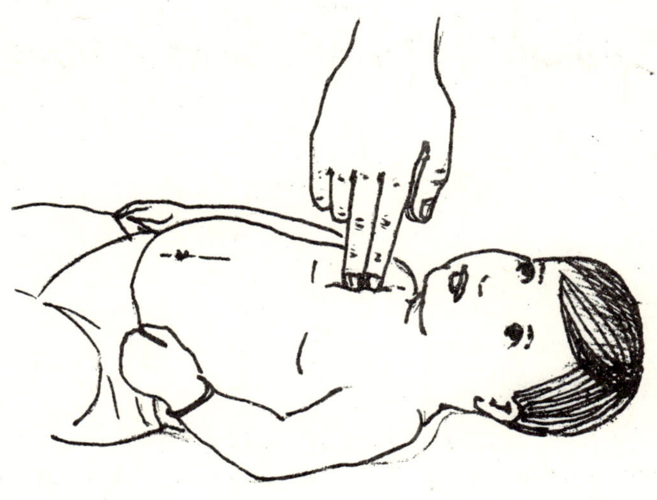

(Fig. 19.13)

fingers (middle and index) and not with the heel of the hand (Fig.19.13).

2. Less force is used to avoid injury to lungs and ribs. The chest is compressed by about ½ to 1 inch only.
3. The fingers used for compression are placed over the middle portion of the breast bone and not at its lower part. You can use an imaginary line joining the two nipples on the child's breast as a guide.
4. Chest compressions are done at a faster rate of 100 times per minute. Mouth-to-mouth breathing is done once after every five chest compressions as usual.

20

CARING FOR A SICK CHILD AT HOME

Most parents feel anxious when faced with looking after a sick child at home. They often find themselves at a loss about the appropriate manner of handling many of his day-to-day problems, like his feeding, clothing, personal hygiene and regulation of his physical activities. They also feel unsure about their ability to make simple observations accurately, like the recording of temperature in a 2-month-old baby. The following guidelines will help parents to attend to their sick child better and with greater confidence.

GENERAL CARE

As far as possible, keep the child's room at a comfortable temperature. Proper ventilation should be provided by keeping windows slightly open but direct strong draughts of air on the child should be avoided. It is better to use cotton sheets for his bed, they are more soothing. These should be changed regularly. Leave a box of tissues or two to three hand towels on his bedside table. Keep a bowl by the bed of a child who is prone to vomiting. If he vomits, tell him not to be anxious. Let him clean his mouth and teeth with water after being sick. A mint or a sweet will help to take away the unpleasant aftertaste. The child may feel comfortable in loose night clothes.

CLEANLINESS AND HYGIENE

Many children dislike full body baths while they are sick. It is not necessary to insist upon such daily baths. It is enough to wash the child's hands and face and brush his hair. The body can be given a general sponging. A quick bath, particularly in the hot and humid season, induces a general feeling of freshness and is welcome by most children. The child's teeth must be cleaned regularly and his mouth rinsed well. The sick child must wash his hands well with soap and water after passing motion and before taking or handling food.

FEEDING THE SICK CHILD

Most sick children have a poor appetite. Be patient and handle this problem with understanding and persuasion. Do not try to force him to have his normal food in its usual quantities. Instead, offer light, appetizing food in small quantities at more frequent intervals. The child may be allowed to occasionally indulge in his favourite foods like ice cream, ice lolly, chocolates, home-made desserts, etc. Some sick children may like to have bananas, mango, *cheeku* and yoghurt. Let them eat these foods, they are good for him. There is absolutely no truth in the widely held view, particularly among the older generation that yoghurt (*dahi*) is harmful for a child with fever On the contrary, it is good, nutritious and easily digested. Some children may actually prefer plain foods such as dry toast, mashed potato or biscuits. Spicy and fatty foods should of course be avoided. If the child is completely off food and refuses to eat for two or even three days, do not get too anxious. He will make up quickly when he gets better. In the meantime try to give him some light snacks. It is important that the child continues to take adequate amounts of fluids. He should be encouraged to take milk, fruit drinks and thin soups. Milk may be more acceptable in the form of milk shakes, egg flip or flavoured with chocolate and other flavouring agents. Squashes of different kinds and fizzy drinks are less preferred choices but may be used to supplement the child's intake of fluids. You should see that the child continues to pass adequate amounts of urine daily. If he vomits or passes motions frequently, the doctor must be informed; the child may need to be given fluids and nutrition intravenously.

REST AND COMFORT

It is not necessary for a child who is not very ill to always stay in bed. It must however, be ensured that he does not exert himself to the point of getting exhausted. He must get adequate rest and necessary steps should be taken to make him comfortable. He can be provided with a comfortable chair or soft cushions to lean on, when not in bed. A child with breathing difficulty and cough will feel better in a propped up position.

SENSE OF SECURITY AND ENTERTAINMENT

Most sick children develop some behaviour changes. Small children feel bewildered; they cling to their mothers, cry for no particular reason and want to be fed much more frequently.

Older children also feel insecure, bored and irritable. You need to stay calm and find plenty of time and patience for your sick child. You may read stories to your small child or help him with his colouring, painting or building blocks. Let the older child be engaged in bedside games, painting, watching TV, or his favourite video games. Above everything else, sick children need your love, company and a sense of security.

ISOLATION OF THE SICK CHILD

The segregation of patients suffering from measles, rubella, chicken pox and mumps is usually not of much practical help in preventing the spread of these infections to other children and family members in the same household. This is because patients carrying these highly contagious infections start transmitting them to others from a few days before they themselves show recognizable symptoms of these diseases. After developing the disease these patients however, further continue to remain infective for some more time. It is then useful to minimize their contact with other susceptible individuals.

School going children affected by these diseases should not be sent to school till their infective period is over and they are otherwise fit to go to school. Children suffering from German measles (rubella) pose a special risk to pregnant women, particularly during the early stage of their pregnancy. While the rubella infection would cause only a mild illness in the mother, it may infect the baby in her womb and cause several serious birth defects in him.

It is very important that a child suffering from chicken-pox and German measles should not come in close contact with a pregnant woman. This has been discussed at length under the respective individual diseases in the section on Common Diseases in Children. The infectious period of a disease is the period during which the child can give infection to others. On the other hand, incubation period is the time interval between a child catching the infection from another person and he himself falling ill. These are shown in the table below for your guidance.

DISEASE	INFECTIOUS PERIOD FROM	TILL	INCUBATION PERIOD
Chicken pox	The day before the rash appears	Until all blisters get covered by scabs (about 7 – 10 days)	11 – 21 days
Measles	4 – 5 days before the rash appears	For 5 days after the rash subsides	10 – 12 days
Mumps	1 day before swelling appears on the face	Upto 3 days after the swellings subside	14 – 21 days
Rubella (German measles)	7 – 10 days before onset of rash	Upto a week after the rash first appears	14 – 21 days
Whooping cough	The beginning of illness with cold and cough	Upto about 6 weeks after the child starts coughing	7 – 14 days

Preventive measures considered useful for avoiding occurrences of the above diseases – and a few others like meningitis –in susceptible contact cases and in general have been discussed in the section on Common Diseases in Children. It must, however, be borne in mind that the truly effective way of preventing these diseases is to have the child fully immunized against them at the right time.

MEDICINES IN CUPBOARD FOR HOME USE

Considering the fact that your child can suddenly fall ill at any time of day or night or on Sundays and holidays when your doctor may not be able to come quickly, you should always keep some medicines and first aid material readily available at home. These medicines must, however, be stored safely so as to be out of reach of small children. The list of desirable medicines and materials is given below:

MATERIALS

1. Mercury thermometer (rectal thermometer, if the baby is below 1½ years of age).
2. Adhesive antiseptic dressing (e.g. Band-Aid).
3. Sterile wound dressings (sterile gauze/cotton).
4. Cotton wool.
5. Bandages of two to three different sizes.
6. Antiseptic cream and antiseptic powder.
7. Crepe bandages.
8. Methylated spirit.
9. Surgical tape.
10. Antiseptic cleansing lotion.

MEDICINES

(i) Paracetamol syrup, tablets or drops.

(ii) Tablet or syrup for control of vomiting as per your own doctor's advice (keep a note of the dose recommended for your child for emergency use only).

(iii) O.R.S. packets. Glucose-electrolyte powder sachets for making oral rehydration solution for emergency use in case the child develops acute diarrhoea or vomiting.

(iv) Any specific medicines recommended by your child's doctor for emergency use in the event of his not being available.

(v) Medicine for relief of intestinal colic (for use in emergency, strictly according to the doctor's instruction).

(vi) Calamine lotion for irritating rashes.

21
CONSULTING YOUR DOCTOR

IMPORTANT TIPS

All parents have to consult a doctor some time or the other, as children do occasionally fall ill. Here are some general guidelines to help you in securing and making the best use of medical advice.

Try to develop a good communication between you, your child and the doctor. Do not use the doctor as a bogey to force your uncooperative child to obey you. You will need to take your child to the doctor sometimes and the fear of doctors instilled in him would make any medical examination by the doctor very difficult. If your older child is to have an injection or some other procedure, it should be explained to him in advance so that he does not lose faith in you and the doctor and continues to cooperate in his medical care. Older girls may prefer to see a woman doctor. Boys may like to have some privacy during the examination of their sex organs. Such wishes must be given due consideration.

You must appreciate that the doctor may not always be in a position to give the exact diagnosis of your child's illness at his very first visit. Some illnesses like typhoid fever or hepatitis, take some time before their symptoms, clinical signs and laboratory investigations enable their precise diagnosis to get established. It is advisable to be patient in such circumstances. Several viral illnesses may be associated with high fever and severe bodyache but they are not helped by antibiotics. Your doctor may, therefore, like to avoid prescribing them in such cases. He may also prefer to let your child get over his minor illnesses on his own and recommend minimal use of drugs. You need to be understanding and patient. However, if you have any reservations or doubts, you should discuss them freely with your doctor.

Understand clearly the treatment advised by the doctor and follow the instructions strictly. If a drug has been prescribed for one week, it must be regularly administered for the whole of the advised period. Do not discontinue it earlier to avoid what you consider to be overmedication. Premature discontinuation of treatment may cause immediate recurrence of the disease or some other problems later.

If your child does not seem to be getting well after a reasonable period of treatment, you may obtain another medical opinion. It is, however, desirable not to switch treatments too frequently as it would not be in the best interest of your child.

VISIT TO THE DOCTOR

You must note the symptoms of your child's illness carefully and in detail. If the illness lasts more than two to three days, you would do well to maintain a written record to ensure accuracy. For example, if the child has diarrhoea, keep a note of the number of motions passed per day, the quantity, consistency and colour of his stools, presence of blood or mucus, accompanying fever, abdominal pain and the amount of urine passed. Your doctor is likely to ask you several questions relating to the child's present illness and about his illnesses in the past. He needs this information to determine the nature and severity of the problem. You should therefore, go to him properly prepared with all relevant information. It would help to carry a written note with you about the things you would like to ask the doctor. You should also keep handy anything you want to show him, e.g., your child's soiled nappy, stool or vomit.

You should obtain detailed advice from the doctor about any particular symptom in your child which he would want you to look out for or especially observe. You should also enquire about the steps which he would like you to take under those specific circumstances, for example in the event of a sudden rise in the child's temperature or his developing a fit. It would be better for you to make written notes of such instructions for your own guidance rather than simply relying on your memory.

22

COMMON DISEASES IN CHILDREN

Most parents wish to know some basic facts about the nature of their child's disease. They feel that such knowledge would help them in coping with their child's illness better and with greater confidence. However, generally they are unable to get the necessary information, as their doctor is far too busy. Besides, the unsolicited advice from the sick child's relatives, family friends and visitors based on their 'own' so-called experiences confuse the parents even more. Several widely held untrue convictions about common diseases act not only as an impediment to taking proper care of sick children but are, not infrequently, positively harmful.

Considering the imperative need of parents to have some essential and accurate information about a few diseases common among children, a brief description of these diseases has been given in this section. Some illneses like diarrhoea or asthma, in the management of which the parents play a very important role, have been discussed in detail. However, it is beyond the scope of this manual to cover the entire range of children's diseases.

ANAEMIA

Anaemia is a condition in which the haemoglobin concentration in the blood of a child is below the normal range for his age. Broadly speaking, a haemoglobin level below 11 g per decilitre of blood in children between 6 months and 6 years of age and below 12 g per decilitre in older children indicates anaemia. The haemoglobin (a pigment) contained in red blood cells carries supplies of vital life-sustaining oxygen to the brain, heart, kidneys and all other organs and tissues of the human body. A fall in the amount of circulating haemoglobin and the oxygen carried by it adversely affects the efficient functioning of several vital organs. The child appears pale and there occurs paleness of the colour of the tongue and the inner surfaces of eyelids and lips. The child gets tired easily, feels weak and lethargic, and does not look well. He may feel short of breath on exertion. He is also more prone to infections. Severe anaemia can have serious harmful effects on the functioning of the heart.

WHY DOES IT OCCUR?

Anaemia can occur due to either (i) deficient production of haemoglobin and red blood cells in the bone marrow, (ii) excessive abnormal destruction of red blood cells in the body or (iii) excessive loss of blood due to bleeding. Among other causes, iron deficiency in the child's diet and hookworm infection in the intestines are two common causes of anaemia in children in India. In iron deficiency anaemia, the production of haemoglobin gets hampered due to insufficient supply of iron, which is essential for the formation of haemoglobin. Excessive destruction of red blood cells due to blood group incompatibility between the mother and baby, certain infections and bleeding are sometimes responsible for causing severe anaemia in newborn babies. A few children who suffer from abnormal haemoglobin disorders, like thalassaemia, develop persistent anaemia. They require frequent blood transfusions and long-term special treatment under regular medical supervision. Leukemia and other bone marrow disorders may also sometimes cause anaemia in children.

WHAT TO DO

In view of the many different underlying causes of anaemia, the doctor carries out a detailed physical examination of the child who is suffering from anaemia. He further advises haemoglobin estimation and certain other blood tests to determine the severity, nature and cause of anaemia. Based on various relevant facts, appropriate treatment is then prescribed.

To prevent iron deficiency anaemia, an older child must take a properly balanced, iron-rich diet. Green leafy vegetables, Bengal gram, lentils, beans, pomegranates, apricots, pineapple, egg yolk, meat and liver are rich in iron and the child should regularly eat some of these foods. Young infants, especially premature babies are given iron supplements to prevent development of iron deficiency anaemia. This has been explained in greater detail in the section on Care of the Newborn Baby.

For the treatment of iron deficiency anaemia, the child is given a suitable iron preparation in a dose appropriate for his age and body-weight. Other types of anaemia need specific treatment according to their causes.

APPENDICITIS

The appendix is a finger-sized tube situated at the junction of the small and the large intestines and lies in the lower right-hand side of the abdomen. (Fig. 22.1) The appendix has one blind end and only a small opening into the intestines. If the narrow passage gets blocked by a lump of hardened faecal matter or a kink it results in a build-up of bacteria inside the appendix. This causes inflammation of the appendix which is known as 'appendicitis'. Appendicitis may occur at any age but it is comparatively rare under the age of two years. It is more common in teenage and the young adult period.

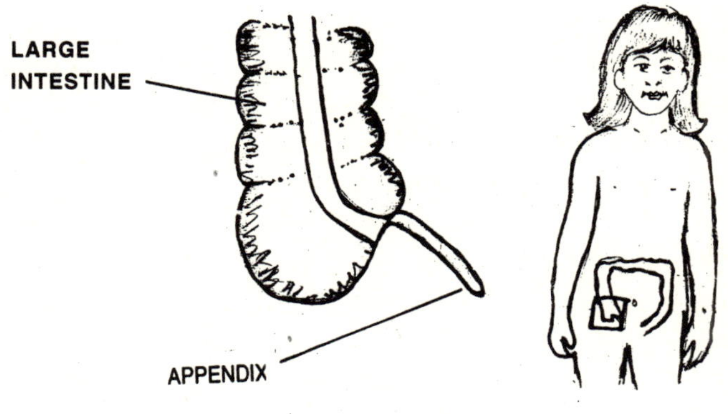

(Fig. 22.1)

An older child with appendicitis initially complains of pain in the abdomen, starting around the navel, which then moves to the lower, right-hand side of the abdomen. The child has vomiting, lack of appetite and generally mild to moderately high fever. Because of variations in the position of the appendix, the pain may be felt at unusual sites such as in the loin region or lower mid-abdomen. A young child may only be able to express himself by holding a hand over the navel. Small children become irritable and may lie with their thighs pulled up.

It is important that if there is any suspicion about the possible occurrence of this disease in your child, a doctor must be consulted quickly. The disease can sometimes progress quite rapidly within a matter of a few hours. Emergency removal of the appendix is the recommended treatment for acute appendicitis and it should not be delayed for more than a few hours. If delayed, the child may develop complications including a burst appendix. Parents need not be afraid about this operation as children tolerate it very well and recover completely.

ASTHMA

Asthma is today a very common disease among children of all age groups. In a majority of affected children, it is mild to moderate in severity and can be managed without much difficulty. Many of these patients grow out of asthma, some by school age and a few before they become adults. The disease can however be severe and persistent in a few cases requiring long-term careful handling.

UNDERSTANDING ASTHMA

For appropriate and successful management of this condition, it is very important for parents to have a basic understanding of the true nature of this disease. They need to be free from undue anxiety and misconceptions about this condition. During breathing in a normal child, the air travels into and out of the lungs with ease through tube-like passages called the 'bronchi'. The bronchi normally remain adequately open throughout the whole process of breathing. However, during an attack of asthma, the muscles surrounding the airways tighten causing narrowing of the air passages. There is also excess formation of thick, sticky mucus. As a result of these changes, the child finds it hard to breathe through the narrowed air passages. He makes a wheezing sound, especially, when breathing out and he coughs persistently.

Children with asthma have air passages which are oversensitive. They react quickly to various irritants (triggers) that do not affect normal children. The triggers that bring on an attack of asthma vary from child to child. The known triggers include:

(i) viral infections (especially common colds);

(ii) allergies;
(iii) cold weather or strong dry winds;
(iv) sudden changes in temperature; and
(v) strong odours and fumes such as fresh paint, white-washing, perfume or tobacco smoke.

The common substances to which a child with asthma may be allergic to include:

(i) house dust mites, which live mostly in the bed and soft furnishings;
(ii) grass and pollen of some flowers; and
(iii) animal fur and feathers.

The pattern and severity of the illness vary from child to child. Some may only cough, especially at night or have breathing difficulty after running around for some time. While some children have moderate difficulty in breathing a few may develop a severe wheeze and breathlessness from time to time, requiring urgent and intensive medical treatment. Each individual asthmatic child has to be managed according to the severity and the recurrent nature of his condition.

MANAGEMENT OF ASTHMA

There is as yet no permanent cure for asthma. But with proper management, the asthmatic child's symptoms can be largely kept under control and he can lead a full and active life. Ian Botham, the well-known English cricketer and an asthmatic, is a good example. Many children also grow out of asthma with age. Broadly speaking, a two-fold approach is employed to tackle this problem: (a) prevention of attacks, and (b) treatment of acute episodes and persistent symptoms.

PREVENTING ATTACKS OF ASTHMA

The following steps help in preventing or reducing the number and severity of attacks of asthma.

A. Avoiding the triggers

It is easier to avoid some triggers than others.

(i) Parents should take steps to avoid the exposure of an asthmatic child to cigarette smoke. They should stop smoking at home and avoid taking the child to smoke-filled places.

(ii) Strong odours such as those of disinfectants, perfumes, wet paints and whitewash and smoke from wood fire can trigger an attack of asthma. The child's exposure to them should be avoided.

(iii) House-dust mites are tiny creatures that live in beds, carpets, curtains, soft toys, quilts and blankets. Many children, particularly of school-going age, are allergic to the droppings of house-dust mite. Steps to control dust and thereby reduce dust mites may be beneficial to some asthmatic patients. Therefore, it is better that the child's bedroom should have no carpets, rugs, upholstered furniture, stuffed toys, calendars or books, etc., which are liable to gather dust and are difficult to keep clean. The mattresses, pillows, quilts and blankets should be inside airtight covers which can be washed. The covers should be washed once weekly in hot water in order to kill the mites. Where feasible, vacuum the mattresses, quilts and blankets once a week or have them dusted outside when the child is not at home. The floors of the house should be wiped with a wet mop and not swept dry, particularly when the child is at home.

(iv) Rooms should be kept aired and humidity should be avoided. Moulds tend to grow rapidly in damp and warm places. Airconditioning helps to reduce humidity.

(v) Do not use pillows with feathers. It is better not to keep pets with furs or feathers, if there is a family history of allergy and your child suffers from asthma.

(vi) Pollen can induce an attack of asthma in some children. It is, however, very difficult to identify or avoid the offending pollen.

(vii) It is better to avoid the use of aspirin and aspirin containing formulations (such as Anacin, Dispirin, etc.) and ibuprofen preparations (such as Brufen, Ibugesic) in asthmatic children. These drugs are known to trigger attacks in some children who are prone to asthma.

B. Drugs for preventing attacks

A few prophylactic drugs like sodium cromoglycate are now available. They exercise some protective effect on the lining of the air passage of asthmatic children and make them less likely to become narrow when exposed to various triggers. They are available in the form of inhalers. The use of these inhalers helps to prevent or reduce the severity of attacks in some children, particularly in those with seasonal and exercise-induced asthma. The protective effect of these preventive inhalers begins about 14 days after the commencement of their regular use. It is, therefore, recommended that in children having seasonal attacks, regular use of preventive inhalers should be started about two to three weeks before the anticipated time of onset of the child's breathing problem. The preventive inhalers should be taken regularly during the vulnerable period even if the child is apparently well.

TREATMENT OF ATTACKS OF ASTHMA

Be calm and reassure the child

Many children are frightened at the onset of an attack of asthma. Some parents also become overanxious and upset on noticing the discomfort of their child. It is, however, important that parents stay calm, assess the situation properly and take necessary action quietly and efficiently. The child should be reassured and encouraged to overcome his agitation. He should be helped to take the necessary medication and the child's mind should be tactfully taken off the attack. Anxiety is liable to worsen it.

MEDICINES FOR RELIEF OF ATTACK

To control an acute attack of asthma, various drugs are used which help in opening up the narrowed-down air passages. These are called bronchodilators. The bronchodilator drugs can be given as tablets or as a syrup by mouth or through inhalation with the help of inhalers. When inhaled, the bronchodilator drugs go straight into the lungs. As such they can be given in low doses, are quickly effective and have comparatively less side effects. There are different types of inhalers. Older children can use aerosols (which are like mini spray cans) or dry powder (in capsules) inhaler devices. Small children below 6 years of age find it difficult to control and coordinate their breathing during the use of aerosol inhalers. They need to use a spacer to fit their aerosol puffer. Very young children will also require a face mask to be placed over their nose and mouth which is attached to the spacer. It is important that parents fully understand from their doctor the correct technique of using a spacer and the face mask. It is desirable that the child first uses the inhaler in the presence of the doctor. The administration of inhaler medication to infants and very young children who cannot use an inhaler can be done with the help of a nebuliser. The use of a nebuliser is generally done in a hospital or at a doctor's clinic; some small models of nebulisers are also now available for use at home. A nebuliser is a machine that turns the liquid medicine into a mist by blowing compressed air or oxygen through it. The bronchodilator-medicine in the fine mist is inhaled by the baby through a mouthpiece or a mask. Different types of bronchodilator medicines are now available in the form of inhalers and the doctor will prescribe them singly or in combination, as per the child's requirements.

Many parents hesitate to let their children have inhaler medication under the wrong impression that inhaler treatment should only be used as a very last resort when nothing else works. Some mistakenly believe they are addictive and that children cannot do without them once they have been put on inhalers. In truth, inhaler treatment is today a very useful and effective tool in the management of asthma.

STEROIDS IN THE TREATMENT OF ASTHMA

The rational use of steroids now plays a very important role in the treatment and prevention of repeated attacks of asthma. Used under close medical supervision, they should not be rejected out of hand on account of fears about their side effects. The steroids given by inhalation and short courses of steroids by mouth, have hardly any side effects to worry about. Steroid treatment can be life saving in a child with a severe and otherwise uncontrollable attack of asthma. It can help children with chronic asthma to obtain satisfactory control of their symptoms and lead an active and normal life. The decision regarding their use should be left to the treating doctor.

EXERCISE AND ASTHMA

Some children do not have any symptoms of asthma ordinarily but become wheezy and breathless after exercise. This is called exercise-induced asthma or exercise asthma. It may sometimes be difficult to tell the difference between normal breathlessness after exertion and asthma caused by exercise, particularly in those children who are otherwise normal. However, if your child develops such symptoms after exercise, you should consult a doctor. The symptoms may become most evident within a minute of stopping the exercise. They may then get worse and last for upto half an hour or longer and may require reliever medication for control. In many children, fast running for five to ten minutes is enough to bring on the problem. Do not stop your child from exercising and taking part in sports simply because he has exercise-induced asthma. It can be largely prevented and effectively treated and the child should be allowed to continue his sports activities. Many athletes and sports persons suffering from asthma have gone on to win laurels in international competitive sports, including at the Olympics. To reduce chances of developing exercise-induced asthma, the child should warm up before playing games. Several short 30-second sprints done over a period of five to ten minutes may protect the child against developing breathing difficulty for an hour or so. In some children, the preventive use of one to two puffs (according to age) of sodium cromoglycate inhaler (Cromal-5 or Fintal), just before exercising prevents the development of asthma. If this does not work, the doctor may prescribe the use of another type of inhaler before exercising. The child is likely to have more wheezing on cold and dry days and when he engages in long spells of exercise instead of short games. It may be better for the child to play in comparatively less active positions in team games. Swimming is a good exercise for children with asthma.

BRUISES, CUTS AND WOUNDS

BRUISES

Injuries by blunt objects sometimes cause bruises in which there occurs damage to blood vessels and bleeding beneath the child's skin. The overlying skin remains intact. The area looks initially red and later changes to blue or black. Thereafter, the colouration gradually becomes lighter as healing progresses. Cold compresses, or ice-pack compresses should be applied to the injured area during the first 24-48 hours. Cooling causes constriction of small blood vessels and may reduce the local bleeding and swelling. Bleeding under a nail can be extremely painful due to the built-up pressure in an enclosed area. Medical help should be sought for its quick relief. You should also consult a doctor if your child tends to bruise repeatedly. He may be suffering from some underlying bleeding or clotting disorder.

CUTS AND WOUNDS

Children often sustain grazes, cuts and wounds during their restless activities or while playing. It is important that these injuries are properly taken care of. You should, however, encourage your child to face minor injuries boldly and not make an undue fuss over them. Older children can even help in cleaning and dressing their own injuries.

Wash your hands before treating injury and avoid coughing or sneezing over a wound. The dirt and debris over the wound can be washed away by holding it under clean running water. Alternatively, it may be wiped away with the help of a clean piece of gauze using plenty of clean water or diluted antiseptic solution. Bleeding also helps to wash out the dirt. Now dry the surrounding skin thoroughly with clean cottonwool or paper tissues. Begin drying the skin at the edges of the wound and then dry progressively outwards. Small wounds can be covered with medicated dressing, e.g., Band Aid, Handyplast, etc. If the wound is on a joint or some awkward site, a sterile antiseptic dressing may be placed over the wound and a bandage applied over it. Do not use a fluffy dressing on the wound. It is likely to get stuck to the wound and later pull off the scab.

It is now considered desirable to leave the dressing on a wound undisturbed for two to three days until the healing is well underway. A too frequent change of dressing interferes with the process of scab formation and healing. However, if the dressing comes off, it should be replaced with a new one. A deep, long or irregular cut may need stitching. It may also be prudent to do fine stitching of small wounds over the face, neck and other exposed areas for cosmetic reasons. The stitching of the wound may reduce the chances of scar formation.

It is important to take suitable preventive measures against the possible development of tetanus following any injury. The first essential step in each case is thorough cleansing of the wound with soap and water or diluted antiseptic lotion. The doctor may decide to give a dose of tetanus toxoid to boost the child's immunity acquired earlier through routine immunization. It is important that the tetanus toxoid injection should be given within 24 hours of the injury. Children with poor immunization status, highly contaminated wounds, puncture wounds or wounds due to crush injuries may need to be given human tetanus immunoglobulin (TIG) besides tetanus toxoid. In children who have not received complete tetanus immunization earlier, the doctor may advise further administration of two doses of tetanus toxoid injection, the first after one month and the second six months later, for providing long-term protection to the child.

CHICKEN POX

Chicken pox is a very common infectious disease of childhood. It is a mild disease which is caused by a virus. Initially, the child develops mild fever and bodyache. The same day or the next day, tiny red spots appear on the covered parts of the child's body (chest, abdomen and back). The spots soon become raised and then change into tiny blisters. Subsequently, the rash appears on the face, arms and legs. As there is hardly any fever and other symptoms initially, many parents become aware of this disease in their child only when the rash appears on his face, arms and legs. The first blisters start drying up quickly and scabs are formed. While the older blisters are quickly scabbed, fresh crops of rash appear for three to four days which also go through the same cycle of changes. Hence at a particular time you may see the rash in all its forms, flat or raised dry spots, blisters and scabbed blisters. Blisters may sometimes also appear in the mouth, eyes, and over the genitals.

WHAT TO DO

The child often has persistent annoying itching over his whole body. He may scratch and break open the blisters which may then get infected. Local application of calamine lotion soothes the itching. Antihistaminic or antipruritic drugs and sometimes mild sedatives are given to relieve the itching and discomfort. The child's nails should be cut short. His clothes and bed linen should be changed daily. Potassium permanganate may be lightly added to the water for his bath to prevent the blisters from getting infected. The child may be given a paracetamol preparation, like Crocin, for relief of headache or fever, if required. DO NOT GIVE ASPIRIN, as it may sometimes cause complications.

There is no need to isolate a child with chicken pox from other children under ordinary circumstances. He becomes non-infective to others when all the blisters over his body get covered over by scabs. This usually happens 7-10 days after the beginning of his illness. He can then be sent to school.

Isolation of the child is however recommended if (a) another child in the family is less than one month old (b) another child is suffering from a serious illness like leukemia or cancer or (c) if there are chances of a pregnant woman coming in contact with him. Besides, the doctor may also advise intramuscular injection of VZIG (immune globulin) to the above mentioned high risk contact cases to prevent development of chicken pox in them.

A safe and effective (but costly) vaccine for protection against chicken pox has now become available. A single dose is given by injection to children from the age of 12 months onwards to 12 years of age. Children aged 13 years and above are administered two doses with an interval of 6 to 10 weeks.

COLIC

Many babies, in the first few weeks, go through several spells of inconsolable crying every day. They may cry almost continuously for variable periods, some lasting several hours at a stretch. This happens usually in the evenings and almost nothing seems to help them. During the crying spell, their legs are usually drawn up on the abdomen and their fists are clenched. The abdomen may occasionally appear to be distended and taut. The attack may end only when the baby is tired out. Sometimes he appears to get relief after passing wind or a small amount of stool.

The cause of this condition, which is distressing for the baby as well as the mother, is not yet clear. Doctors generally feel that it is a sort of stomach cramp and the baby apparently gets waves of stomach pain, which make him cry repeatedly. The much tormented mother of a baby with this problem needs to face it calmly and boldly. She can draw some comfort from the fact that this condition is temporary in nature and generally passes off by the time the baby is three months old. The baby may get some relief if he is made to lie face down across the lap on a warm water bottle or is held up against the shoulder. In some babies administration of a small amount of a home-made traditional digestive like *saunf ka pani* (prepared with aniseed and water) may be worth a try. If the problem persists seek your doctor's advice. He may prescribe some medication for providing relief during the attack. Using proper feeding techniques, burping the baby during and after feeds, avoiding underfeeding or overfeeding and making trial changes in the mother's diet may help in reducing the attacks of colic.

COMMON COLD

Colds are caused by viruses. The child normally develops a runny or blocked nose, sneezing, sore throat, cough and bodyache. A small baby may have associated loose motions. The reason why children get colds so often is that there are a large number of cold causing viruses and that the immunity acquired through infection against one virus does not protect against another virus.

Because colds are caused by viruses and not bacteria, antibiotics are ineffective and should not be used under ordinary circumstances. Nasal drops, steam inhalation and local application of menthol rub or vaporizer are generally enough to relieve the child's symptoms. Nasal drops should be discontinued after a few days. Steam inhalations are very effective in relieving irritation and congestion in the nose, throat, nasal passages, sinuses and the upper respiratory tract. Bring water to boil to form steam in an electric kettle or in one of the home-use steam generators now available in the market. The child should have steam inhalations two to three times a day for 10 minutes on each occasion. There is no particular advantage in adding any drug to the boiling water. In severe cases, the doctor may prescribe an oral decongestant to alleviate nasal obstruction and congestion and paracetamol for relief of bodyache and fever. Use of aspirin should be avoided.

Sometimes a child with a common cold may develop secondary superimposed bacterial infection. The nasal secretion may then become yellow, and foul smelling. The child's temperature may rise further and he may become more ill. The bacterial infection may occasionally spread to the ear leading to earache and ear discharge. It may extend down into the lower air passages causing bronchitis and pneumonia. If your child develops any symptoms suggestive of bacterial infection, you should consult your doctor quickly for prompt control.

CONSTIPATION

The problem of constipation in children is unduly magnified in most Indian families. Often there is an overuse of laxatives and suppositories. It is important that parents should know some essential facts about the true nature of this problem.

Constipation hardly ever occurs in breast-fed babies who receive an adequate amount of milk. Although babies on bottle feed tend to have firmer and larger stool than breast-fed babies, true constipation is rare so long as their intake of milk is adequate. The nature of the stool and not its frequency is what is important. A healthy infant may occasionally pass a stool of normal consistency at intervals of as long as 36 to 48 hours. If such a baby has no discomfort or other symptoms, nothing needs to be done. However, if the baby is constipated right from birth or soon thereafter, the baby must be examined by a doctor. A tight anal passage or some other organic cause may sometimes be responsible for constipation during the first few months of his life, though this is rare.

Generally, constipation in babies is because of insufficient intake of food or fluids. The addition of extra sugar and more fluids, like fruit juice in the diet, should help. Constipation in older children may be due to their diet being deficient in fibre content or due to faulty bowel training. Too many aggressive efforts by parents to make their child pass stool every morning, when he may not be inclined to do so, or the commencement of toilet training much before he is ready for it, may be responsible for the child's constipation. A child may initially develop constipation due to poor food intake during an illness associated with fever. The passage of hard stool may cause cracks around the child's anus (anal fissure). Subsequently, the intense pain felt by the child in the area of anal fissure while trying to pass hard stone-like stool makes him avoid passing stool. A vicious cycle is thus created, perpetuating the constipation. An application of local anaesthetic cream in the region of anal fissure would reduce the child's discomfort during passage of stool and encourage him to pass stool. These children should also eat high-residue foods containing plenty of fibre, such as *chapati*, rice and other cereals, fruit and vegetables and take plenty of fluids. Parents may sometimes introduce a suppository in the child's rectum or give him a dose of mild laxative for relief from constipation. It should not be done on a regular basis as it can be harmful. A child with persistent constipation should be properly examined by a doctor.

DIARRHOEA

A child with diarrhoea passes loose stool with increased frequency. He may sometimes have associated vomiting and fever and his stool may occasionally contain blood and mucus. Most cases of acute diarrhoea in children are caused by viral and bacterial infection of the intestines.

These infections are caused by consuming contaminated water and food and by using utensils infected by disease-causing organisms (bacteria/viruses). Flies play an important role in carrying infections to the child's food and drink.

During acute diarrhoea a child may quickly lose a lot of body fluids and minerals in his stool resulting in dehydration. In the intitial stages of diarrhoea, a child with mild dehydration feels thirsty and likes to take plenty of water. As the dehydration becomes more marked, he becomes irritable and drowsy, his mouth and tongue become dry, the skin loses its elasticity and his eyes get sunken. The quantity of his urine reduces. In a small baby the soft spot on top of its head (the fontanelle) gets depressed. If the child does not receive adequate fluids and the dehydration is allowed to become severe, it may lead to a fall in blood pressure, malfunctioning of the kidneys and several other complications which may be fatal.

HOW TO COPE

The most important elements in the management of a child with diarrhoea are:

a) to prevent the development of dehydration and

b) to correct dehydration quickly and effectively, if it has already occurred.

Both these objectives can be achieved by giving the child plenty of fluids at the earliest to replace the water and minerals being lost by the child in his stool. The various types of fluids which can be used for this purpose and the methods for giving them are discussed later.

Antibiotics have only a limited role in the treatment of diarrhoea. They are ineffective in a large number of patients where the diarrhoea has been caused by viruses. However, antibiotics help in the early control of diarrhoea due to bacterial infections. You should promptly begin giving plenty of fluids to the child to drink soon after he develops diarrhoea, without waiting for a doctor. You may begin with any one of the following :

(i) ORS or oral rehydration salt solution;

(ii) home-made rehydration solution; and

(iii) lentil water (*dal ka pani)*, rice *kanjee (chawal ka maand), lassi, chach,* and lemon water (*shikanjivi*). The amount and manner of giving the fluids is discussed later.

ORS

The basic ingredients of the oral rehydration solutions are water, sodium chloride, sodium bicarbonate, potassium chloride and glucose. A standard composition for ORS has been laid down by WHO. These ORS packets can be obtained free of cost from government hospitals or dispensaries or purchased from the market. The marketed ORS packets are generally available in two sizes, one in which the contents of the whole packet have to be reconstituted in one litre (5 glasses approximately)of water and the other in 200 ml (one glass approximately) of water.

When buying an ORS packet you should choose a product like Electrobion, Prolyte or Quicksol, which contains the salt-glucose combination in accordance with the standard WHO formula. This may be done with the help of the chemist and by checking the label on the ORS packet. It is desirable to do so, because although some of the ORS packets which are being sold in the market make a more palatable solution, they are not constituted properly and are not suitable for use.

The ORS solution should be prepared by adding the ORS powder to boiled and cooled water or filtered clean water strictly according to the manufacturer's instructions. If the baby is less than 3 months old, the ORS packet should be reconstituted in a more dilute form. A packet meant for one litre of water should be made up for these babies in 1½ litres of water.

The prepared solution should be kept properly covered and it must be used within a maximum period of 12 hours, after which it should be discarded. Once the ORS solution has been prepared it should not be boiled again for further use.

HOME-MADE SALT SUGAR SOLUTION

If ORS is not readily available, you may instead begin with home-made salt and sugar solution. The home-made solution can be quickly prepared by using readily available clean home salt and sugar. Pour 200 ml (a medium-size glass holds about 200 ml) of boiled and cooled water or safe filtered water in a clean container. Take a pinch of common salt, using your finger and thumb, add it to the water and stir well with a clean spoon. Check the taste of this mixture; it should taste less salty than your tears. Now add a heaped teaspoon of sugar and stir the mixture until the sugar is dissolved. A few drops of fresh lemon juice may be added to make the solution more palatable.

HOW MUCH FLUIDS TO GIVE?

The child should be encouraged to take as much fluids as he likes without any restriction. This should, however, be offered to him in small quantities at a time, in the form of a few sips or teaspoonfuls. He may have this small amount of fluid every few minutes or at intervals of ½ hour or so to ensure adequate intake. If given in glassfuls or cupfuls at a time he is likely to bring it up. You should see that the child continues to pass sufficient quantities of urine. The chart below indicates broadly the amount of fluids to be given to the child to replace its loss through loose stools:

Child's age	Amount of fluid to be given for each stool passed
Below 2 years	50-100 ml (¼ to ½ glass approximately)
2 to 10 years	100-200 ml (½ to 1 glass approximately)
Above 10 years	As much as the child can drink

He would further need extra fluids to replace the fluids already lost before treatment is started, and to meet his routine body requirements.

WHEN DOES HE NEED ACTIVE MEDICAL ASSISTANCE?

While continuing to give fluids to the child you should keep a close watch on (a) the state of his diarrhoea and vomiting; (b) the amount of urine passed; and (c) his general condition. If the child shows any one or a combination of the following features he should be taken to a doctor or a hospital without any delay as he may need intravenous fluids administration and other treatment under close medical supervision:

(i) The child continues to have persistent vomiting and does not retain the fluids given by mouth.

(ii) He is too sick and lethargic and does not have enough fluids.

(iii) He has several loose watery motions within one to two hours.

(iv) He is passing blood and mucus in his stool and has fever.

(v) The urine has become very scanty or he has not passed it for over 6 hours.

(vi) The child shows symptoms of severe dehydration. He looks ill, his eyes are sunken, the mouth and tongue are dry and the skin looks wrinkled and inelastic.

(vii) He develops abdominal distension with sudden diminution in the passage of stools and wind.

(viii) He has fits or shows an altered level of consciousness.

The situations indicated at (v) to (viii) above occur due to insufficient replacement of fluids lost in the child's stools and its consequent complications. These can be quite serious and must be treated promptly under close, regular medical supervision.

FEEDING DURING DIARRHOEA

You should continue to breast-feed a baby with diarrhoea and not stop it for fear of aggravating the loose motions. In the case of a bottle-fed baby dilute the formula milk or animal milk which he was taking earlier to half the strength by adding to it an equal amount of water. Fruit juices and aerated drinks should preferably be avoided. Some babies who are particularly fond of aerated drinks may be given these drinks after the fizz in them has been allowed to go off by shaking and allowing the drink to stay in a glass for some time. Coconut water is a useful drink. Older babies can have khichri, *moong dal,* curd, egg-white and mashed banana (which should not be overripe). It is particularly important to continue feeding a baby, who is malnourished. In certain situations, the doctor may advise a specific diet or a type of milk, such as soya milk, to be given to him for a temporary period. You should seek advice from the doctor as to when the child can go back to his normal diet.

DIPHTHERIA

Diphtheria is a serious, highly infectious disease of childhood. In the common tonsillar form of diphtheria, the germs invade the tonsils and the adjoining area causing severe local inflammation. The infected child develops fever, bodyache, pain in the throat, difficulty in swallowing and develops a muffled voice. Sometimes there is a marked swelling and pain in the upper part of the neck due to inflammation of lymph glands. This disease can at times be mistaken for an ordinary tonsillitis. It is, however, potentially much more serious. The toxins liberated by the germs can severely damage the patient's heart and nervous system resulting in abnormalities in the functioning of the heart and widespread paralysis. In another form of diptheria, the larynx (voice box) and the upper respiratory passages may get involved causing hoarseness of voice and severe respiratory difficulty.

In the event of any symptoms suggestive of the disease, it is very important that the child is got examined quickly. The outcome of this disease is closely related to the speed with which it is treated. Throat swab smear and culture examination are done for confirmation of diagnosis of this condition. This disease requires intensive treatment under close medical supervision. A highly effective vaccine is available for the prevention of this disease. It is usually administered as a constituent of DPT (triple antigen). Initially, three doses of DPT are given at 4-week intervals, beginning at the age of 6 weeks. Booster doses are given at the age of around 18 months and 5 years. The details are given in the section on Immunization.

Diphtheria is a highly infectious disease. The child

needs to be segregated. Besides medical examination, throat swab cultures and other tests are performed on all family members and close contacts. Some of the contacts may require preventive or active treatment.

EPILEPSY

In epilepsy, an individual has a tendency to have recurrent fits or seizures. There are several different types of seizures, depending upon which part of the brain is affected. But basically all of them are the manifestation of a sudden excessive activity of a group of brain cells. The abnormal spasmodic activity of the brain cells is revealed on the EEG (electroencephalogram) tracings, which record the electrical activity of the brain.

WHAT HAPPENS? WHAT CAN PARENTS DO?

In the generalized tonic-clonic (grand mal) type of epilepsy, the child develops generalized stiffening of the body and jerky movements with loss of consciousness, which may last for a few minutes. If faced with such a situation, the parents should avoid the temptation of trying to revive the child by pouring water into his mouth, as the child may choke. He should be protected from getting injured and turned over to one side to help his breathing and to allow the excessive froth at his mouth to flow out.

In another form of epilepsy, called the absence seizure, the child, usually around six years of age, suddenly looks blank and stares vacantly. He may also make blinking movements with his eyes. The whole episode lasts for only a few seconds and the child soon resumes his usual earlier activity. Unaware of the true nature of this illness, it may be missed by parents and school teachers. It is sometimes passed off as the child being inattentive or careless. However, it is important to recognize this problem and get it treated properly. In another form of epilepsy, the child may have jerky movements in only one limb or some other part of the child's body. There are a few other types of epilepsy too.

HOW IS DIAGNOSIS ESTABLISHED?

The most important factor which helps to recognize and diagnose epilepsy is the description of the attack as given by the parents, the school teacher or any eyewitnesses. Further help in making the diagnosis is obtained by carrying out some tests. An EEG is performed to make a recording of the electrical activity occurring within the brain. It is particularly useful in helping the physician to determine the type of epilepsy and the selection of appropriate drugs for treatment. The recent availability of CT scan has enabled a diagnosis to be made of the underlying disease process responsible for causing epilepsy in a significant number of cases. CT scan, or computerized tomography scan, is a special form of X-ray in which a computer produces pictures of the brain at different levels. This is particularly important for India and other developing countries where tuberculosis and some other infections of the brain are responsible for causing fits. In such cases the eradication of the underlying causes of the disease is highly effective in the treatment of epilepsy.

Another new technique of imaging, called the MRI (magnetic resonance imaging), which employs magnetic waves to create pictures of the brain, has been found to be very helpful. It is used to study some areas of the brain which are difficult to assess on the CT scan.

WHAT MUST PARENTS KNOW ABOUT DRUG TREATMENT

Many different drugs are now available to control epilepsy. It is important that the treatment of this condition should not be delayed. The drugs must be taken regularly as prescribed. The drugs which have to be taken once, twice or thrice daily must be taken at the same time each day. Generally, it does not matter whether the drugs are taken before or after meals. If a dose is missed, the child should be given that dose as soon as it is realized but do not give him a double dose to make up for the missed one. If treatment is missed over a few days, simply restart the earlier prescribed dose. Some drugs, either because of overdosage or because of the child's oversensitiveness, may produce side effects like drowsiness, nausea, double vision and unsteadiness in the legs. You should seek advice from your doctor regarding the possible side effects of the drug being given to your child. The child should be given medication for as long as recommended by the doctor and not changed or stopped abruptly as this may result in severe and prolonged epileptic fits. In general, the doctors prefer the child to be free from fits for a period of two years or more before they withdraw the drugs. Drug withdrawal has to be done gradually.

CHILD NEEDS ENCOURAGEMENT

The child should be encouraged to participate in the normal academic and extra-curricular activities in the school. He should, however, not be allowed to take part in swimming, motor cycling and such other competitive sports activities which may endanger his life. At the same time he should not be unduly protected and treated as an invalid. Modern investigations and management with new drugs have brought about a marked improvement in the treatment of epilepsy.

FEVER

It must be first understood that there is no single fixed degree of temperature (for example 98°F or 37°C), which can alone be considered normal for each and every child. The normal body temperature ranges from 36°C-37°C (96. 8°F - 98.6°F). It also varies in the same child during the course of a day; it is generally lower in the morning and higher in the afternoon due to accelerated body metabolism following the child's day-long activities. A normal child's temperature may rise temporarily even upto 100°F after a strenuous game of football.

RECORDING TEMPERATURE CORRECTLY

The temperature can be recorded by using a mercury thermometer. The commonly used clinical thermometer can well be used in children aged six to nine years and above by placing it in the mouth. A rectal mercury thermometer (with a round short bulb) is primarily for use in children below 1-1½ years of age. Any mercury thermometer can be used for recording the temperature in the armpit. Strip thermometers (made of liquid crystals), which are placed on the child's forehead, are far less accurate than mercury thermometers. These should be used only as a rough guide. In India, these strip thermometers are of particularly limited value because they get out of order quickly due to high environmental temperature.

TAKING TEMPERATURE IN THE MOUTH

Ask your child to open his mouth and raise his tongue. Place the thermometer under his tongue and ask him to close his lips. He must keep his mouth closed throughout the recommended time for recording the temperature. Make sure he does not hold the thermometer with his teeth. It is generally advisable to keep the thermometer in the mouth for two minutes although a shorter time may be indicated by the manufacturer. The temperature must not be taken shortly after the child has taken cold or hot food or fluids.

USING A RECTAL THERMOMETER

Lubricate the bulb of the thermometer with some vaseline, baby-cream or oil. Remove the baby's diaper and lay him on his back. Now lift up the legs and gently insert the rectal thermometer into his rectum by about one inch (2.5 cm) and hold it in place (Fig. 22.2). The baby should be held gently but firmly. Keep the thermometer in place for two minutes, remove and read the temperature.

(Fig. 22.2)

RECORDING TEMPERATURE IN THE ARMPIT (AXILLA)

Remove the child's clothing from over one of his armpits. If you are right-handed, you will find it easier to use the child's left armpit. Place the thermometer properly into the armpit and lower his arm over it. Hold it securely in place for two minutes, then remove and read. In babies below 1 month of age, you need to keep the thermometer in position for three minutes.

WHAT TO DO

Every child with relatively high fever requires close observation, particularly if the temperature approaches 39.5 C (103 F). His temperature should be checked initially every 20 minutes to assess its progress. If the temperature approaches 40 C (104 F) you should immediately start wet towel sponging of his whole body with cool water. It may be better not to use very cold water as it may sometimes cause shivering. During the body sponging, check his temperature every five minutes. Sponging should be stopped when the child's temperature falls to 38 C (100.4 F). The temperature should be taken by mouth, or in the rectum, or in one of the armpits where cold sponging has not been done. Subsequently keep a check on his temperature every 20 minutes or so as it may again rise and require further sponging.

The child may be given a dose of paracetamol (Crocin, Metacin) syrup or tablets in a dose appropriate for his age to reduce his fever. It is preferable to avoid the use of aspirin on your own. Give him plenty of fluids to drink. The child would feel more comfortable in loose night clothes. Cover him with a light sheet. Do not make the mistake of heavily overclothing your child with fever so as to protect him from catching cold or getting 'chest congestion'. It would do him more harm than good by preventing loss of his body heat, as a result of which his temperature will rise further. In hot weather you should also make sure the room is adequately cool. A light draught of air helps evaporation of water from the wet skin during sponging, thereby hastening the lowering of the child's temperature.

HEPATITIS

Jaundice occurs in children chiefly due to viral hepatitis. Hepatitis is a medical term which means inflammation of the liver. There are mainly two types of viral hepatitis: (i) viral hepatitis A (commonly known as infectious hepatitis); and (ii) viral hepatitis B. In children, viral hepatitis A is much more common than type B.

INFECTIOUS HEPATITIS (VIRAL HEPATITIS A)

In this disease, the functioning of the liver is disturbed as a result of inflammation. This results in the accumulation of bile pigment – bilirubin – in the patient's blood. The raised bilirubin level causes a yellow discolouration of the eyes and skin – a characteristic feature of jaundice. Jaundice, however, appears late during the course of illness in a patient of infectious hepatitis. For the first few days, the child may just have an aversion to food, a tendency to vomit, moderate fever, fatigue and a vague abdominal pain. Subsequently, the child or his mother may notice the dark yellow or dark brown colour of his urine, which leaves deep stains on his underclothing. His eyes and skin will look yellow and his stool may become pale or grey coloured. When a doctor suspects viral hepatitis, the child's urine and blood are examined to confirm the diagnosis and for assessment of severity of the disease. The disease is generally mild, the jaundice and the child's symptoms gradually abate.

HOW DO YOU GET THIS INFECTION?

A child acquires viral hepatitis A (infectious hepatitis) mainly by consuming unhygienic food, milk or water which has been contaminated by the causative virus. Epidemics of this disease have occasionally occurred due to contamination of water supply by sewage.

DRUGS, DIET AND REST

There are no specific drugs for the treatment of infectious hepatitis and the child does not generally need any antibiotics. The child should rest in bed for as long he feels tired and unwell. As he recovers, he can resume mild to moderate activity at home but he should not overexert to the point of getting exhausted. His nutrition must be kept up by giving him a nourishing diet, which should be rich in carbohydrates. The child can have his favourite home foods but the use of butter, fats and oil should be restricted. In view of the child's poor appetite he may be given palatable preparations like home-made ice cream prepared from skimmed milk, hygienically prepared sweets and desserts, and ice candy. He can have practically all seasonal fruits like banana, *cheeku*, mango, grapes, oranges, papaya, etc. Sweetened fruit juices, squashes, drinks are also good. It must however be ensured that the drinks are prepared in a clean, strictly hygienic manner in order to prevent the child from getting diarrhoea and other infections.

INDICATIONS FOR SPECIAL CONSULTATION

If the child has persistent vomiting or his food and fluid intake are very poor, he may need to be given intravenous fluids. You must not use drugs to curb the child's vomiting without consulting the doctor. A child may, in rare, cases, have a fulminant (very severe) attack of hepatitis. If the jaundice continues to deepen, and the child becomes progressively drowsy or restless, he would need urgent hospitalization.

HEPATITIS B

Another form of hepatitis caused by infection with hepatitis B virus is now assuming increasing significance. The manifestations of hepatitis B in older children as well as its treatment are generally similar to those of infectious hepatitis (viral hepatitis A) described above. A child may get infected by this virus through the use of needles contaminated with the blood of a hepatitis B positive individual or by receiving blood transfusion or blood products contaminated with this virus. It is, therefore, important to ensure that the needles and syringes used for giving injections to children are absolutely sterile and that the blood and blood products, if given to him, are free from this infection. Adults and adolescents can acquire this infection through sex with an infected individual.

Some babies many acquire this infection during pregnancy from their hepatitis B positive mothers. Infected new born babies and children are liable to develop serious chomic liver damage, cirrhosis and liver cancer later in life. For protection of children against this infection, 3 doses of hepatitis B vaccine are administered to them as a constituent of regular immunization schedule. It is also recommended that all pregnant women should be tested for hepatitis B infection. If an expectant mother is found to be hepatitis B positive, her newborn baby is administered a protective dose of hepatitis B immunoglobulin along with first dose of hepatitis B vaccine within 12-18 hours of his birth. For details, see under section on 'Immunization'.

HERNIA

A developmental defect in some babies in the groin region allows the passage of a small portion of the intestine from the child's abdomen into the scrotum. This happens particularly when the child coughs or runs around for some time (Fig. 22.3). In these situations a swelling is noticed in the scrotum. The swelling may disappear when the child sleeps. This condition is called inguinal hernia and it can be easily and permanently corrected by a simple operation. The operation must not be delayed because the intestines may sometimes get caught in the narrow passage in the groin region. The resultant complication of intestinal obstruction can become life threatening.

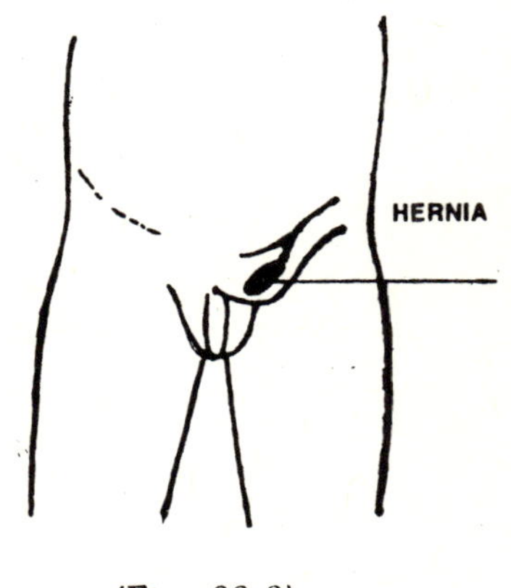

(Fig. 22.3)

In some instances, a bulge may appear in the region of a baby's navel some time after his birth due to protrusion of his abdominal contents. This condition is called umbilical hernia. It has been discussed in the section on Understanding Your Newborn Baby.

MALARIA

Malaria is widely prevalent in many parts of India. It is transmitted through the bite of a specific species of mosquito – the female anopheles mosquito. The infective mosquito carries the plasmodium parasite in her saliva, which is responsible for causing malaria. As a result of its bite the parasite gets injected into a child, who subsequently develops malaria after a gap of about one to three weeks.

A child with malaria usually develops high fever after a bout of chills and shivering. He complains of headache, nausea, malaise and pain in the limbs. After a variable period, the fever subsides rapidly along with considerable sweating. Thereafter, depending upon the type of malarial infection, fever may recur on alternate days or on every third day. However, these features of malaria are not encountered in every child. A child may have no shivering, he may have fever every day without a break or the temperature may be very high. On the other hand, a child with a serious type of falciparum malaria may not develop very high fever, but may have fits and loss of consciousness.

Considering the high incidence of malaria in India it is prudent to exclude malaria in almost every case of fever. A few drops of blood, drawn by pricking the finger with a needle, are taken on a glass slide, stained and examined for the presence of malarial parasites.

Malaria is a preventable disease. The following steps will help prevent or reduce the chances of its occurrence in your family. As mosquitoes breed in stagnant water, you should avoid any long-standing accumulation of water in and around your house. Desert cooler water tanks and any other open water storage chambers in the house should be drained dry once a week.

Mosquitoes mainly bite human beings in the evening and at night. The use of appropriate mosquito repellents and mosquito killer sprays, making the children wear long-sleeved shirts and stockings at night and the use of mosquito nets would help to reduce bites by malaria carrying mosquitoes.

When the incidence of malaria is high, your doctor may advise you to give your child a dose of anti-malarial drug (generally chloroquin) once every week as prophylaxis against malaria. He will advise you about the exact dose appropriate for your child.

Worldwide efforts have been in progress for the last several years to develop a safe and effective vaccine against malaria. It now appears that such a vaccine may become available in the not too distant future.

Generally, malaria is treated with chloroquin given over a period of three days. However, some newer drugs or a combination of drugs are sometimes needed to treat resistant cases of malaria. You should follow the doctor's instructions carefully in this regard.

MEASLES

Measles is a highly infectious viral disease. At its onset in a child this disease looks like a severe attack of common cold. The child develops high fever, running of the nose, a dry hacking cough and red watery eyes. A rash appears on the fourth day of illness and along with it the temperature rises sharply to as high as 40°C (104°F). Tiny pinkish spots of rash appear behind the ears, on the forehead, face and neck. Within the next three days, the rash spreads over the entire body and becomes more pronounced, giving the skin a blotchy look. After about three days of the onset of the rash, those over the face starts fading. The fading progresses downwards, leaving a brownish discolouration. The child's temperature starts dropping around the fifth day of his illness and usually touches normal by the seventh or eighth day. Throughout this period, the child is very ill, irritable and restless. He also suffers from lack of appetite and an annoying hacking cough. But within a day or two after his fever has gone he shows a sudden improvement and starts feeling better.

MYTHS ABOUT MEASLES

Measles is probably the most misunderstood illness in India, even among the educated. Some of these beliefs are positively harmful. For instance, measles is believed to be the manifestation of a goddess called *mata* or *mariama* in different parts of the country. The faithful believe that any medical interference with the child during the course of this illness is a sin against the deity and harmful to the child. As such, many seriously ill patients with measles, especially in the rural areas of India, are denied medical assistance. Many educated parents also believe that the administration of allopathic medicine causes undesirable suppression of the rash in measles. The lack of measles rash is wrongly presumed to be highly injurious to the child. Some even recommend magic potions to bring out the rash. It is hence extremely important that parents should understand the true nature of this condition.

THE FACTS

Measles is a self-limiting viral disease and it passes off without causing serious harm in most healthy children. Many serious complications can, however, develop during the course of the disease, particularly in malnourished children. If not handled promptly, these complications can lead to several permanent disabilities in the affected child or may even be fatal. An attack of measles, however, provides lifelong protection and a second attack of this disease hardly ever occurs. There are several viral infections which cause a rash in children, with or without much fever and they are wrongly labelled by parents as second or third attack of measles.

WHAT TO DO

A child with measles requires total attention and care till he fully recovers. The sick child should rest in bed. His room should be comfortably warm, but not cool. While he should be protected from the strong light because of discomfort to his eyes, his room must not be made dark. Bathing his eyes with lukewarm water with a moistened cottonwool thrice daily will provide some relief to his sore eyes. The child should brush his teeth and have regular mouth washes. His body should be kept clean and his clothes and bed linen changed daily. Covering him with heavy warm clothes should be avoided. Although the child does not feel hungry, make sure he takes sufficient fluids by providing him small but frequent drinks. A light, bland diet may be supplemented with home-made desserts, like *kheer,* custard, sweets, ice cream and other palatable preparations. His fever, bodyaches and general discomfort should be eased by giving him paracetamol and sedatives as advised. Some children may occasionally need tepid water sponging to lower their fever. Steam inhalations given for 10-15 minutes each, three to four times a day will provide relief to his voice and cough.

Ordinarily, a child with measles does not require any antibiotics. It may, however, become necessary to use them judiciously, if the child develops pneumonia, middle ear infection or some other infection elsewhere in the body.

WHEN SHOULD YOU CONSULT THE DOCTOR AGAIN?

The progress of a child with measles must be watched very closely and if any one of the following features are noticed, a doctor must be consulted without delay:

1. Usually the child's temperature comes down to normal in about three to four days after the first appearance of the rash. If a child develops fever again after its having settled down or the fever continues beyond the eighth day of the beginning of the disease, a doctor must be consulted. He may have developed pneumonia or a secondary bacterial infection elsewhere. The child may then need antibiotics as an essential part of his treatment.
2. Unduly fast breathing or laboured breathing,

combined with indrawing of the chest wall suggests that the child may have developed pneumonia or some other respiratory tract complications. This must be attended to promptly.

3. A child may develop severe diarrhoea as a complication of measles. Do not delay treatment as it can be life-threatening. The child may need intravenous fluids and other drugs for the control of diarrhoea.

4. Consult the doctor if the child complains of pain in the ear or if he develops a ear discharge. These symptoms suggest middle ear infection and perforation of the ear drum. He will then need prompt treatment with antibiotics.

5. Very rarely, a child may develop swelling of the brain (encephalitis) following an attack of measles. This complication generally develops towards the end of the original attack of measles. The child may develop fever again, become drowsy and start having fits. He would need urgent hospitalization, investigations and intensive treatment.

HOW TO PREVENT THE SPREAD OF MEASLES

Isolating a child with measles is of no practical benefit in preventing its spread to other children in the family. This is because a child with measles is most infective and passes on his infection to others much before he himself develops the rash and his own disease gets recognized. Special protection is needed for another child in the family who is suffering from a long-standing illness, is in poor health and who has not had the measles vaccine or suffered from measles. Such a child needs to be protected by giving him an intramuscular injection of gammaglobulin. This either prevents measles or the child may develop measles in a mild form. He would subsequently need administration of regular measles vaccine 3 months later in order to provide him long-term protection.

PREVENTING MEASLES

A dose of measles vaccine is recommended for administration to children at 9 months of age as part of routine immunization schedule. It prorides them life-long protection against this disease. This vaccine is now available free of cost in Government hospitals and child welfare centers, For details, see in the section on 'Immunization'

GERMAN MEASLES (RUBELLA)

German measles is a mild viral disease and although similar in name it is entirely different from measles. This disease starts in a child like an attack of mild cold. The child develops a runny nose, a sore throat and a temperature of around 38°C (100°F). A rash consisting of small pinkish spots appears on the face on the second or third day and quickly spreads over the whole body. The child also develops a few small painful swellings due to enlarged lymph nodes behind the ears and at the back of the neck. The rash fades in two days but the swellings may persist for about a week. Since the illness does not cause much discomfort it is often missed or ignored.

WHAT TO DO

The child himself does not need much treatment. Give him paracetamol if his temperature rises above 38°C and do not send him to school for a week from the time the rash first appears. More important, he must not come in contact with a pregnant woman.

While this illness is not serious in so far as the child is concerned, it is of crucial significance to any pregnant woman who comes in contact with him. If she acquires this infection during the first four months of her pregnancy, she is very likely to pass on the infection to her baby in the womb. In that event, the infected baby may be born with serious birth defects like deafness, mental retardation, blindness and heart defects. It is therefore, absolutely necessary that the child with German measles should not be allowed to come in contact with a pregnant woman, especially if she is in the early stages of her pregnancy. If this happens, inform her of your child's infection so that she can promptly get proper medical advice regarding the continuation of her pregnancy, etc.

HOW TO PREVENT IT

Rubella vaccine is recommended for routine administration to all children at around 15 months of age as a constituent of MMR (mumps-measles-rubella) vaccine to confer on them long-term protection against the disease. It is especially important for girls so that they are protected against this disease before reaching the child-bearing age. The details about this vaccine are given in the section on Immunization.

MENINGITIS

Inflammation of 'meninges', the sheet-like membranous lining of the brain and spinal cord, is called meningitis. It occur at all ages – in newborn babies, infants, children and can be caused by several different types of bacteria and viruses. Meningococcal meningitis and pneumococcal meningitis are two common types of bacterial meningitis in children. Tuberculosis can also cause meningitis in some cases. Meningitis is a serious disease. It can occur at all ages–in newborn babies, infants, children and adults. A patient of meningitis is liable to become very ill over a period of one or two days. Sometimes it can develop even more rapidly in a matter of a few hours.

A child with meningitis may have the following symptoms:

(i) fever; (ii) headache; (iii) vomiting; (iv) stiffness in the neck and pain on bending the neck; (v) dislike of bright lights and a desire to keep the eyes closed; (vi) drowsiness, irritability and confusion. A rash of tiny red and purple spots or bruise-like patches may appear on the skin in cases of meningococcal meningitis and meningococcal blood infection. The symptoms in small babies with meningitis who cannot complain of headache and other discomfort are slightly different. These are: (i) lethargy, being too sleepy and difficult to wake up; (v) a vacant, staring look; (vi) the fontanelle (the soft spot on the top of the baby's head) may be tense or bulging; (vii) pale or blotchy skin. A rash of red and purple spots or bruises may appear over the body in babies with meningococcal meningitis.

It is, however, important to bear in mind that all symptoms listed above may not appear together all at once in a child or baby with meningitis. But if you have any suspicions about meningitis in a child, do seek expert medical assistance promptly without any hesitation.

WHAT SHOULD PARENTS DO?

If this disease is diagnosed early and treated quickly, most children recover completely. But in some cases, especially when there is a delay in treatment, the disease can result in permanent disabilities, such as deafness and brain damage and may even be fatal. Recognizing the symptoms of meningitis by parents at an early stage of the disease and prompt treatment of the child are therefore, extremely important.

TREATMENT

A child who is suspected to be suffering from meningitis needs to be hospitalized. He would firstly need a sample of his spinal fluid to be examined to establish the diagnosis of meningitis. The spinal fluid is obtained by doing a lumbar puncture. In this simple procedure, a needle is inserted in the lower part of the child's back in the mid-line and a small amount of spinal fluid is withdrawn. This procedure is entirely safe. Parents should have no anxiety or doubts about this procedure, which is essential to confirm a diagnosis of this disease. Cases of bacterial meningitis require regular intravenous administration of antibiotics and careful supportive treatment for a minimum period of 10 days.

CAN MENINGITIS BE PREVENTED?

Meningitis is caused by a large number of different bacteria and viruses. There is as yet no one vaccine to protect a child against all types of meningitis. Vaccines are currently available only against three types of bacterial meningitis. Hib vaccine protects children against meningitis caused by Haemophilus influenzae type B organisms and it is now being recommended for routine immunization of children below 5 years of age. The details about this vaccine are given in the section on Immunization. The meningococcal vaccine is administered for protection of children during an epidemic of meningococcal infection in the community. It is not given as a part of the routine immunization schedule. The third type of vaccine against pneumococcal meningitis is only recommended for use in certain high-risk situations, such as, children with sickle-cell disease or whose spleen has been removed.

MUMPS

Mumps is a viral disease of salivary glands. The child initially develops fever, malaise, headache and loss of appetite. Within a day or two, he complains of pain near the lobe of the ear and difficulty in chewing. A swelling appears around the ear lobes in front and on the side of child's face, below in the angle of the jaw, as well as behind the ear due to inflammation of the parotid salivary gland. The swelling may be quite mild or very marked and painful to the touch. The parotid swelling may appear either on one side or both sides of the face. Swellings of other salivary glands may occasionally appear below the jaw. The fever and swelling generally subside within three to seven days.

WHAT TO DO

The child should have bed rest when he feels ill. His mouth should be kept clean by frequent mouth washes. He should have fluids or a semisolid diet to reduce the pain during chewing. Avoid sour liquids such as lemon juice as these make the pain worse. He can be sent to school four days after the parotid swellings (around the ear) have subsided as by then he is non-infective to others.

In a small number of adolescent boys, one or both testes may become swollen and painful, together with redness of the skin and fever. The swellings and fever usually subside in about four days. The swollen testes should be held up with supports and not allowed to hang loosely to provide some relief from pain. The child should rest in bed and paracetamol may be administered to alleviate his pain and fever. A few adolescent girls with mumps may sometimes develop inflammation of ovaries resulting in pain in the lower part of the abdomen. A doctor should be consulted for advice.

HOW TO PREVENT MUMPS

Administration of a single dose of mumps vaccine to a child confers almost lifelong immunity against this disease. It is usually given as a dose of MMR (measles-mumps-rubella) vaccine at 15 months of age as a part of the routine immunization schedule for children. If this vaccine has been missed at that age, it can be given later under a doctor's advice to a child who has not suffered from mumps earlier.

NAPPY RASH

Many babies get soreness or a rash in the buttock region where the napkin is tied (nappy rash). Some babies tend to have it more because their skin is extra sensitive. This also happens if the soiled nappy remains in contact with the skin for a long time. You should take care that the baby's nappy is changed soon after its soiling. Clean the baby's bottom well with water but do not apply soap. Allow your baby to remain without a nappy. The free flow of air over the child's skin will help the rash to subside quicker. If the rash persists or gets worse, consult your doctor. He may advise a cream for its quick relief and the subsequent use of a protective cream to prevent its recurrence. If the baby's nappy rash tends to persist, the doctor would also check if your baby has developed a mild fungus infection of the skin, 'thrush', which responds quickly to local application of anti-fungal skin creams.

PNEUMONIA

Pneumonia is an inflammatory condition in which there occurs inflammation and solidification of air sacs (alveoli) in the patient's lungs. A part or the whole of one or both lungs may be affected. The inflammation may be caused by different types of viruses, bacteria and other organisms. Pneumonia can develop at any age, including in infants below one year, for whom it is particularly serious in nature.

During the normal process of breathing, purification of blood occurs through the removal of carbon dioxide and its replacement by oxygen by a process of diffusion within the air sacs which are situated deep inside the lungs. As a result of these air sacs being diseased in pneumonia, the affected child's respiratory function gets disturbed. His breathing becomes fast and shallow and he develops fever. In small babies there may also be 'grunting' noises and indrawing of the chest wall during breathing. In a child with severe pneumonia his lips and face may turn greyish-blue due to the low level of oxygen in his blood. He may also become drowsy because of the poor supply of oxygen to his brain.

Pneumonia is a serious disease and it demands prompt and effective treatment. A child with severe pneumonia would need to be hospitalized for the administration of oxygen, effective control of infection with suitable antibiotics, regular monitoring and management of complications, if any.

POLIOMYELITIS

Poliomyelitis is an acute infectious disease caused by the polio virus. It occurs more frequently during the summer months. The polio viruses which are excreted by patients in their stools, gain entry into the human body through ingestion of food and water which has been contaminated by these viruses. Infection by the polio virus causes a broad spectrum of illnesses in those affected, ranging from unrecognized illness to extensive paralysis of various muscles and involvement of the brain.

WHAT TO DO

There is as yet no specific treatment for poliomyelitis. During the acute stage of poliomyelitis patients are advised to have complete bed rest with proper positioning of affected limbs to avoid deformities later. Symptomatic relief is provided for muscular pains and spasm. Injections are avoided at this stage as they may induce paralysis in the limb where the injection is given. Severe cases of polio with extensive muscle paralysis and complications involving lungs and other systems need hospitalization. Following the child's recovery from the acute stage, active physiotherapy is instituted for improvement of muscle power and prevention of deformities. Some cases later need occupational therapy and psychological support for the restoration of their functional capacities and return to active life, despite some residual handicaps. The only truly effective method of handling the problem of poliomyelitis in children is to prevent it. The details about prevention with the help of polio vaccine are given in the section on Immunization.

SINUSITIS

The sinuses are air-filled spaces which are situated around the nose in the cheek-bones and around the eyes in the forehead region of a child. These air spaces normally serve the function of providing resonance to an individual's voice. Since these sinuses are connected to the nose and the upper part of the throat, common colds and other infections of the throat can spread to the sinuses and cause sinusitis. In these cases, the 'cold' tends to persist. The child may have fever, a persistent cough, headache and a yellowish green pus discharge from the nose.

WHAT TO DO

In case of symptoms suggestive of sinusitis, the child should be shown to a doctor for proper treatment. The doctor may like to have an X-ray of the sinuses and other investigations done to confirm the diagnosis and to advise suitable antibiotics for the eradication of infection.

TETANUS

Tetanus is a very serious disease. It is largely caused through contamination of a person's skin abrasions, cuts and wounds by dust, dirt and animal faeces containing the tetanus germs. Puncture wounds due to rusted nails, splinters, thorns, etc., in dirty fields and on dusty roads are particularly liable to cause this disease. The use, particularly in rural areas, of improperly sterilized instruments for cutting the umbilical cord in newborn babies at birth and subsequent application of cow-dung to the navel area for its alleged purifying properties are responsible for causing tetanus in many newborn babies.

This disease in older children is characterized initially by an inability to open the mouth and chew properly due to spasm of muscles of the jaw. The child may have a fixed sardonic grin on his face because of the persistent contraction of his facial muscles. He later develops a stiff neck, arching of the back, and repeated fits. During extremely painful fits the arms bend and become stiff, the fists become clenched and the legs straighten out rigidly. However, the child remains conscious throughout the whole illness. He may develop breathing difficulty and several other complications which may prove fatal. A child with tetanus needs to be hospitalized for proper treatment.

Tetanus in the newborn is particularly serious and carries a very high mortality rate. A newborn baby develops excessive crying, difficulty in swallowing and may tend to choke while taking feeds. Inability to open the mouth (lower jaw) is followed by stiffness of the limbs, arching of the back and difficulty in breathing. The fits are characteristically induced by jerking of his bed, noise and bright light. The condition of these babies is often extremely serious, requiring intensive treatment at a major hospital.

It is extremely important to take adequate preventive measures against this serious disease. To prevent tetanus in the newborn baby, the mother is given two doses of tetanus toxoid at an interval of four weeks during her pregnancy. For later protection the baby is given three doses of DPT, which contains tetanus toxoid as one of its constituents. The first dose of DPT is administered at the age of six weeks which is followed by two doses at an interval of four to six weeks. Booster doses of DPT are later given at around 18 months and 5 years of age. Tetanus toxoid (TT) injections are given at the age of 10 years and 15 years for continued protection of the child against tetanus.

The appropriate manner of management of skin abrasions, cuts and wounds as well as the administration of preventive immunization against tetanus has been discussed separately.

THALASSEMIA

Thalassemia is a form of hereditary anaemia. A child with this blood disorder is unable to make enough amounts of the desired type of haemoglobin. The red cells in the patient's blood are smaller than usual and contain less haemoglobin.

There are two forms of thalassemia:

(i) thalassemia minor or thalassemia trait and

(ii) thalassemia major.

A child with thalassemia major appears normal at birth but becomes anaemic, irritable and sluggish between the age of 3 months and 2 years. His anaemia does not improve with any drugs and he has to be given blood transfusions almost every month throughout his life. He also needs daily administration of a drug to remove excess iron from his body. The procedure of bone-marrow transplant which is performed in an effort to provide a permanent cure, is very costly and is still very risky.

Children and adults with thalassemia trait (minor) are not ill and may not even know that they have any disorder. However, if both parents have thalassemia trait, there is one in four chance that their child may suffer from thalassemia major. It is, therefore, recommended that when there is a family history of thalassemia on the side of either parent, both parents should get themselves tested for the presence of thalassemia trait prior to the woman becoming pregnant. In the event of the mother having already become pregnant, she is advised to undergo tests for detection of this disease in her baby between 9 and 18 weeks of pregnancy. If the baby in the womb is found to be suffering from thalassemia major, the mother is offered the option of undergoing an abortion. The facilities for carrying out some of these special tests on the baby in the mother's womb are available at the All India Institute of Medical Sciences, New Delhi and a few other major medical centres in India. A list of some of these centres is placed at appendix 8.

TONSILS AND ADENOIDS PROBLEMS

ENLARGED TONSILS

The so-called 'enlarged tonsils' are often wrongly blamed by many parents for their children's lack of appetite, failure to thrive and inability to gain height. They therefore, consider removal of the child's tonsils as an appropriate solution for these problems. It must, however, be understood that the two tonsils, located on either side at the back of the throat, are designed by nature to act as guards to trap and prevent entry of disease causing organisms into the lower respiratory passages and hence serve a very useful purpose. It is difficult for a lay person to assess the state of health of a child's tonsils merely by peeping into his throat. The decision regarding retention or removal of tonsils must be left to the doctor.

ENLARGED ADENOIDS

In some children, the adenoids get enlarged and interfere with the passage of air through the nose. They develop mouth breathing and persistent nasal discharge and tend to snore at night with their mouth open. Their voice may become nasal and muffled and they may have foul breath. Persistent mouth breathing over a long period may result in the child developing a typical facial appearance with a pinched nose and a long lower jaw. Some children may develop repeated attacks of middle-ear infection. You should consult your doctor for advice. The child may need removal of the enlarged adenoids, if medical treatment fails and his problems persist.

TONSILLITIS

The two tonsils placed on either side of the back of the throat and the two adenoids placed on either side in the back portion of the nose, act as filters to trap germs.

However, in the course of catching various germs (bacteria and viruses), the tonsils themselves may sometimes get inflamed. In acute tonsillitis, the child develops fever, pain in the throat, difficulty in swallowing, headache and bodyache. Tonsillitis caused by virus infections does not require antibiotics. The child is provided symptomatic relief with paracetamol and bed rest, as required.

STREPTOCOCCAL TONSILLITIS

Acute tonsillitis is sometimes caused by streptococcal infection, sometimes called 'strep-throat'. The child usually has high fever, a pain in the throat and difficulty in swallowing. The diagnosis of this condition is confirmed by performing a throat swab culture examination. In this condition some complications like middle-ear infection and sinusitis can develop. The child may also occasionally suffer from kidney disease and rheumatic fever one to three weeks later. The condition therefore requires to be treated quickly and effectively. The antibiotic prescribed for its treatment (generally erythromycin, penicillin) must be taken regularly for the entire recommended duration for proper eradication of this potentially bad infection.

In certain situations where the child has very frequent recurrent tonsillar infection or middle-ear infections, the removal of tonsils may become necessary. However, this should not be rushed into. The ENT surgeons are much more cautious these days in taking this decision than before.

TUBERCULOSIS

HOW DOES THE CHILD GET IT?

Tuberculosis can occur at all ages – in infants, children and adults. Although it is more common among the poor and the malnourished living in crowded conditions, no social class is exempt. Children acquire this infection through contact with an adult suffering from lung tuberculosis. At home a domestic help, a relative, a gardener or a neighbour and at school a canteen bearer or some other employee having infectious lung tuberculosis may act as the source of this infection for a child. Some of these adult patients of tuberculosis may even themselves be ignorant about the true nature of their disease. The adult infectious cases of lung tuberculosis cough out a large number of tuberculosis causing germs in their sputum (phlegm). A child gets infected by inhaling those germs contained in the contaminated air. A child suffering from tuberculosis is, however, generally not infectious to others because of the different nature of his disease.

HOW DOES IT MANIFEST?

Tuberculosis in children may affect the lungs, lymph glands, meninges (membranes covering the brain), intestines, bones and other organs. Infants and young children are particularly prone to suffer from tuberculous meningitis and miliary tuberculosis, which are the more serious types of tuberculosis. The manifestations of this disease in children are quite different from the commonly held image of an extremely sick adult patient of tuberculosis coughing out blood in his sputum. An affected child may just suffer from prolonged unexplained fever, lack of appetite, lethargy and failure to gain weight. A baby or a young child may sometimes suddenly show up as a case of tuberculous meningitis with fever, irritability, headache and vomiting. In some children, this disease may manifest itself as glandular swellings in the neck. The symptoms of this disease vary, depending upon the organ and nature of involvement.

WHAT TO DO

Tuberculosis is today a treatable disease. Highly effective and safe drugs are now available to cure this condition and the duration of treatment has been reduced to about six to nine months in most cases. It is, however, absolutely essential that the patient is given a regular full course of treatment as recommended, under proper medical supervision.

Irregular administration of drugs and failure to continue treatment for the entire recommended duration, even when the child looks well and appears to have recovered earlier, lead to poor control of disease, recurrence and complications.

HOW TO PREVENT IT

Tuberculosis is a largely preventable disease. The BCG vaccine provides reasonable protection, particularly against serious forms of tuberculosis. Every newborn baby should be given BCG vaccination within one month of his birth. If BCG vaccination has been missed during that period, it can be given at a later stage. In that case, the doctor would, however, first like to examine the child and do a Mantoux test (a skin test) to assess the need and advisability of giving BCG vaccine.

A very important preventive step is the avoidance of the child's close contact with an infectious case of tuberculosis. Towards this end, it is advisable that every new household member or employee, who is likely to come in contact with the child and who has not been keeping well or has been suffering from cough or fever, be screened to exclude tuberculosis. Such precautions should also be taken by the school and hostel authorities and those running creches and day care centres for children. If an adult contact of the child is found to be suffering from infectious tuberculosis, immediate steps should be taken to segregate the child. Further, even if the child looks apparently well, he should be investigated to make sure that he has not already contracted the tuberculosis infection. If so, he would need to be properly treated. In certain situations, the doctor may like to prescribe prophylactic medication to a child to prevent the development of this disease.

TYPHOID FEVER

Typhoid fever is quite common among children and adults in India and several developing countries. Paratyphoid fever is a similar disease but is usually milder than typhoid fever.

The disease occurs through the intake of unhygienically prepared food, milk or milk products and water contaminated with typhoid causing germs. Ice, particularly, is very often highly contaminated. The contamination takes place through the hands of typhoid patients, typhoid carriers and through flies. Some typhoid patients continue to excrete typhoid germs in their stool for as long as two to three months after they have recovered and even when they themselves are apparently quite well and back to work. They are called typhoid carriers and are often instrumental in transmitting infection to others, especially when they work as food handlers. Typhoid fever is more common in the hot summer months due to frequent breakdowns of safe water supply, larger number of flies and increased consumption of unhygienically prepared food, ice, cold drinks and exposed foods.

The child with typhoid suffers from bodyache and lack of appetite. The fever is generally quite high and persistent but can also be intermittent. There may also be abdominal pain and constipation. Some children develop loose motions instead of constipation. If the child is neglected for long, he may develop various complications involving the intestines, brain, lungs and other organs.

The diagnosis of this disease is established by performing a blood culture examination. The specific drugs prescribed for the control of typhoid infection must be given to the child for a minimum period of 10-14 days, as advised. If discontinued prematurely he is liable to have a relapse. It is wrong to starve the child because of misconceived fears about the harmful effects of food in a patient of typhoid fever. He needs adequate nutrition and fluids to assist his early recovery. The child may have light home-cooked food.

There is no need to restrict his intake to just milk, juices or a bland diet.

The patient should wash his hands thoroughly with soap and water after toilet and before handling food. The family attendant who handles him and his soiled linen should also wash his hands well.

For the prevention of typhoid fever in general, all children above two years of age should receive regular prophylactic doses of the typhoid vaccine. Details about the use of typhoid vaccine are given in the section on Immunization. It is also important to avoid consumption of unhygienic food and fluids, which are liable to be contaminated with typhoid germs by flies and the use of contaminated ice.

UNDESCENDED TESTES (ABSENCE OF TESTES IN THE SCROTUM)

In a boy, the testes are initially formed in the abdomen. They subsequently descend into the scrotum about a month before birth. When a boy is born, one or both testes may not be felt in the scrotum. (Fig. 22.4) In a premature baby, an undescended testes may occasionally come down without treatment over the next few months. This happens less often in full-term babies. The parents must however be conscious of the fact that sometimes, while the boy's testes have actually come down into the scrotum, they may not appear to have done so. This is because when

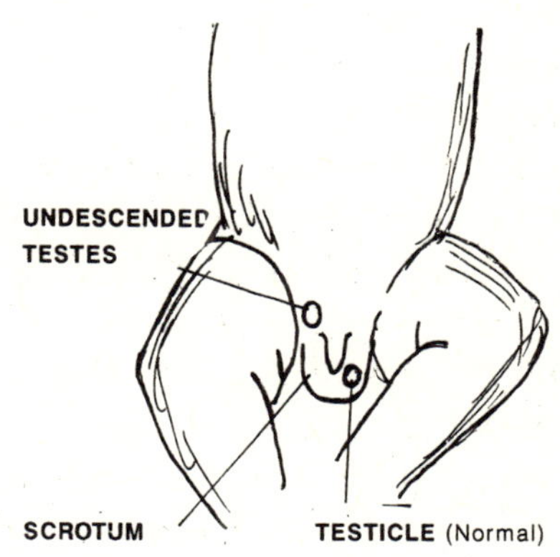

(Fig. 22.4)

the baby is either nervous or feeling cold, the testes may get drawn up into the groin region by involuntary muscular pull. A doctor, therefore, sometimes needs to examine the child more than once to confirm the diagnosis.

WHAT TO DO

It is important for the testes to be placed in the scrotum. If not in the proper position, the testes are liable to suffer from damage and loss of function, which may result in infertility later.

A child with a problem of undescended testes must be got examined and treated early in the second year of life. The child would generally need surgery to bring down the testes into the scrotum. The treatment must not be delayed so as to avoid irreparable damage to the functioning of the testes.

URINARY TRACT INFECTIONS

Urinary tract infection is quite common in infants and children. Children older than two to three years sometimes complain of a burning sensation in the urinary passage and pain in the lower abdomen while passing urine and for some time thereafter. They also tend to pass urine very frequently in small amounts. The urine may also be foul smelling. Children with kidney infection may, in addition, develop fever with chills. Children less than three years old are however unable to express themselves and may not show any obvious urinary symptoms. They may just have fever, diarrhoes and a deficiency of weight gain. The following steps must be taken for every child who develops urinary tract infection:

1. The child must be adequately treated with appropriate antibiotics, according to urine culture and sensitivity findings, for 7-10 days.
2. There should be a proper investigation to exclude an obstruction or abnormality in the urinary tract which may predispose the child to recurrent infections.

3. Urine examination should be repeated after a suitable interval by the doctor to make sure that the urinary infection has not recurred even though the child may have no obvious symptoms.
4. Some babies and children with an inborn obstruction or physiological dysfunction in the urinary passage may require surgical correction to prevent recurrent urinary tract infection and kidney damage.

WAX IN EARS

The presence of wax in the ear of a child is normal. Wax is a normal secretion produced by glands in the outer part of the ear canal. It helps to trap dust and other small particles. When it is first produced by the glands, it is colourless and semi-liquid. Later it becomes yellow to brown in colour and becomes hardened. Being a normal secretion, the presence of wax should normally be ignored. However, very occasionally a large wax plug in the ear canal may cause local irritation or hearing difficulty. If so, you should seek medical advice. The doctor may need to do syringing to remove the wax. He may advise local instillation of a wax softener drops (like Waxsolve) for a few days to make subsequent removal of the wax by syringing easier.

WHOOPING COUGH (PERTUSSIS)

Whooping cough is a serious childhood disease, more so when it occurs in babies under one year. It is caused by bacteria (B. pertussis). The disease begins innocuously like an ordinary cold with a mild cough. The cough gradually worsens and after about two weeks the child starts having repeated bouts of prolonged and severe coughing. Sometimes, there is a whooping noise as the child draws in breath after coughing, hence the name of the disease. The bouts of cough are exhausting, hence the child often finds it difficult to breathe. He may vomit after prolonged bouts of coughing. He is unable to take feeds properly, which, along with the vomiting, makes him very debilitated. This stage continues for two to four weeks after which he takes another two to four weeks to gradually recover. Serious life threatening pneumonia and other lung complications may occur. He may develop bleeding in the eye and even a rib fracture due to intense forceful coughing. Patients may have fits and other complications.

Consult your doctor. He may like to do some tests to confirm the diagnosis. Follow his advice scrupulously. Your child may need prolonged treatment and observation for several weeks.

HOW TO PREVENT

For prevention, pertussis (whooping cough) vaccine is given as a component of DPT (diptheria -pertussis-tetanus) vaccine to children as a part of regular immunization schedule. It has been explained in detail in the section on 'Immunization'

WORMS IN CHILDREN

Worm infestation of different types is quite common among children and they cause a wide variety of symptoms. Amongst them, the roundworm, threadworm and hookworm are the most frequently encountered.

Your knowledge of some basic facts about these worms and the disorders caused by them will help in understanding them better and in taking suitable measures to prevent your child from getting infected.

THREADWORM

Lots of children get threadworm infection. The tiny, white, thread-like worms live in the patient's intestines. At night, the female worms come out and lay their eggs around the anus. This makes the child scratch his bottom frequently, especially at night. He may sleep poorly, grind his teeth and sometimes develop bed wetting. In girls, it may cause irritation around the vulva and vaginal discharge. The child's hands, especially the nails, get contaminated by scratching the skin around the anus. His underclothing and bedding also get contaminated with these eggs. Although the treatment of this infection is simple, it is important that the whole family is treated simultaneously. This is necessary to stop the vicious cycle of spread of infection from one family member to another. Scrupulous attention to personal hygiene, of cleaning the child's bottom after defecation, daily change of the underclothes, adequate attention to his bed linen, keeping his nails short and clean, avoidance of itching around the anus, and washing hands well after passing stool and before taking food are important measures for avoiding this infection and its recurrence.

ROUNDWORM

The adult roundworms resemble earthworms, and are about 6 to 12 inches long. They live inside the patient's intestines and their infective ova are passed out in the faeces. Roundworm infection occurs through the intake of food, water, or soil which has been contaminated by their ova. The adult roundworms residing in the intestines consume the food meant for the child, thereby causing the child to become malnourished. The child may also have pain in the abdomen, lack of appetite and poor digestion. In rare cases, a large bunch of worms may block the intestinal tract and cause total constipation, abdominal distension and vomiting.

A child with roundworm infection may notice the passage of these worms in his stool. Occasionally, roundworms may be vomited out. The presence of this infestation is otherwise diagnosed by the detection of ova of roundworms on microscopic examination of the patient's stool. To avoid missing the diagnosis of this infestation the stool samples of the child should be examined on three successive days.

Roundworms cause a relatively mild disease and can be quickly and well treated with modern drugs. The child's stool should, however, be examined after completing the prescribed course of treatment to make sure that the infection has been eradicated. It is also advisable to ensure that all other members of the household, particularly the domestic cook, are free from this infection, even if they may have no obvious symptoms, to prevent the child from getting re-infected.

The following steps should be taken to prevent a child from getting roundworm and threadworm infection in the first place and if infected from disseminating it to others:

1. Wash thoroughly carrots, radishes, onions, salad leaves and other vegetables meant for eating raw, because the soil in the field may be contaminated with the ova of roundworms.
2. Make sure that the drinking water is clean. Where in doubt, use boiled water. Care should be taken that prepared food as well as drinking water do not get contaminated through unhygienic handling by a person carrying the ova in his finger nails.
3. The child should be discouraged from eating soil as it may be contaminated with ova. It is also desirable that he does not go round passing his stool everywhere and that his faeces are disposed off properly.
4. He should wash his hands thoroughly after passing stool and before taking food.
5. Nails should be cut short and kept clean. Scratching of the area around the anus should be avoided. If there is itching in this region (due to threadworms), your doctor will prscribe a suitable cream for local application. He should also have daily baths with thorough washing of his bottom. The underclothes should be changed daily and bed linen kept clean.

HOOKWORM

A child acquires this infection as he moves about barefoot in fields and grounds where the soil is contaminated with the larvae of these worms. The larvae penetrate the skin of the foot, enter the bloodstream and finally reach the intestines where they grow into adult worms. The adult worms, about 10 cm long, attach themselves to the wall of the patient's intestines and suck the host's blood. When a child has a heavy load of worms, continuous daily loss of blood results in the child becoming severely anaemic. He may also develop abdominal discomfort and loss of appetite. This disease is diagnosed by detecting eggs of hookworms in the patient's stool. Modern drugs are highly effective in treating this infection. To avoid getting hookworm infection, children should wear shoes while playing in the fields and in the open grounds likely to be contaminated with the infected faeces.

APPENDIX: 1

IMMUNIZATION TIME TABLE

Age	Name of Vaccine	Dose
Birth to 2 Weeks	BCG	1 Dose
	Polio	1st Dose
	Hepatitis B	1st Dose
6 Weeks	Polio	2nd Dose
	DPT	1st Dose
	Hepatitis B	2nd Dose
	Hib	1st Dose
10 Weeks	Polio	3rd Dose
	DPT	2nd Dose
	Hib	2nd Dose
14 Weeks	Polio	4th Dose
	DPT	3rd Dose
	Hib	3rd Dose
At 14 weeks or at 6 months	Hepatitis B	3rd Dose
9 Months	Measles	1 Dose
15-18 Months	Polio	5th Dose
	DPT	1st booster dose
	Hib	Booster Dose
	MMR	1st Dose
2 Years	Typhoid	1 Dose
5 Years	Polio	6th Dose
	DPT	2nd booster
	Typhoid	booster
	MMR	booster
10 Years	Tetanus Toxoid (TT) or Td	Booster (1)
16 Years	Tetanus Toxoid (TT) or Td	Booster (2)
Pregnant Woman	Tetanus Toxoid (TT)	2 doses at 4 Weeks interval

APPENDIX: 2

TEMPERATURE EQUIVALENTS

Centigrade (C)	Fahrenheit (F)
36.0	96.8
36.2	97.2
36.4	97.6
36.6	97.8
36.8	98.2
36.9	98.4
37.0	98.6
37.2	99.0
37.4	99.4
37.6	99.6
37.8	100.0
38.0	100.4
38.2	100.8
38.4	101.2
38.6	101.4
38.8	101.8
39.0	102.2
39.2	102.6
39.4	103.0
39.6	103.2
39.8	103.6
40.0	104.0
40.2	104.4
40.4	104.8
40.6	105.0
40.8	105.4
41.0	105.8
41.2	106.2
41.4	106.6
41.6	106.8
42.0	107.6

APPENDIX: 3

AVERAGE HEIGHT AND WEIGHT OF CHILDREN AT DIFFERENT AGES

Boys			Girls		
Age	Weight (Kg)	Height (cm)	Age	Weight (kg)	Height (cm)
Birth	3.0	50.0	Birth	2.9	48.5
6 months	7.2	66.0	6 months	6.6	64.2
1 year	9.5	75.0	1 year	9.0	72.5
2 years	11.5	85.5	2 years	11.0	84.0
3 years	13.5	94.0	3 years	13.0	93.0
4 years	15.4	100.0	4 years	15.0	99.0
5 years	17.2	106.5	5 years	16.5	105.5
6 years	19.0	112.5	6 years	18.0	111.5
7 years	21.0	118.0	7 years	19.8	117.0
8 years	22.0	123.0	8 years	22.0	122.0
9 years	25.4	128.0	9 years	25.3	127.8
10 years	28.0	133.4	10 years	28.7	133.6
11 years	31.2	139.0	11 years	32.4	140.0
12 years	35.0	144.5	12 years	36.5	147.0
13 years	40.0	150.5	13 years	40.5	152.8
14 years	45.2	157.0	14 years	44.5	156.0
15 years	51.0	163.0	15 years	47.8	157.0
16 years	56.0	168.5	16 years	50.0	157.8

APPENDIX: 4

WEIGHT, VOLUME, AND LENGTH EQUIVALENTS

Weight

1 ounce (oz)	= 28.4 grams (g) approx.
1 pound (16 ozs)	= 453.6 g
2.2 pounds	= 1 kilogram (kg)

Liquid measure

1 fluid oz	= 30.0 millilitre (ml) approx.
16 fluid oz	= 480.0 ml
33 fluid oz (approx.)	= 1 litre

Length

1 inch	= 2.54 centimetre

APPENDIX: 5

RECIPES OF WEANING FOODS FOR BABIES

1. SUJI KI KHEER

Suji	25 gm
Sugar	10 gm
Milk	250 ml (¼ litre)

Method: Boil milk and add suji. Cook on a slow fire till it becomes semisolid. Add sugar. Cool and serve lukewarm to the baby.

2. RICE KHEER

Rice	10 gm
Sugar	10 gm
Milk	250 ml

Method: Wash rice after cleaning and picking it. Boil milk and add rice. Cook on a slow fire till it becomes semisolid. Add sugar. Serve at lukewarm temperature.

3. KHICHRI

Rice	50 gm
Dehusked moong dal	25 gm
Spinach (optional)	50 gm
Oil	2 teaspoons
Salt	to taste

Method: Cook rice and dal together and mash. Boil spinach, mash and strain. Add the spinach puree, salt and heated oil to the rice-dal mixture and stir. Cool and serve lukewarm.

4. BENGAL GRAM DAL KHICHRI

Rice	50 gm
Green gram dal	25 gm
Roasted Bengal gram	50 gm
Green leafy vegetable	25 gm
Oil	1 teaspoon
Salt	to taste

Method: Boil rice and green gram dal and mash them. Boil, mash and strain the spinach/other leafy green vegetable. Add vegetable puree, powdered roasted Bengal gram, oil and salt to the rice and dal mixture and cook on slow fire for a few minutes. Serve lukewarm.

5. KHICHRI OF WHEAT DALIA

Wheat dalia	50 g
Lentil	50 g
Potato	in amounts desired
Any green vegetable	in amounts desired
Oil	3 teaspoons
Salt	to taste
Onion	1 small
Ginger	2 g
Bay leaf and cardamom (optional)	1 each

***Method*:** Clean and wash dalia and lentil separately and cut vegetables. To boiling water add onion, ginger, bay leaf, cardamom and dalia. Cook until half-cooked. Then add lentil and vegetables and cook until soft. Season with salt and oil.

6. RICE UPPUMA

Rice	25 g
Green gram dal	25 g
Onion	1 large
Any vegetable	10 g
Mustard	½ teaspoons
Groundnut oil	4 teaspoons
Salt	to taste
Water	2 cups

Method: Roast rice and dal and grind into granules. Cook green gram dal with 3/4 cup water and mash. To hot oil, add mustard, onion and fry and then add water and salt. Add the rice granules and vegetables to the water and stir cook for 10 minutes and add the green gram dal paste. Drumstick leaves may also be used instead of vegetables.

7. POHA

Rice
Onions
Potatoes or other vegetables

Method: Brown onions and cumin and mustard seeds in oil. Add vegetables and cook till tender, adding minimum quanity of water. Finally add rice, cook for 2-3 minutes.

8. KHAMAN DHOKLA

Bengal gram dal	50 g
Black gram dal	25 g
Rice	50 g
Amaranth leaves	50 g
Curd	25 g
Oil	1 teaspoon
Salt	to taste
Mustard	a few seeds

Method: Soak Bengal gram dal, black gram dal and rice separately for a few hours. Grind them separately and mix. Add curd and salt and ferment the mixture overnight. Add amaranth leaves, season with oil and mustard seeds and pour the batter into idli moulds and steam.

9. RAGI ADAI-SWEET

Ragi flour	30 g
Roasted Bengal gram dal	3 teaspoons
Jaggery	15 g
Coconut scrapings	1 teaspoon
Oil (groundnut)	2 teaspoons
Water	3 teaspoons

Method: Dissolve jaggery in water. Add Bengal gram flour, ragi flour and coconut scrapings to the jaggery water to make thick dough. Prepare the adai on a greased iron pan or tawa.

Source: Selected Nutritious Recipes – *1983 National Institute of Public Cooperation and Child Development, New Delhi.*

APPENDIX: 6

INSTITUTIONS FOR THE HANDICAPPED

NAME AND ADDRESS OF MAJOR INSTITUTIONS.

	Telephone No.
(1) Federation for the Welfare of the Mentally Retarded (India) 1 Shaheed Jeet Singh Marg Special Institutional Area Katwaria Serai New Delhi 110 067	(011) 651 3432
(2) Regional Centre National Institute for Mentally Handicapped Kasturba Niketan Lajpat Nagar II New Delhi 110 024	(011) 683 1012
(3) NIMH Regional Centre AYJ NIHH Campus Bandra Reclamation Near Bandra Tel. Exchange Bandra West Bombay 400 050	(022) 644 2880
(4) Regional Centre National Institute for the Mentally Handicapped B.T.Road Bonhoogly Calcutta 700 090	(033) 557 1357
(5) National Institute for the Mentally Handicapped Manovikas Nagar Secundrabad 500 009	(040) 775 9267 (040) 775 9268

(6) NIMH Regional Centre (0612) 420 910
IAS Colony
Bailey Road
West of Nehar
Danapur
Patna 801 503

(7) Spastic Society of Northern India (011) 669 107
Near General Raj's School (011) 696 6331
Hauz Khas
New Delhi 110 016

(8) The Institute for the Physically Handicapped (011) 323 4309
(011) 323 9690
4, Vishnu Digamber Marg (011) 323 2403
New Delhi 110 002

(9) Ali Yavar Jung Rashtriya Shravan (022) 640 9176
Viklang Sansthan (AYJNIH) 442 2638
Kishanchand Marg
Bandra (West)
Bombay 400 050

(10) National Institute for the Orthopaedically Handicapped
B.T. Road
Bon Hoogly
Calcutta 700 090

(11) National Institute for the Orthopaedically Handicapped
116 Rajpur Road
Dehradun 248 001

(12) National Institute of Rehabilitation Training & Research
Olatpur Bairoi
Cuttack 754 010

(13) National Institute for the Hearing Handicapped (011) 693 5093
Northern Regional Centre
Kasturba Niketan
Lajpat Nagar II
New Delhi 110 024

(14) Ali Yavar Jung National Institute for the Hearing Handicapped EPBAX No. 640 0215, 640 0228, 640 9176
Bandra (W)
Bombay 400 050

(15) National Institute for Visually Handicapped (0135) 24491, 24578
116, Rajpur Road
Dehradun 248 001

(16) Regional Centre for Visually Handicapped 572 505
Poonamille
Madras 600 056

Note: Parents can obtain more information about these and other institutions for the handicapped and the facilities provided by them from:

National Information Centre on Disability and Rehabilitation CACU-DRC Scheme
Ministry of Welfare
4 Vishnu Digamber Marg
New Delhi 110 002

APPENDIX: 7

PARENT GROUP BODIES

Thalassemics India Tel : 661 199
C-1/59 Safdarjang Development Area Fax : 685 5721
New Delhi 110 016

APPENDIX: 8

MAIN CENTRES FOR GENETIC STUDIES

1. All India Institute of Medical Sciences
Genetics Unit
Department of Paediatrics
Old Operation Theatre Building
Ansari Nagar
New Delhi 110 002

2. B.J. Wadia Hospital for Children & Institute of Child Health
Parel
Mumbai 400 012

3. Institute of Immunohematology
13th Floor Multistoried Complex
KEM Hospital
Parel
Mumbai 400 012

4. Vivekanand Institute of Medical Sciences
Ramakrishna Mission Seva
Pratishthan
99 Sarat Bose Road
Calcutta 700 026

5. B.J. Medical College
Pune 411 001

6. Institute of Genetics & Hospital for Genetic Diseases
Osmania University
Begumpet
Hyderabad 500 016

APPENDIX 9

INDEX OF MEDICAL EMERGENCIES

INDEX